STAR WARS

A Question of Initiative

NOTE TO THE READER

Within the text of each chapter, you will find references to the time at which it was written, and there is acknowledgement of the original location of publication. To allow each chapter to stand on its own, some facts have been referred to more than once, but I also have cut overlaps within the context of this book, and rewritten text that had been prepared for a particular magazine or conference. In general I have tried to make this book an entity in itself without changing the state of mind, or the view of the facts, with which each of its various parts was written. The introduction, written in late July 1986, appears here for the first time. I am grateful for the editorial assistance of Gaynor Redvers-Mutton and Deborah Hooper of John Wiley and Sons.

STAR WARS
A Question of Initiative

Richard Ennals

JOHN WILEY AND SONS

Chichester · New York · Brisbane · Toronto · Singapore

Library of Congress Cataloging in Publication Data:
Ennals, J.R. (John Richard), 1951–
    Star wars.

    Includes index.
    1. Strategic Defense Initiative. 2. Great
Britain—Military policy.   I. Title
UG 743.E56 1986   358'.1754   86-22373

ISBN 0 471 91293 X

British Library Cataloguing in Publication Data:
Ennals, J.R.
    Star Wars: A Question of Initiative.
    1. Expert systems (Computer Science) 2. Strategic Defence Initiative
    I. Title
    006.3'3   QA76.9.E95

ISBN 0 471 91293 X

Typeset by Inforum Ltd, Portsmouth
Printed and bound in Great Britain
by Biddles Ltd, Guildford

Contents

Introduction

This is a personal account of highly complex technical and political issues in which I have been involved. In the summer of 1985, I was approached by senior Civil Service colleagues who told me of their concern over the planned but unannounced involvement of British government, industry and universities in the Strategic Defence Initiative. My personal campaign to change this policy was first conducted as a civil servant on a contract from the Department of Trade and Industry. When Michael Heseltine and Caspar Weinberger agreed the Memorandum of Understanding for British Participation in the Strategic Defence Initiative on 6th December 1985 I resigned my post, announcing my decision at a meeting on 13th December 1985 which was called by the British Computer Society to consider the professional implications of participation in projects such as SDI, whose technical feasibility was in doubt.

President Reagan's Strategic Defence Initiative, launched in March 1983, (known popularly as Star Wars) has served to raise old issues, but with a new urgency: at stake has been not only the use of British and European advanced information technology, which prior to my resignation it was my job to manage, but the very future of human life on our planet, whose defence was to be entrusted to automatic computer systems.

The papers collected in this book have been part of a campaign to raise awareness of complex technical, economic, strategic, political, legal and moral issues, representing an attempt to understand and explain rapidly changing events – as they occurred – to a variety of audiences.

The book is organised in five sections, addressing different aspects of strategic initiatives in advanced research.

In the first section, I address issues of research management in advanced information technology. The same enabling technology – extending the effective power of human thinking – can support a wide range of possible applications, and choices have to be made regarding the management of scarce resources of expertise and finance.

The second section concerns SDI, and consists of a series of speeches, lectures and articles written in 1986 as part of an international campaign, involving scientists, civil servants, the peace movement and politicians from across the political spectrum. The chapters are printed in chronological order, and are substantially unrevised since they were first written, though some elements of duplication have been removed. Some degree of repetition remains, as certain points have had to be explained in different ways to different audiences who have been discovering shared concerns.

It is all too easy to attack mistaken policies put forward by others: the third section offers constructive alternative uses for advanced information technology in the fields of education, training and health, building on practical experience of experimental projects and approaches to management.

The fourth section addresses technical issues concerned with the development of intelligent systems, whatever their area of application. It is important to be aware of the limits of technology, and of our dependence upon a sound basis of knowledge if we are to build knowledge-based systems.

The final section introduces the field of computational politics, of which this book is a case study. The methodology described in this section has been employed in the writing of the book. The Reykjavik Summit which took place in October 1986 is a clear illustration of computational politics. We are concerned both with the politics of computing and the light that computing concepts can cast upon politics.

So, this is also an historical work, a record of recent events, many of which have not been reported. The chronological chart at the end of this introduction shows when each of the papers was written in the context of events in the US, UK, Europe and Japan. At the time of writing, secret negotiations are under way between the United States and the Soviet Union over the reduction of nuclear weapons, and the Strategic Defence Initiative is part of the bargaining, despite assertions by the President and the Pentagon up to and including July 1986 that SDI would go ahead unrestricted.

The Washington correspondent of *The Guardian*, 23rd July 1986, wrote:

Although the Pentagon hawks won a round over the State Department when the US repudiated the Salt II Treaty in May, the impression is growing that the tide is turning against Star Wars. In its search for budget cuts, the Senate and House of Representatives are moving towards a 1987 Star Wars research budget of between $1.5 billion and $2 billion below the White House's $5.3 billion request.

Senate sceptics, including the influential Democratic defence specialist Sam Nunn, are seeking to redefine its goals as being to defend missile silos rather than provide an "astrodome" over whole populations, as President Reagan alone appears to believe is still technically feasible. The scientific community is deeply divided over the wisdom of SDI and its supporters are frequently accused of contradictory and exaggerated claims.

As this book goes to press we do not know the outcome of the argument in Washington. We do, however, have some understanding of the position of the British government. One of the central issues surrounding Star Wars is whether its promises to British industry (via the representatives of the Department of Trade and Industry in the British SDI Participation Office) of contracts worth millions of dollars would actually hold true. The leading article in *The Financial Times* for 15th July 1986 which was entitled "UK role in Star Wars" states:

The Reagan Administration appears unlikely to obtain more than about $3.9 billion for the anti-missile project for the year beginning in October, compared with the $5.4 billion which it has requested.

Furthermore, the longer the Star Wars project goes on without UK concerns gaining a foothold, the harder it will be for them to build up enough momentum to obtain substantial contracts in later years. Many of the important decisions about the direction of the programme have already been taken. Teams from US aerospace and defence companies have been working on the main technical thrusts for a couple of years. They are bound to be in a better position to win the significant contracts than UK groups which are becoming acquainted with the nuances of the programme relatively late.

Were it not for the high expectation of UK involvement in Star Wars which both Whitehall and the US Defence Department have encouraged, the current state of affairs would not be surprising. British concerns were always going to find it difficult to break into a programme whose centre is 8,000 miles away in Los Angeles, the focal point of the US defence systems industry.

More realistically, however, the UK Government may have only itself to blame. Ministers should take a hard look at the motives which caused them to sign last December's agreement in the first place. On the face of it, the US won implicit political support for its controversial programme by getting a major ally to agree on participation in the research. The UK, as events have turned out, gained relatively little in return.

Some new light may also be cast on controversies such as those over Westland Helicopters and the proposed sale of British Leyland to General Motors and Ford, which suggests the need for a reassessment of, for example, the resignation of Michael Heseltine from Mrs Thatcher's Cabinet. I quote from the Third Report of the House of Commons Defence Committee on *The Defence Implications of the Future of Westland plc*, published on 23rd July 1986:

> The starting point for Mr Heseltine's argument was that collaboration between a large American firm and a smaller European firm would lead to the domination of the latter by the former . . . Mr Heseltine acknowledged it and described it in terms that went much wider than the helicopter industry: "It is quite right that . . . there is practically nothing you cannot buy cheaper from the United States because they have huge production runs, huge resources, huge research programmes, funded by the taxpayer, and if we want to cut down Britain's industrial capability all we have to do is to go to the United States of America and they will enable us to buy the products cheaper, and they are very good products, which would satisfy most of our demands, I might add with defence as well. But it would be, in my view, totally unacceptable as a judgement, both in the strategic concept that you should never allow the strategic control over your essential defence requirements to be outside your hands, and, secondly, because the consequences in the acceleration of the brain drain, the loss of jobs, the destruction of the high technology base and the civil implications would be wholly unacceptable."

There is nothing anti-American in the analysis which follows. This is a book about the complexity of human affairs, not about heroes and villains. Recent events have the richness of Shakespearean tragedy mingled with the science fiction fantasy of *"The Hitchhiker's Guide to the Galaxy"*.

In a Shakespearean manner, I must introduce some of the principal players in our tragedy: the "dramatis personae". Their names will become familiar in the papers and speeches which follow, in the real-life plots and sub-plots.

Americans   *President*, Ronald Reagan
                       Secretary of Defence, Caspar Weinberger
                       Assistant Secretary of Defence, Richard Perle
                       Pentagon official, Paul Hopler
                       Pentagon consultant, Clarence Robinson
                       Secretary of State, George Shultz
                       State Department official, David Schwartz

Director of the SDI Office, Lt-Gen. James Abrahamson

Senator, Barry Goldwater

British Government *Prime Minister*, Margaret Thatcher
Foreign Secretary, Sir Geoffrey Howe
Defence Secretary, (1) Michael Heseltine
       (2) George Younger
Industry Secretary, (1) Leon Brittan
      (2) Paul Channon
Leader of the House of Commons, John Biffen
Minister of State, Information Technology and Aerospace, Geoffrey Pattie
Minister of State, Agriculture, John Gummer
Minister of State, Education, Chris Patten

British critics *Labour Party leader*, Neil Kinnock
Liberal Party leader, David Steel
Social Democratic Party President, Shirley Williams
Labour Foreign Affairs spokesman, Denis Healey
Liberal Industry spokesman, Paddy Ashdown
Labour MP, Tam Dalyell
Labour MP, Chris Smith
Chairman, Parliamentary Information Technology Committee, Sir Ian Lloyd
Chairman, Select Committee on Trade and Industry, Kenneth Warren
Former Prime Minister, Edward Heath

British officials *Director, SDI Participation Office*,
   (1) Kenneth Hambledon
   (2) Stan Orman
SDIPO University liaison, George Gallagher-Daggitt
SDIPO Industry liaison, George Chantry
Director, Alvey Programme, Brian Oakley
Director-General, NEDO, John Cassells
Chief Scientific Adviser, John Fairclough

Academics Professor David Parnas, Victoria University, Canada
Professor Manny Lehman, Imperial College
Professor John Darlington, Imperial College
Professor Bob Kowalski, Imperial College
Professor Margaret Boden, Sussex University

Professor Des Smith, Heriot-Watt University
Dr Henry Thompson, Edinburgh University
Dr Alan Bundy, Edinburgh University

Peace Movement   Edward Thompson, European Nuclear
                         Disarmament
                         Colin Hines, Greenpeace Disarmament
                         Campaign
                         Paul Walton, The Strategic Research Initiative
                         Dr Jeremy Leggett, Scientists Against Nuclear
                         Arms
                         Professor John Humphrey, Medical Campaign
                         Against Nuclear Weapons
                         Dr Andy Haines, FREEZE
                         Bruce Kent, Campaign for Nuclear
                         Disarmament
                         Malcolm Harper, United Nations Association
                         Dr Chris Moss, Computing and Social
                         Responsibility
                         Maxwell Bruce QC, British Pugwash Group

In addition, following the example of Lamb's *Tales from Shakespeare*, and commentaries on Chaucer's *Canterbury Tales*, I must offer a brief summary of events: (see overleaf).

We can make our own choice from the titles of Shakespeare's plays: there are ingredients here from *King Lear*, *The Tempest*, *The Taming of the Shrew*, *Twelfth Night* and *All's Well That Ends Well*. My own role has been uncomfortably close to that of Hamlet, but I have been more fortunate in my friends.

This is not a complete and objective account of the issues and events surrounding Star Wars. I have not had access to classified information and I have been personally close to the events I describe. The book may serve to cast some light on a dark period, and on issues which governments have not wished to discuss in public. The reader is invited to find his or her own way through the maze, and to ask further questions.

The broader scientific community is now expressing its concern.

Richard Ennals

CHRONOLOGY

* indicates when a chapter was written

Date	USA	UK	Rest of World
1983			
March	President Reagan announces SDI	Alvey Directorate established	ESPRIT taskforce established
1984			
September		SRI Cambridge conference	
* 1.1 1.2			
December	Reagan and Thatcher discuss SDI at Camp David		
* 3.1			
1985			
March	Negotiations start on British involvement in SDI Prof David Parnas resigns from SDI Computing panel	Sir Geoffrey Howe criticizes strategic basis of SDI	President Mitterand announces EUREKA
July			
* 3.3			
October	Weinberger and Heseltine meet on SDI	United Technologies visit Imperial College	
* 4.4		Pentagon visit to Imperial College cancelled	
December	Nuclear tests for X-ray laser	Cabinet split over Westland	
* 4.1		Alvey Logic Programming	

Date	USA	UK	Rest of World
1986 **January** * 2.1 3.2		Alvey FLAGSHIP Project launched Pugwash conference on militarization of space Heseltine signs MoU on SDI R.E. resigns from Imperial College and Alvey Programme Westland crisis continues Michael Heseltine resigns END launches Campaign Against Star Wars Leon Brittan resigns British Leyland affair House of Commons debates SDI Clarence Robinson caught by GEC Kenneth Hambledon replaced by Stan Orman	German MoU for SDI Israel MoU for SDI Chirac elected in France
February	Challenger shuttle explodes		
March * 2.2 2.3 4.3 4.5	Weinberger apologizes over Robinson misunderstanding British companies feted in Pentagon		

Date	USA	UK	Rest of World
April			**Rest of World**
			American bombing of Libya
*— 2.4			Chernobyl disaster
2.5			Tokyo Economic Summit
May		International Appeal Against Militarization of Space	
*— 5.1			
June	Challenger report published	Strategic Research Initiative	Nakasone wins Japanese
	Congress cuts funds for SDI	seminar launch of Coalition	election
*— 2.6		Against Star Wars	
2.7			
July	US and USSR agree to discuss	Publication of report on	new EUREKA projects
	nuclear tests	Westland	
*— 4.2	Breakthroughs in East-West		
2.8	talks		
4.6			
October	Reykjavik Summit	500 scientists pledge to	
		oppose Star Wars research	

SECTION 1

THE RESEARCH MANAGEMENT CONTEXT

1.1
Research Perspectives and National Strategies

Introduction

Research in advanced information technology has become a matter for general concern in recent years. Combined with the enormous increase in computer power, the sudden fall in costs brought about by the development of microcomputers has meant that computer use is now within the reach of the ordinary citizen of an advanced nation. Applications that had previously been thought to be in the domain of science fiction are discussed by computer scientist and layman alike. The veil of mystery and secrecy that partly protected the high priests of computer science from outside scrutiny has begun to be pulled aside. Issues of research perspectives and national strategy are now recognized to be worthy of discussion by politicians and industrialists. When the accompanying new infrastructures for research and development are considered, as they will be in Chapter 1.2, the context of discussion broadens to include potentially all citizens participating in a democracy.

This chapter draws on the contributions made by speakers at the Cambridge conference on "Advanced Information Technology: Applications, Achievements and Prospects", organised by SRI International at Churchill College, Cambridge in September 1984. It also seeks to broaden the discussion in the light of subsequent events, and of points of view which were not represented in Cambridge. The area

First published in *Intelligent Machinery: Theory and Practice*, ed. Ian Benson. Cambridge University Press, 1986.

of research perspectives and national strategies combines issues of politics, economics and science. We must not expect to find universal agreement, but the events of recent years have brought us nearer to consensus: not on the answers, but as to the questions that are worth asking.

Continuity in computer science

Many of the technical issues are not new. Professor Roger Needham has been at the Computer Laboratory of Cambridge University since 1956, and stated:

> It is fashionable to think that the information technology scene is in some very fundamental ways different now from what it was a rather small number of years ago. There is said to be such a thing as a fifth generation computer. I have never seen one.

Needham likes to emphasize the continuity of work in computer science:

> If you look at what goes on, there is indeed a pretty good degree of continuity with the past at all points, but nevertheless there have been changes which taken together can be regarded as very serious.
>
> It is not as if somebody has made an invention which changes the face of the world, it is a conjunction of things that have happened separately.

Changing emphases in new generation computer science

The peace and tranquillity of the computing world was rudely disturbed in the autumn of 1981 by the arrival of invitations to attend a conference in Japan on the proposed development of a new generation of computers.

The Japanese were determined to set the lead in the next stage of developments in computer science, rather than continuing to be subordinate to American academic and commercial direction. They proposed an explicit scientific revolution in contrast to previous minor design changes in computer technology. The proposals were spelt out in a May 1982 publication of the Japanese Institute for New Generation Computer Technology (ICOT): (Moto-oka, 1982)

> The changes from one generation to the next in computer technology have so far been made to accommodate changes in device technology, that is from vacuum tubes to transistors, then integrated circuits, and recently to large-scale integrated circuits. Such hindsight tells us, then, that there have been no major changes in the basic design philosophy and utilisation objectives of computers.

With fifth generation computers, however, the expected generational change is more like a "generic change" which involves not only a change in device technology, to very large scale integrated circuits (VLSI), but also simultaneous changes in design philosophy and in fields of application.

A new approach to the use of computers was proposed for a number of application fields in the 1990s, involving a change from machines centred around numerical computations to machines that can "assess the meaning of information and understand the problems to be solved."

To accomplish this change a number of developments are required; in the words of the ICOT report:

1. To realise basic mechanisms for inference, association and learning in hardware and make them the core functions of the fifth generation computers.
2. To prepare basic artificial intelligence software to fully utilise the above functions.
3. To take advantage of pattern recognition and artificial intelligence research achievements, and realise man-machine interfaces that are natural to man.
4. To realise support systems for resolving the "software crisis" and enhancing software production.

Dr Kazuhiro Fuchi is Director of ICOT. In his paper "Aiming for knowledge information processing systems", published in 1981, he was explicit about the central thrust of the Japanese initiative, which is summarized in Figure 1.1.1.

Logic programming and its research tradition were assigned a central role in hardware and software terms:

PROLOG (PROgramming in LOGic) seems to be the best suited as the starting point in considering new base languages for knowledge information processing.
PROLOG machines could represent the first step toward inference machines.

Fuchi, while emphasizing the radical nature of their strategy, also acknowledged the continuity with past research traditions:

While the route to knowledge information processing is an advance to a new age, it can also be viewed as representing the inheritance and development of the legacies of the past from the viewpoint of research efforts.

Significant among the research traditions on which Fuchi and his colleagues have drawn has been that of work at Stanford Research

Figure 1.1.1: Organization of the Fifth Generation Project

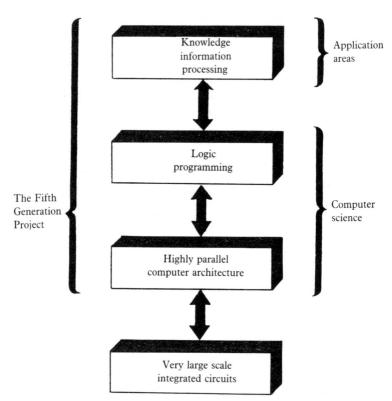

Institute, where some of the ICOT team were visitors in the research study stage of the project. Not only did they work there on expert systems, but it was through SRI that the first copy of PROLOG reached Japan. SRI researchers place on emphasis on logic, rather than on logic programming, and LISP remains as their dominant artificial intelligence programming language.

Responses to the Japanese initiative

Professor Needham was the sole academic representative on the British Alvey Committee which was formed to consider a British response to the Japanese Fifth Generation Initiative in 1981, and the invitation to British researchers to collaborate. The Japanese presentation of a considered national strategy provided a model for others to follow or reject. Whether or not inventions are involved which "change the face of the world", we must accept that, in the words of Bob Muller of SPL-Insight:

> At the very least, Japan has set the world computing targets for the rest of the decade and beyond.

In the early years of the Japanese programme, there was some confusion among overseas researchers as to the research perspective adopted by the Japanese. There was sufficient respect for the Japanese national strategy in other areas of economic and technical endeavour for governments and companies to be spurred into initiating their own programmes of research and development. Unsurprisingly, research groups deployed the Japanese initiative as an argument to secure improved funding for their own preferred perspectives. At the time of the submission of the Alvey Report to the British Government, Professor Max Bramer observed (Bramer, 1984):

> Although the envisaged fifth generation is not a continuous development from the previous four, there is much substance to the claim that it arises naturally from existing research into artificial intelligence. The difference is that, whereas the Japanese project will be well-funded and nationally organised and supported, artificial intelligence work in the West is usually carried out in small and badly-funded research groups, especially in universities, with little or no national co-ordination. It is possible that, largely as a result of the Japanese proposals, this position may now change.

Over three years have passed since the Japanese initiative. New national research programmes have been established in most developed countries, in both East and West. They have not solely concentrated on artificial intelligence, nor have they all preserved the Japanese central emphasis on logic programming. One purpose of this chapter is to assess how the different programmes have progressed, starting with a review of progress on the Japanese Fifth Generation Programme.

Progress in the initial stage of the Fifth Generation Programme

At the Cambridge conference reports were given by Kinji Takei, Managing Researcher in the Research Planning Department at ICOT, and Professor Hideo Aiso, Chairman of the Technology Forecasting Committee at ICOT. Further reports were given at the Fifth Generation Computer Systems conference in Tokyo later in 1984, planned as the culmination of the initial stage of the project. The overall plan is summarized in Figure 1.1.2.

Figure 1.1.2: The FGCS plan

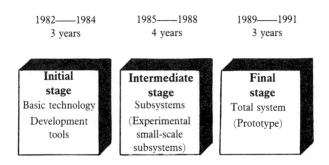

Takei described progress as being more rapid than expected in the research and development efforts that have taken a practical approach, but rather slower in those that have chosen a more sophisticated course. This judgement would be accepted by most of the delegates at the Tokyo conference, where there was a lack of surprise at what was demonstrated – a lack of surprise due to the openness with which work in progress has been discussed.

At the end of the initial stage ICOT was able to demonstrate the new personal sequential inference machine (PSI); an enhanced version of PROLOG (KL0) (the first of a planned series of kernel languages for fifth generation systems); their prototype relational database machine (DELTA); and a series of example expert systems on the PSI. The work of ICOT is broader than expert systems or artificial intelligence, but expert systems are among the earliest demonstrable applications. One, called LOOKS, was developed with Tokyo University as a medical system to diagnose glaucoma. Another system, from Fujitsu, automates the design process of integrated circuits from a given set of specifications. A Harmonizer system arranges a four-part chorus based on a given melody.

Aiso described the project as being on course so far. He emphasized the importance of the developments with PROLOG:

> PROLOG is becoming very popular in Japan among computer scientists and it seems to be that PROLOG has grown up to a new culture in Japanese computer scientists, alongside LISP. Many researchers are proposing new ideas on the language and PROLOG machines.

The intermediate stage is clearly going to be difficult, designing computational models, basic architectures and algorithms, and building basic subsystems. Aiso sees the final stage as being devoted to improving and enhancing the results obtained in the previous stages, and integrating them to form a knowledge information processing system.

In recent months ICOT researchers have been at pains to point out the limits of their aspirations over the timescale of the project. Aiso said in Cambridge:

> In my opinion, it will be almost impossible to realise such an ideal knowledge information processing system in ten years. So the present Fifth Generation Computer Project should be devoted to basic technology required for future knowledge information processing systems.

Furthermore, although it is envisaged that future machines should have graphics, image devices and voice recognition, these are not the concern of the Fifth Generation Project, which is merely one of many government-coordinated research and development projects, based on long-term planning. It is almost impossible, in Aiso's view, to "expect drastic and sophisticated evolution or breakthroughs in a short term project".

At the Tokyo conference Aiso chaired a panel discussion on "Parallelism in New Generation Computing", an issue central to the development of a new computer technology. Ehud Shapiro, of the Weizmann Institute in Israel and a regular visitor to ICOT, warned that the development of parallel computing would not be easier than that of sequential computers. All the important machine-dependent concepts of computer science have to be rediscovered in a new context. In the existing technology both computers and programmers are too slow, and although a parallel machine with an appropriate language could provide the solution the perspective is clearly long-term.

The European Strategic Programme for Research and Development in Information Technologies (ESPRIT) — progress report

At the Cambridge conference a report on the ESPRIT Programme was given by Horst Hünke, who is in charge of Programme Coordination in the Directorate for Information Technology and ESPRIT of the Commission of the European Communities. Since that conference there have been further developments such as the publication of the 1985 ESPRIT workplan, approval of further projects, and public discussions of the complementarity of the ESPRIT and individual national programmes.

Hünke stated the case for ESPRIT very much in economic terms:

> Overall there is a need for ESPRIT because the leading companies'

activities are much smaller than those of overseas companies, and their revenue in a number of cases can clearly not support the necessary research and development. Whilst also in the internal markets, the foreign controlled and foreign owned companies are very important. That is, they further reduce the home base for the companies for which they could produce products that can then successfully compete on the world market.

He described the historical context whereby the centre of innovative activity, which used to be in Europe in the nineteenth and early twentieth centuries, had now moved to the United States and Japan. He cited the problem of a shortage of skilled manpower (to which we will return in Chapter 1.2), which compounded with the consequences of being organized in small separate nation-states means that on a European level duplication of efforts cannot really be afforded. At present European industry was developing products with too low a level of technology.

Figure 1.1.3: Japanese national projects for future computer technology

Very-high-performance computer systems	1966–1971
Pattern information processing systems	1971–1980
VLSI technology	1976–1979
Basic technologies for fourth generation computer systems	1979–1983
Optoelectronics application system	1979–1986
Basic technologies for next generation industries	1981–1990
Very-high-speed scientific computing systems	1981–1988
Fifth generation computer systems	1982–1991
Intelligent robots	1984–1991

The problem was broader than that of industrial research and development, for there was also an application lag, in that users are more conservative in their habits of buying equipment than in the USA.

The ESPRIT Programme addresses the area of pre-competitive research, aiming to build a technological base that will make it competitive on the world market within the next five to ten years. Hünke's analysis of American programmes in the field suggested that those that were especially successful not only initiated a technology push, but also provided an initial market, so that then the normal industrial market forces took over. A similar process would be required in Europe.

Although one of the stimuli for the ESPRIT Programme has been the Japanese Fifth Generation Initiative, Hünke was at pains to emphasize how the ESPRIT Programme differed:

> It is not, as for instance the Japanese programme is, focused along one idea, namely the Fifth Generation Computer system. . . . The idea of the Fifth Generation computer is not a goal, but rather it is a means to focus thought. What you can see in the Fifth Generation Programme, is the use of PROLOG as a basic paradigm. This is, of course, a very useful thing in providing a common semantic basis for people doing research. They understand each other's problems much more easily than if they all followed a different school.

The ESPRIT Programme does not adopt such common paradigms, and the interests of the researchers are more diverse.

Whereas the Japanese Fifth Generation Project, like other advanced research projects in Japan, is organized by the Ministry of International Trade and Industry (MITI), and coordinated by the specialist Electro-Technical Laboratory (ETL), collaboration in ESPRIT is much looser. To quote Hünke:

> The ESPRIT Programme is the organisation of a process of collaboration, between industrial partners, between industry and academia; a process that is mediated but not run in that sense by the Commission. It is strongly influenced by its participants.

A survey of the ESPRIT Programme (Frederiksson, 1984) made the contrast in terms of research strategies:

> Whereas the Japanese MITI directs research and development within an overall strategy, ESPRIT and other programmes merely back industry proposals.

The area covered by the work programme, which itself constitutes an invitation to make proposals, is much broader than that covered by the Japanese Fifth Generation Project. ESPRIT seeks to remedy a wider range of research and development deficiencies, and includes areas covered by other Japanese projects. Figure 1.1.4 is the outline of the programme taken from the 1985 Workplan:

The area with which we are most concerned is that of "Advanced Information Processing" (AIP). This is described in the workplan as follows:

> This subprogramme is seeking means for improving the performance and efficiency of computing systems by making use of advances in four key areas, namely knowledge engineering, including the development of knowledge acquisition, representation and manipulation techniques; external interfaces, dealing with the recognition, understanding and

Figure 1.1.4: The ESPRIT Programme

1	Subprogramme R & D areas	1: Advanced microelectronics 1.1 Submicron MOS 1.2 Submicron bipolar 1.3 Computer Aided Design (CAD) 1.4 Compound Semiconductor integrated circuits 1.5 Optoelectronics 1.6 Advanced display technologies
2	Subprogramme R & D areas	2: Software technology 2.1 Theories, methods and tools 2.2 Management and industrial aspects 2.3 Common environment
3	Subprogramme R & D areas	3: Advanced information processing 3.1 Knowledge engineering 3.2 External interfaces 3.3 Information and knowledge storage 3.4 Computer architectures 3.5 Design and systems aspects 3.6 Focusing projects
4	Subprogramme R & D areas	4: Office systems 4.1 Office systems science and human factors 4.2 Advanced workstations 4.3 Communication systems 4.4 Advanced filing and retrieval systems 4.5 Integrated office system
5	Subprogramme R & D areas	5: Computer integrated manufacture 5.0 Manufacturing company strategy and organizatio 5.1 Integrated system architecture 5.2 Computer Aided Design and Engineering (CAD/CAE) 5.3 Computer Aided Manufacturing (CAM) 5.4 Machine control systems 5.5 Subsystems and components 5.6 CIM systems applications

---

synthesis of signals; information and knowledge storage. These advances are the developments in data and knowledge bases as well as the techniques of access to these bases, and deals with architectural characteristics and physical properties of advanced storage devices; computer architecture, i.e. the development of new computer architectures and their associated programming environments where particular emphasis will be placed on the use of concurrency.

The ESPRIT Programme was approved by the EEC Council of Ministers for an initial period of five years in February 1984, and 120 projects were under way by the end of 1984. Each proposal must come from a consortium made up of at least two companies from different member states, with research and higher education institutions able to participate. Successful proposals receive 50% funding.

It is too early to judge the technical outcomes of the ESPRIT Programme, but it is worth noting that PROLOG, the language adopted by the Japanese as their principal paradigm, was first implemented and developed in Europe. Researchers in logic programming, and in artificial intelligence in general, have had little funding for their work until recently, and a small but influential European academic community has developed for mutual support, some of whom have taken temporary residence in the United States.

The United Kingdom Alvey Programme in advanced information technology — a progress report

The Alvey Programme was represented at the Cambridge conference by its Director, Brian Oakley. He drew attention to the similarities between the Alvey strategy and that of ESPRIT and the Japanese Fifth Generation Project. Referring to technical directions, he said:

> You could just scratch out the bit which says "ESPRIT" and write in "Alvey" and nobody would notice the difference in many ways.

Concerning the general approach to research planning, he said:

> The Alvey Programme is quite unashamedly copying what we see as the best features of the Japanese programme as well as we can in transplanting it to the British scene. This is particularly true of the administrative arrangements. In many ways, when we wonder what to do, we look up the Japanese Fifth Generation plans and then we see how to organize ourselves. Let me assure you that to copy in Europe is recognized as an extreme form of flattery.

The Alvey Programme was set up in 1983 following the British Government's acceptance of the majority of the recommendations of the Alvey Committee (chaired by John Alvey of British Telecom). Whereas in Japan MITI coordinated the work of eight collaborating companies focused on the ICOT research centre, in the United Kingdom the Alvey Directorate coordinates a much wider collaborative programme. Three government ministries are involved (the

Department of Trade and Industry, the Ministry of Defence, and the Science and Engineering Research Council of the Department of Education and Science), together with industry and academic research groups.

Like the ESPRIT Programme, the Alvey Programme is broader and less focused than the Fifth Generation Project. It is concerned with the development of what are described as the four crucial enabling technologies for advanced information technology:

> Very large scale integration (VLSI);
> Software engineering;
> Man-machine interface (MMI);
> Intelligent knowledge based systems (IKBS).

The Directorate is organized into corresponding sections, though as Oakley concedes that "the distinction between the areas is no more than a device that human beings use to try to administer such things."

He noted, however, that there do appear to have been barriers between academic communities with apparently related interests:

> It does seem to us to be very important to try to bring these communities together. It is a strange thing that they intermingle so closely, and yet the barriers between them are really very extreme. It's terribly easy, I find, to say a man belongs to the AI community or he belongs to the software engineering community. It is remarkably difficult to find the people who cross these two communities.

It may be useful to outline the work of the different sections of the Alvey Programme, in summary form:

VLSI: Work has been led by the large computer manufacturers, and concerns:

> silicon whole-process development;
> cmos;
> bi-polar;
> silicon on insulator;
> 1.5 micron features in year 3;
> 1.0 micron features in year 5;
> equipment for same;
> CAD for VLSI standard design codes;
> silicon brokerage to serve immediate needs of smaller companies.

MM: This section represents an uneasy coalition of the concerns of previously separate academic communities, and deals with i.e.:

speech recognition;
pattern analysis;
ergonomics;
better displays;
links with cognitive sciences, psychology, etc.

Software engineering: This part of the Alvey Programme builds most explicitly on the methods of conventional computer science. It is an area given relatively little emphasis in Japan, where the view is that new software technology should overcome many current software problems. British companies have been somewhat reluctant to make the investment in software engineering research under Alvey or ESPRIT. Work has concentrated on the production of integrated programming support environments:

First generation:
    file-based tool set;
    Unix.
Second generation:
    database-based tool set;
    distributed operating system;
    formal specification methods:
Third generation:
    IKBS-based tool set.

IKBS: The IKBS area has had the greatest academic contribution, and much of the strategy stems from an SERC working party which preceded the Alvey Report. It is organized around the following research themes:

parallel architectures;
declarative languages;
intelligent database systems;
expert systems;
intelligent front ends;
inference;
natural language;
image interpretation;
intelligent computer-aided instruction.

Apart from projects in the separate areas, a number of large "demonstrator" projects were established, drawing on the different enabling technologies, such as a project for knowledge-based decision support with the Department of Health and Social Security, two

companies and three universities; and a voice-driven desktop workstation, exploiting new parallel computer architecture and work in
phonetics and linguistics, involving two companies, three universities
and an associated research consortium.

According to figures cited by Oakley at the Cambridge conference in
September 1984, 93 projects had been approved from 274 proposals.
There were an average of 4.3 partners per project. A total of 45
companies, 38 universities, 4 polytechnics and 5 other establishments
were involved. Further projects were to be approved before the spring
of 1985, leading to 80% of the budget being committed. The majority
of contracts went to large companies, and ten leading universities
were the academic partners in over half of the projects.

There were increasing complaints in the early part of the programme along the lines of "Where is the Fifth Generation in the Alvey
Programme?" In the summer of 1984 an initiative was launched in
Declarative Systems Architecture, administered through the IKBS
section but underlying the whole programme. This focused attention
on parallel architectures such as the ALICE machine at Imperial
College, to be made initially from a delta network of Inmos trans-
puters. A compiler target language (CTL) was agreed for the implementation of declarative languages. New programmes were launched
in large knowledge bases and in logic programming languages, applications and architectures.

Brian Oakley is reluctant to make mid-term assessments of the
progress of the programme:

> The proof of the pudding is in the eating. It is no damn good, really,
> taking the pudding out of the oven and having a look to see how it is
> getting on at this stage.

A brief survey of national strategies in other countries

The United States: In the United States the Defence Advanced
Research Projects Agency (DARPA) has launched a Strategic Computing Programme, with a budget of $600m over five years. The main
demand has come from the military, with artificial intelligence applications such as autonomous vehicles, expert associates, and large-
scale battle management systems.

IBM has taken an increasing interest in fifth generation computer
systems and logic programming, having been publicly dismissive at
the time of the Japanese initiative. They have been recruiting leading
international researchers in logic programming for their Yorktown
Heights research centre.

In response to the perceived threats from both Japan and IBM, 18 computer manufacturers have united to form the Microelectronics and Computing Technology Centre (MCC) based in Austin, Texas, which will be discussed further in Chapter 1.2. This necessitated changes in the existing anti-trust legislation in the 1984 Joint Research and Development Act.

West Germany: Following the 1984 Riesenhuber Report on information technology, a programme of $1bn over five years has been established, placing a special emphasis on cooperation between research establishments and industry in order to achieve a faster application of research and development results to new products. Research was to be encouraged in knowledge engineering, new computer structures, and CAD for computers and software.

In addition to participation in the ESPRIT Programme, West Germany is host to the new European Computer Industry Research Centre (ECRC) in Munich, involving Siemens, Bull and ICL, which will be discussed further in Chapter 1.2.

France: In France, research and development initiatives relating to the facets of the Fifth Generation Programme appear as a set of distinct projects that complement each other technically as well as in their scientific and industrial objectives. Government felt that the French information technology industry should master the full range of technologies, and in 1983 initiated seven major technology transfer projects. These complement a series of Joint Research Projects in fields such as advanced programming, various facets of artificial intelligence, and concurrency, cooperation and communication.

The Soviet Union and Eastern Europe: Recent reports suggest that the Soviet Union is planning a "low budget" Fifth Generation Programme along similar lines to those in Japan, the United Kingdom or the United States. The Communist countries intend to leapfrog our present fourth generation computers from the third generation of computers which they now employ. This is to be part of the third computing (five year) plan.

The Soviet Commission for Computer Engineering (CCE), based at the Moscow Academy of Sciences, has agreed the five principal goals of the plan:

Very large scale integration microprocessors for storage and processing, including fabrication techniques, to give advanced hardware;

parallel and multiprocessor computer architectures;
intelligent databases and methods of operation;
software methodologies;
logical programming basis for computer operation.

A major part in the Soviet plans will be played by the Institute for
Computer Coordination (SZKI) in Budapest, which was the first
group to write applications programs in PROLOG, in 1977. Over 250
expert systems have been produced, for everything from running
collective farms to manipulating molecules in three dimensions. In
1982 the Japanese researchers from ICOT purchased the Hungarian
MPROLOG, which is available commercially in Western Europe and
North America. Soviet scientists have also been taking increasing
interest in this research area, as have their colleagues in Bulgaria, East
Germany, Poland and Rumania.

Some notes of scepticism

A large number of national research programmes have been assembled in a very short time, and no advanced country can feel complete
without one. Indeed, the spread of computing technology is such that
research programmes are no longer the monopoly of advanced countries. In addition to the countries mentioned above, major research
centres are being established, to my knowledge, in Canada, Australia,
Portugal, Sweden, Israel, China, Brazil and India. Is this a wise use
of money and resources?

At the Cambridge conference, Dr Jeremy Bray MP expressed his
unease about certain aspects of fifth generation computer developments. He looked at other areas of science, and wondered if there were
not a number of unexploited scientific openings in other fields, and
whether among the many projects now being refused funding by the
British Science and Engineering Research Council there were not a
large proportion which have better formulated problems and far less
adequate resources than we are trying to marshal in the artificial
intelligence field. He also questioned the concepts which at the
conference were taken as points of reference: the fetch and carry robot
and the personal information assistant. In his view:

> these are more in the nature of the medieval philosopher's stone than
> objectives in a modern Popperian science and technology. It also seems
> to me that they are rather inadequate conceptions of behaviour, whether
> individual or social.

Dr Bray had a further worry, that research programmes such as the

Alvey Programme were technique driven rather than application driven. This is of course implicit in the emphasis on enabling technologies. Dr Thomas Garvey to a certain extent shared his view, when he said:

> There is a phenomenon in artificial intelligence at least, and I suspect in computer science generally, that you start to solve a problem by first inventing a language that will enable you to express it better or quicker or whatever. It appears that what we like to do best really is to invent tools rather than necessarily solving the problems, and sometimes we have to first invent problems which will then require these tools.

Conclusions

Professor Ted Elcock has observed with respect to the Fifth Generation projects that "between the expectation and the reality lies the shadow". We can describe what we want to achieve, using a declarative language such as PROLOG, but to obtain the desired outcome is less straightforward, and many technical issues remain unresolved.

We are now in the shadow. Those who are expecting quick results may well be disappointed. Serious researchers are reconciled to many years of hard work, and success is not guaranteed for all participants. This is not, in the words of Lewis Carroll, a "caucus race".

Professor Alan Robinson, now of Syracuse University, but like Elcock and many others a British expatriate in North America, has reviewed the problem of research strategies in his paper "Logic programming – past, present and future", first presented at ICOT in 1983. He was the originator of the Resolution principle in 1965, preparing the way for logic programming, and is the founding editor of the *Journal of Logic Programming*. Addressing his Japanese audience, he said:

> I sometimes have a twinge of anxiety about your having made logic programming the central theme in your Fifth Generation Project. I wonder whether your great confidence in this idea is going to be justified. There are some risks involved, as you well know, in putting this idea in the centre.

On the other hand, on looking to the future, he sees more hope in the Fifth Generation approach than in the traditional American approach based on expert knowledge engineers:

> I think we can expect expert systems to be in general use. Once the tools are available, I do not believe that a special kind of expert – the "knowledge engineer" – will be needed to implement such systems. The

point of the Fifth Generation revolution is to eliminate, as far as possible, the role of such a go-between. Today's situation, in which the professional expert is not necessarily able to express his expertise in suitable computational form, is not the model for the future. We must expect that "logic programming literacy" will become widespread.

References and suggestions for further reading

Alvey, J . (1982). *A Programme for Advanced Information Technology. The Report of the Alvey Committee*. London; HMSO.

Bramer, M. (1984). The Japanese Fifth Generation Computer Project. In *New Information Technology*, ed. A. Burns. Chichester; Ellis Horwood.

Campbell, J.A. (ed.) (1984). *Implementations of PROLOG*. Chichester; Ellis Horwood.

Clark, K.L., Darlington, J., Kowalski, R.A. & Ennals, J.R. (1984). *Research Plan of the Declarative Systems Research Group Department of Computing*. London; Imperial College.

Commission of the European Communities (1984) *Draft Council Decision adopting the 1985 Work Programme for the European Strategic Programme for Research and Development in Information Technologies (ESPRIT)*. COM(84)608 final.

Elcock, E.W. (1983). The Pragmatics of PROLOG. In *Proceedings of Logic Programming Workshop*, ed. L. Pereira. Lisbon; University of Lisbon.

Feigenbaum, E.A. & McCorduck, P. (1983). *The Fifth Generation*. London; Addison-Wesley.

Frederiksson, E. (1984). Overview of national strategies. *Future Generations Computer Systems*, Vol. 1, No. 1. July 1984.

Fuchi, K. (1981). *Aiming for Knowledge Information Processing Systems*. Electro-Technical Laboratory, Japan and in *Logic Programming and its Applications*, ed. D. Warren & M. Van Caneghem. San Francisco: Ablex, 1986.

ICOT (1984). *Proceedings of Fifth Generation Computer Systems Conference Tokyo*. November 1984.

Kowalski, R.A. (1984). Software engineering and Artificial Intelligence in new generation computing. *Future Generations Computer Systems*, Vol. 1, No. 1, July 1984.

Moto-oka, T. (ed.) (1982). *Fifth Generation Computer Systems*. Amsterdam; North-Holland.

Muller, R. (ed.) (1984). *Impact 84*. Abingdon; SPL-Insight.

Robinson, J.A. (1983). Logic Programming – past, present and future. ICOT TR-015.

Simons, G.L. (1983). *Towards Fifth-Generation Computers*. Manchester; NCC Publications.

Walton, P. (1984). An account of research strategies in the Soviet Union and Eastern Europe, with special attention to Hungary. *Computing*, 24 May 1984.

1.2
New Research Infrastructures

Introduction

Governments and commercial companies have more than an academic interest in the outcomes of research and development programmes in advanced information technology. They regard a strong capability in this area as essential for economic reasons. The Alvey Report in the United Kingdom put forward arguments for a national collaborative programme that were repeated in many other countries:

1. The world IT market is growing. The UK needs a large share, but is declining at present.
2. We need competitive levels of achievement in certain fundamental enabling technologies.
3. These enabling technologies are the necessary supporting infrastructures and can be identified now.
4. We require a strong domestic capability in these technologies.
5. A national collaborative effort is required. This means government backing.

The choices were summed up in clear terms:

> The issue before us is stark. We can either seek to be at the leading edge of these technologies; or we can aim to rely upon imported technology; or we opt out of the race.

A large proportion of the recommendations of that report were accepted. The challenge now, in each of the programmes of research

First published in *Intelligent Machinery: Theory and Practice*, ed. Ian Benson. Cambridge University Press, 1986.

and development around the world, is to construct a solution to the problem whose description has been accepted.

Different solutions in terms of new research infrastructures have emerged in different programmes, influenced by historical, economic and political circumstances, as well as by what are taken as appropriate models of experience elsewhere. One such model has clearly been SRI International which has been established for 30 years. The degree of influence of technical researchers has varied, as has the experience and competence of those faced with responsibilities of research management. Whatever new research infrastructures are established, some of the same issues have to be faced.

In this chapter we will examine case studies of new infrastructures, identifying some of the common issues, and conclude with some suggestions as to how we may proceed from academic research to industrial applications that can be of general social and economic benefit.

At the conference on "Advanced Information Technology: Applications, Achievement and Prospects" held in Cambridge in September 1984, speakers dealing with this subject were presented with six questions to assist in structuring their presentations and the ensuing discussion. They were not always answered, but they were as follows:

1. What is new about your research institution?
2. Do we need long-term planning?
3. How can we cope with problems of manpower?
4. How can we take account of the social and economic implications of our work?
5. Can there be such a thing as precompetitive research in a competitive world?
6. What scope is there here for international cooperation?

The traditional relationship between academia and industry

Dr Geoffrey Robinson of the IBM UK Science Centre gave a cogent account of the relationship between academia and industry, without taking into account recent initiatives and changes. Motivating interests, he said, are different:

> In academia one is very interested in pursuing knowledge, one's work is entirely in the public domain, and one is interested in long-term research. In industry, traditionally, we are very oriented by products. In IBM in particular, and in industry in general, there is an obsessive air of secrecy and confidentiality about what you are up to. Naturally, one

tends to focus much more on short and mid-term goals than long-term ones.

In the real world, both sides suffer shortages. IBM sees it as possible for both sides to benefit from some kind of relationship:

> In industry we find ourselves with some quite specific skill shortages, particularly in some scientific disciplines, in new application areas, and so on . . . In universities there is a shortage of money, there is a shortage of computer equipment and one can imagine that the reasons for academia and industry to get together and collaborate on research are much stronger in IT than perhaps in many other disciplines.

One should not expect collaboration to be easy, according to Robinson:

> The driving forces of research in academia, the pressures from the academic environment, are on openness, on scientific truth, pursuit of knowledge, on peer reputation from one's peer researchers. In industry we have problems of confidentiality, timing, product leads, and so on, and the pressures on us tend to pull us apart rather than together. Then on top of all that we have the dreary logistic problems of organization and of finance. Even geography can be a terrible problem if you are trying to collaborate with people.

There is in this last sentence an echo of Professor Needham's identification, at the same conference, of the weak link in present and past computer systems: people. Needham observed that:

> A very important component of the system has not changed whatsoever, and shows no sign of doing so, and that's us. We are no better than we ever were at understanding complex systems that have got to work.

Systems here should be taken to include research programmes.

New research infrastructures in Japan

In one sense the Fifth Generation Project is nothing new for Japan. As outlined in Chapter 1.1, it is simply one in a series of national or government-funded projects which have covered wide areas of information and associated technologies. Long-term planning is seen as inherent to high technology research and development.

As Professor Aiso stated in Cambridge, such a project is not based on the assumption of financial profit. The facilities of high quality government laboratories are available, together with a supply of well-qualified researchers. The official view is that "the success of the project partly depends on whether or not there are well qualified people who are working for the project really hard."

Aiso acknowledged the importance of the tradition of cooperation:

> We have already established very good tripartite cooperation of university, industry and government. In particular, Japanese computer manufacturers have had long experience cooperating with each other on official projects. It is quite natural that when there is government funding cooperation between companies usually takes place in Japanese industry.

This tradition is reinforced by the high costs of fundamental research in this field, which make collaboration essential. The eight leading Japanese computer manufacturers have seconded staff to the ICOT research centre, while also retaining separate company research laboratories which undertake related work. Coordination is provided by staff from the government Electro-Technical Laboratory. The project is seen to be the responsibility of industry, and though university academics serve on advisory committees and engage in related projects in areas such as expert systems, there are no staff at ICOT seconded from academia.

We will return frequently to the question of manpower. Japan is unusual in that there is a tradition of extensive in-house or continuing education which is seen as an excellent substitute for a formal research education at university. Furthermore, the commitment to lifelong employment enhances the capacity of the individual and the company to take on long-term research projects. ICOT itself is regarded as making a major contribution to the advanced education of young researchers from industry.

There have been criticisms from Western observers that the structure and management style of the Fifth Generation Project has been rigid and hierarchical. A visitor to ICOT will notice that the structure of the Institute reflects the structure of the project as described in its published reports, with separate laboratories and research subgroups working in parallel and communicating their results and requirements. The results of the initial stage suggest not only that the technical programme is on schedule, but that the commercial exploitation of the Mitsubishi PSI machine may be imminent, followed by applications systems and a high-specification low-cost super personal computer at the end of the decade.

ICOT has welcomed visiting scientists, and has sought to apply their ideas. It has developed links with foreign research groups, but has been less inclined to form alliances with foreign companies.

Professor Aiso proposed a continuing programme of information exchange, international workshops and conferences, and scientific visits and exchanges.

David Brandin of SRI was chairman of a US Department of Commerce panel on Japanese Technology, which concluded that much of the Japanese strength in advanced information technology derived not from a world lead in basic research, but from their unrivalled expertise in technology transfer. If other countries are to emulate their success in developing industrial applications, they will have to pay more attention to the appropriate mechanisms for technology transfer, and not focus merely on the technical research issues. It will not be enough to simply copy the "Japanese model", or for instance the "SRI model" of technology transfer, as circumstances vary greatly.

Research infrastructures in the Alvey and ESPRIT Programmes

There is not a tradition in the United Kingdom, or in Western Europe generally, of collaboration between companies, between companies and government, between companies and universities, or between groups across national boundaries. In that sense, therefore, the infrastructures of the Alvey and ESPRIT Programmes have a wider significance than merely that which is implied by the technical content of their programmes, important though that is. They constitute experiments in themselves, extending the frontiers of management and administrative science. All of the participants are to differing degrees feeling their way, and the sponsoring governments have expressed no long-term commitment to what might be perceived as an interventionist approach in a key economic area.

In both programmes human resources are severely stretched. In the Alvey Programme, for example, the Directorate has a focal role in policy and strategy generation and implementation, placing contracts and conducting relations with ESPRIT. The eight directors have been seconded from industry, the Department of Trade and Industry, the Ministry of Defence and the Science and Engineering Research Council. They can call on the services of various advisory bodies, but are limited to a maximum of 30 support staff.

The Alvey Programme does not follow all of the recommendations of the Alvey Report. In particular, whereas the report recommended that fundamental research projects should enjoy 90% government support requiring industry to meet only 10% of their costs on long-term research, in the programme companies are obliged to

26   STAR WARS

contribute 50% of their costs, though the costs of academic participants are met in full. Furthermore, it is not now possible to engage in
fundamental research in information technology without an industrial
sponsor, or "uncle".

The Alvey Directorate are playing a coordinating role, providing
support in terms of hardware and communications, and seeking to
form new research consortia and clubs in accordance with the overall
objectives of the programme in enabling technology.

There are undoubted tensions, with varying perceptions as to the
purpose of the programme. Some large companies see it as a programme of government aid to industry, under which they can have
arrangements for contract research with universities on easier terms.
University research groups such as those at Imperial College and
Edinburgh University, whose work is regarded internationally as
central to fifth generation computing, have had some difficulty in
achieving recognition with companies who have not themselves
undertaken research activities.

British expenditure on research and development, apart from in the
military field, has declined significantly by comparison with her
industrial competitors. The Lighthill Report of 1973 led to the
cessation of most government funding for research in artificial intelligence, and companies have continued to disband research groups in
recent years. Many leading firms either are unprepared to plan
beyond the current products under development, or prefer to
accumulate cash reserves, even buying back shares from shareholders.

Brian Oakley complained about short-term thinking in the British
software industry, which has a good international reputation. He
described problems in developing projects in software engineering:

It is very difficult because the software industry is working flat out. It's
growing very fast. The good people can all earn their keep all too easily
and it's a very great temptation, I believe, for the firms not to make the
investment in this field which they know that they should.

The same problem is experienced at ESPRIT with the same firms
and their European counterparts. Penalties are also being paid for the
change that obliges even small companies to meet 50% of their costs.
Oakley observed:

There is no doubt that it is difficult for a small firm to take a proper part
in the Alvey Programme at 50% funding. Frankly I think the real
problem is whether a small company can spare the high quality man-

power that is inevitably required for such work if the time horizon is reasonably long.

Although Oakley has stated the debt the Alvey Programme owes to ICOT in administrative techniques, it is worth noting that the decision was made to set up no equivalent research centre in the United Kingdom. He argues that:

> There is always a danger in the West that if you set up a research centre it then does its own thing and nobody takes any notice because they haven't invented it.

At the same time, an attempt is being made to build up centres of excellence where a critical mass of researchers in enabling technologies has been reached, and to develop means whereby the work of strategically-important groups can be fed into a variety of collaborative projects. This is particularly true of Imperial College, and Edinburgh, Cambridge and Manchester Universities. Particularly in the IKBS area, the Directorate are coordinating specialist national initiatives in an unprecedented manner.

The Alvey Programme has to live with the consequences of previous research approaches and infrastructures, rather than following an established tradition as in Japan. This has surfaced particularly in the negotiation of collaboration agreements for research contracts. Few companies have experience of similar contracts (which in itself has led to the failure of many of their proposals to ESPRIT), and there is little case law on which to build. Critical difficulties remain in the areas predicted above by Geoffrey Robinson. His own company, IBM, is itself the cause of some controversy, having managed to secure funded participation in both the Alvey and ESPRIT Programmes.

Precompetitive collaboration underlies the concept of enabling technologies enshrined in the Alvey Report. It is not so evident in the detailed negotiation of collaboration agreements, many of which turn on the allocation of percentages of royalties to be paid on the sale of "deliverable" items during the progress of the project. Perhaps it is unsurprising in a project with an assured life of only five years, but there is little evidence of long-term thinking among commercial participants. A notable exception would be the research consortium formed to develop the ALICE machine from Imperial College, a highly parallel computer that would appear to have a world lead, initially using the Inmos transputer, and providing a declarative programming environment for logic and functional programming.

The consortium includes ICL, Plessey, Imperial College and Manchester University.

The Alvey Directorate have sought international collaboration, not merely as the British representatives of ESPRIT, but between companies in Britain and Japan. ICL and Logica have also separately established contacts. The Directorate remain sceptical about overseas industrial collaboration with British academics, leading to exploitation of their ideas by Britain's industrial competitors. Researchers from Edinburgh and Imperial College have been visiting scientists at ICOT, and their work with appropriate acknowledgement has been incorporated into ICOT research results.

Industrial collaboration: the European Computer Industry Research Centre (ECRC)

The work of the Centre was presented by its director, Dr Hervé Gallaire, involving the principal computer manufacturers from West Germany (Siemens), France (Bull) and the United Kingdom (ICL). Despite their size they were dwarfed in their home markets by IBM and other overseas companies, and had little experience of the European market outside their own home countries. The Centre exists to help gain an understanding of how each of the companies operate, and how they could develop into new markets.

The principal reason why the collaborating companies established this separate initiative, apart from participating in ESPRIT and their separate national programmes, was that programmes such as ESPRIT did not provide for collaborative research in a common research centre (on the model of ICOT). This seemed to diminish the practical degree of collaboration that was possible, despite the ESPRIT criterion that projects should foster collaboration between companies and countries in the EEC.

The Munich research centre is a meeting place for the companies where they discuss long-term programmes on a regular basis. Collaboration is not seen as precluding competition, especially when one of the goals is to penetrate one another's market.

The Centre has had no public funding, and is concerned with work which may bear fruit in five or ten years. It has 50 researchers, many of them seconded by their companies as a means of technology transfer and exchange. The research themes correspond to those of ESPRIT and Alvey, and some of the researchers may come from universities or public research bodies. Overall, the Centre should be seen as complementary to the other European programmes described, but also tailored to the needs of the company "shareholders" in the Centre.

Industrial collaboration: the Microelectronics and Computer Technology Corporation (MCC)

The work of the MCC was described by Palle Smidt, its Senior Vice President, Programs and Plans. He set MCC in the context of American expenditure of $90bn per annum on research and development, 50% government-funded and 50% industrially funded. Of government-funded research, two-thirds was devoted to defence, of which 90% was development and some 10% applied and basic research. On the industrially funded research, only some 4% was basic research, while 96% was applied research and product development.

MCC was established as a totally private-sector initiative, dealing exclusively in long-term research. It was established for the profit of its shareholders, initially 10 and now 18 in number, who seek to use it to improve their competitiveness. Smidt emphasized that:

> MCC could be the most efficient developer of excellent research results, but if the results can't fast be brought into the commercial environment there would be absolutely no justification for MCC.

Planning was clearly involved in the corporation; for cooperative ventures, for normal business environments and in planning for states and federal governments.

Problems of research infrastructures: just a matter of profit and loss?

As a purely profit-motivated corporation, MCC could take a straightforward approach to issues which seem more complex for those concerned with the other research infrastructures discussed above.

When faced with the question of manpower, Palle Smidt replied:

> We have a very simple issue from an industrial point of view. We have certain requirements and we need certain profiles of experience, and certain profiles of performance, and if they are not available we would take whatever action is required to get them.

By contrast, Brian Oakley, speaking as a director of a programme coordinated by government, found the problem of manpower extremely worrying:

> I have to say that I do not think that we are providing at the moment the

necessary manpower which we will need both to pursue, satisfactorily, programmes like ESPRIT and Alvey, and really, what is more important, to feed the IT industries as they expand. In my view if there is a race for the Fifth Generation it will go to the country which concerns itself most with the provision of high quality manpower.

When asked about the social and economic implications of the work of MCC, Palle Smidt said:

You have to appreciate that, coming from the private sector, the social and economic implications outside our industry are really not that relevant. We have a very simple vision, and that goes both for MCC and our shareholders. If we cannot increase the wealth of our owners, we have no relevance as participants in the business.

The Master of Churchill College, Professor Sir Herman Bondi, expressed a worry about the implications of the information that could now be provided:

What happens to the information that becomes available and accessible through the new technologies? You have to have customers for it who are prepared to pay the very real costs of absorbing information however palatably and nicely it is presented.

Dr Jeremy Bray MP was concerned with the support of intelligent decision-making:

I would also expect us to give strong support to linked decision support systems in government, business, public authorities, education and to individuals, with a high degree of autonomy to the individual persons and agents in the system.

Finally, on considering the scope for international cooperation, Smidt took an equally straightforward approach:

It would be necessary to understand in broad international cooperation, that if one gives something, what will he get in return? If that's not clearly understood, I think the foundation for international cooperation may be less, especially if it is undertaken within the private sector. The political or common view may be somewhat different from that.

In his closing address, David Brandin of SRI explored the case for cooperation between the various research programmes. He observed what they have in common:

They constitute a science race among a collection of handicapped contestants all suffering from the same disability. For example, they all suffer from limited resources. There is not enough money in every programme. There are not enough facilities. There is a duplication of effort in most programmes in most countries, there are overlaps and there are gaps as well. The most serious problem of all is a lack of qualified people. Everybody suffers from a lack of qualified people, and yet all the programmes have the same objectives.

Recognizing the political reasons that would prevent cooperation between all the overlapping programmes, he suggested that the real need in each programme was "to get more people to develop the technology". "Technology transfer", he observed, "takes place primarily with people."

Advanced information technology as if people mattered

Max Bramer, in his review of the Japanese Fifth Generation Computer Project, (Bramer, 1984) notes the emphasis placed there on people:

> People are regarded as the key national resource. The Japanese workforce is probably the most highly educated in the world; ninety-four per cent of children attend school to age eighteen, compared with twenty-two per cent in the UK, and thirty-seven and a half per cent subsequently enter higher education, as against twelve per cent in the UK. Whereas the funding of UK universities has been drastically cut in recent years, the declared long-term aim of the Japanese government is to provide university education for every child.

While education is regarded by government simply as an expense, rather than as an investment in the next generation of citizens, the chances of developing a new generation of technology, let alone of applying it intelligently, are limited. Knowledge-based systems, above all previous technologies, should exploit the expertise of their users and lead them into further learning.

The spread of microcomputers has possibly compounded the problems of education and training, in that it has encouraged the growth of the myth "Teach everyone how to program or make computers and this will generate people who can make better computers". Governments have seized on the attraction of the quick available solution, and have installed large numbers of microcomputers in schools, colleges, and training institutions. Igor Aleksander, Professor in the Management of Information Technology at Imperial College, has examined the problem, and is critical of conventional approaches (Aleksander, 1984):

> Teaching people to make current computer structures and to program them when the research community is endeavouring to alter such

structures out of recognition and to replace programming by more "natural" means of communication (speech, vision, natural language) seems sheer lunacy.

Instead Aleksander recommends a twofold educational focus. Firstly students should be given a heightened understanding of the potential of ideal machines so that they can press for technological improvements rather than feeling threatened by them. Secondly, the kind of managerial opportunities which are created by information technology should form the foundation of most new business studies as well as forming the basis of re-education for current business people.

Re-education is a major problem for computer scientists, programmers and users. The conventional assumptions which have governed computer design and use are being called into question and radically revised. A view of computing that is based on sequential programs for single-processor machines is not adequate to deal with declarative programming of parallel machines. Courses that provide an ill-structured and outdated view of the subject do little service to their students. Experience suggests that a well-educated student in another area of specialism may fare better in knowledge based computing than the product of such a course. As the Alvey Report notes, university departments of computer science in the United Kingdom find it necessary to provide remedial courses for freshman undergraduates who enter with an Advanced Level qualification in computing.

The research community in advanced computing is small, and in its early years has been drawn from a variety of backgrounds. Workers in artificial intelligence, for example, come from the fields of computer science, psychology, linguistics, philosophy, mathematics and logic.

Many of the ablest researchers had early training and professional experience in a different discipline, such as management science or engineering. In order to take an active part in conferences and international collaborations, researchers need a facility in at least one foreign language, even if their first language is English. The argument at researcher level is then strongly in favour of a broadly based education, with experience in formal reasoning; in short, the best of our cultural tradition over the centuries.

A similar account can be given of the educational needs of less academically advanced users of computers. As knowledge-based systems develop further, the user will be more concerned with the correct description of his problem area than with the precise way in which the computer sets about finding a solution. In a declarative programming system, the user will provide a description, or specification, which the system will transform into an efficient program. Many of the traditional roles of the programmer are likely to disappear as the system becomes more intelligent. Programmers, like hand-loom weavers before them, are likely to be displaced by the advancing technology.

The experience of industrial computer users working in advanced research centres on a "technology transfer" basis is similar. It is important to identify a focal problem area, and to develop progressively more effective ways of describing it.

The same knowledge-based technology that is the object of the courses and research projects can be a uniquely powerful tool for education and training. Doubts may be expressed as to the efficacy of today's expert systems as replacements for human experts. Few patients would prefer to be treated by MYCIN instead of a doctor, and few mining companies would rely exclusively on the advice of PROSPECTOR. On the other hand, many American medical schools are making use of MYCIN for teaching diagnostic skills, providing valuable practice and advice to students without necessitating the presence of a human patient or a busy consultant. Systems in PROLOG that represent pieces of legislation can provide information for the lawyer and his client, support for the legal draftsman or training for the student of legal reasoning or civil servant. Such systems are now available on low-cost microcomputers, and are accessible to students from secondary school age.

The same microcomputer technology is now appearing in schools, colleges and commercial companies. The same software is being used to develop expert systems for power stations, to provide intelligent interfaces to large software systems such as statistical models, and to develop classroom materials for the teaching of history and humanities in secondary schools. Experience in the variety of applications areas feeds back to the core research group at Imperial College, and advances in one project can benefit others.

The potential in the field of industrial training is becoming apparent. For some time courses presented to multinational companies have used materials developed in the school classroom. Now that the companies are using the same personal computer hardware, but lack the experienced manpower to direct its use in expert systems applications, they are turning to colleges of further education where joint courses can be developed to meet the education and training needs of both sides, in collaboration with university research groups.

A further pressure on manpower thus develops, for the same small group of researchers concerned with key enabling technologies is also charged with contributing to applications projects both directly and indirectly, and with a technology transfer role working alongside seconded industrial researchers. Furthermore, a university research group will be involved in undergraduate and postgraduate teaching, and with the development of distance learning materials. In such research infrastructures, a great burden of necessity falls on few shoulders, and management systems have to be designed to maximize the effect of their work.

Conclusions

The issue is far broader than research groups and the manpower needs of particular companies. Fifth generation computers are not yet with us, but already powerful expert systems technology is available on low-cost machines. The technology has already partially escaped the control of its erstwhile political and commercial masters. How is it to be used, and by whom? Information technology is not of itself political, but in its use it is a powerful political tool. Wealthy political parties have used computer facilities for sophisticated opinion polling and election mailings. Such facilities could be provided for all. Governments use computers to help minimize their social security expenditure. They could also be used to help claimants obtain their full entitlements.

In one sense the issue does not just concern our relationship with computers and expert systems. It concerns our relationships with experts, and the way we solve problems in society. In the field of expert systems we have learnt to ask our system to explain its reasoning and conduct an intelligible dialogue. We have all encountered human experts who have been reluctant to do either. If we receive clear explanations from a legal or medical expert system, how will this affect our relationship with a human lawyer or doctor? Will some major professions be obliged to change their methods of working, affecting the social and economic infrastructure?

Interactive problem-solving systems, of which we have some glimpses with small example programs, raise further questions. To be most effective there will be an exchange of questions and answers between the user and the system, using perhaps symmetry between the two as a design principle, with the system drawing on large databases and collections of rules. Are there some questions which we are not prepared to answer, or which we wish to prevent the system or user from being able to ask? Will we revise our views of Freedom of Information legislation if access to information really is in the hands of the ordinary citizen? Do we live in a democratic society if knowledge and consequent power are concentrated in the hands of a minority?

Computer scientists are not accustomed to dealing with issues of politics and philosophy, which have not normally formed part of their education or professional background. The new generation of computers is too powerful to be left in the hands of the computer scientists. The new research infrastructure, if it is to produce the industrial applications for the social and economic benefit of society, must progressively broaden informed access to the technology.

References and suggestions for further reading

Aleksander, I. (1984). Myths that are spoiling Britain's IT chances. *Guardian*, 12th September.

Alvey, J. (1982). *A Programme for Advanced Information Technology. The Report of the Alvey Committee*. London; HMSO.

Benson, I. & Lloyd, J. (1983) *New Technology and Industrial Change*. London; Kogan Page. New York; Nichols.

Bernal, J.D. (1954). *Science in History*. London; C.A. Watts.

Bramer, M. (1984). The Japanese Fifth Generation Computer Project. In *New Information Technology*, ed. A. Burns. Chichester; Ellis Horwood.

Ennals, J.R. (1985). The importance of PROLOG in *The role of programming in Teaching Informatics*, ed. M. Griffiths & E.D. Tagg. Amsterdam; North Holland.

Ennals, J.R., & Cotterell, A. (1985). *Fifth Generation Computers: Their Implications for Further Education*. London; Department of Education and Science.

Hayes, J.E. & Michie, D. (eds.) (1983). *Intelligent Systems: The Unprecedented Opportunity*. Chichester; Ellis Horwood.

Servan-Schreiber, J.-J. (1981). *The World Challenge*. London; Collins.

Toffler, A. (1980). *The Third Wave*. London; Pan.

THE STRATEGIC DEFENCE INITIATIVE

2.1
Changing British Government Policy on the Strategic Defence Initiative

The computer science community, with the lead taken from Edinburgh University and Imperial College, have made it clear in letters to Vice-President Bush and Mrs Thatcher in the autumn of 1985 that they are vigorously opposed to participation in the Strategic Defence Initiative (SDI). The Imperial College letter to Mrs Thatcher gave three principal reasons:

1. Enormous dependence will be placed on computer decision-making tools which, by the nature of the project, can never be adequately tested in realistic conditions.

   We do not currently have the tools to construct such large and complex systems with the necessary reliability, knowing that a false alarm could trigger off a nuclear war, and do not believe that these tools will be developed in the proposed duration of the SDI project.

   It is therefore our judgement that the project is infeasible.
2. The SDI could divert much of our very scarce human and technological resources away from the much-needed rejuvenation of UK industry that we would all like to see.

   There is already a shortage of trained personnel for current projects in advanced IT which money alone will not overcome.
3. Although we are speaking as scientists, we cannot ignore the impact of our participation on the political process.

From *END Journal*, February 1986.

Should the project ultimately prove to be infeasible, as we believe it will, its very continuance could by that time have led to an abandonment of existing treaties and to a new "Star Wars Race" between East and West.

Moreover, we are concerned that promises of neutralization of the nuclear threat may inflate people's hopes beyond the stated goals of the project so that it develops an unstoppable momentum, regardless of its merits.

The letter was not to my knowledge acknowledged or answered.

Computing and Social Responsibility groups have been formed on many campuses, drawing on the experience of the American Computing Professionals for Social Responsibility. They have sought to raise the awareness of the broader scientific and political community regarding SDI. Despite this, there was no discussion of SDI in the House of Commons before December 1985. In this paper I want to review the limited Parliamentary discussion of SDI since the signing of the Memorandum of Understanding on 6th December 1985, and to then concentrate on the way ahead, on the strategy to be adopted to ensure that the Government's policy is changed.

The policy of "open government" that became a feature of the Westland affair is beginning belatedly to spread to the issue of SDI. There follows an extract from the text of a letter from a senior official in the Department of Education and Science in response to a letter from a senior industrialist who had expressed concern regarding the effects of SDI participation on civil research programmes such as the Alvey Programme:

May I start by saying that we are becoming aware from a number of sources, including your letter, that there is a degree of misunderstanding in the academic community about the nature of the Memorandum of Understanding (MoU) agreed between the US and UK Governments last month. We shall shortly be writing to inform universities of the actual situation, and we shall also take steps to ensure that higher and further education institutions in the public sector are informed.

The MoU is a facilitating agreement, one of whose purposes is to safeguard the position of UK firms, academic researchers and government research establishments if they wish to become involved with SDI contracts. It allows them to participate on a clearly defined basis in contracts that will be on offer, and safeguards British interests in relation to the ownership of intellectual property rights and technology transfer arising from SDI-related work. The MOU neither commits any UK institution or individual to become involved with SDI, nor does it commit the US Department of Defence to offer any particular level of contracts to the UK.

In order to provide advice within the UK on SDI contracts a small SDI Participation Office (SDIPO) has been set up in the Ministry of Defence. One of the SDIPO's staff, Mr George Gallagher-Daggitt, has been provided by this Department. His task is to give help and advice to any academic research group considering tendering for an SDI contract, especially on aspects such as the need to ensure that the contract's terms are based on full economic cost, and embody satisfactory arrangements for the ownership of intellectual property rights.

There is no intention to phase out the Alvey Programme in favour of SDI. Indeed we are aware of the risk that SDI might attract so many UK groups that progress on other important work such as the Alvey Programme might be slowed down. No single organization can be responsible for preventing this happening, but we are taking steps we can to that end . . . I might add that I know that the Department of Trade and Industry and the Ministry of Defence are also well aware of it.

But there is another side to the coin. The opportunity to participate in SDI contracts is likely to benefit the UK economy, civil as well as military. In this connection I would draw your attention to Mr Michael Heseltine's answer to Mr Piers Merchant in the House of Commons on 9 December, which is on the same Hansard page as, and immediately below, the exchange between Mr Chris Smith and Mr Heseltine to which your letter drew attention.

The passage in Hansard (9th December 1985, column 633) referred to was as follows:

Mr Chris Smith (Islington South and Finsbury):
Can the Secretary of State give the House any guarantee that the agreement will not divert resources, time and research capacity into military purposes from the extremely important civil work on advanced information technology, at present being carried out under the Alvey programme, which could promote the future of British industry and jobs?

Mr Heseltine:
No one could be more enthusiastic about the Alvey Programme than I am; the Government are wholly involved in the concept, which we created. We give it great priority. I cannot technically give the categorical answer which the hon Gentleman seeks. However, there is as much ground for believing that the civil spin-off from the sort of programmes about which I am talking today will be at least as big as, if not bigger than, any diversion of resources in any one company which might occur.

Mr Piers Merchant (Newcastle upon Tyne, Central):
Will my right hon Friend confirm that the SDI research proposals are neither about stars nor wars, as the Opposition would seem to have us believe, but are about scientific advance and peace? Will he further

confirm that the spin-off in jobs and industrial advance for British industry could be as great as the advance which flowed from the original United States space program?

Mr Heseltine:
My hon Friend raises an important historical precedent. For the United States of America, the advance in terms of military and industrial capability in technology will undoubtedly be of the order of magnitude associated with that earlier programme. Therefore, the issue for Britain is whether we wish to share in this research opportunity in a way that we did not on the earlier occasion. My belief, without the slightest shadow of doubt, is that in sharing in it, and gaining the civil and military benefit from it, we shall be taking the sort of opportunity that we would have been wise to take on that earlier occasion.

Another issue alluded to during the 9th December 1985 question and answer session (column 634) concerned the opening of the new National Space Centre, sharing premises in Millbank Tower with the Alvey Directorate, which was announced on the final day of the Geneva summit (see *The Times* and *The Guardian* for 21st November 1985):

Sir Eldon Griffiths (Bury St Edmunds):
As one who saw at first hand how much Britain lost by rejecting the opportunities that President Kennedy offered us in space exploration, I greatly welcome what my right hon Friend and the Prime Minister have achieved to ensure that we do not lose out on the next half-century's development.

What is to be the relationship between the new SDI Participation Office and the National Space Agency recently set up? Will my right hon Friend confirm to the Opposition that the project is going ahead, and that the only question is whether it will be with us or without us?

Mr Heseltine:
As my hon Friend rightly says, there is no question but that the Americans are determined to pursue the research programme, and we shall not have any opportunity to prevent it, for the very best of reasons – that we are already doing it ourselves and do not want to prevent it. As my hon Friend says, the issue is whether we do it in partnership. I believe him to be correct, because the opportunities for Britain are considerable.

The Space Agency is sponsored by the Department of Trade and Industry, and there are representatives of the Ministry of Defence on it, just as, within the Strategic Defence Initiative Office, there will be representatives of the Department of Trade and Industry. There will be a very close relationship, if it is relevant, and it could well be.

Michael Rowan-Robinson, in his speech on 16th January, noted that vast areas of astronomy, past present and future, have been declared to be "part of SDI research".

On 9th December 1985, technical issues were raised in the House of Commons (column 631):

Mr Tam Dalyell (Linlithgow):
Does the Secretary of State agree that Edinburgh University probably has the most distinguished department of artificial intelligence in Europe, and, indeed, in the world, including the United States? Did he hear the public doubts raised by Edinburgh University scientists, not only about the difficulty of testing any such system, which is a thousand times more complicated than any personal computer, but on other grounds? Is the Secretary of State prepared to have his chief scientist or senior scientists meet those who have doubts at Edinburgh University about the militarization problem? Is the complaint of British scientists who may have expected to be consulted but who were not consulted fair or unfair?

Mr Heseltine:
I shall make arrangements for any meetings to give effect to the hon Gentleman's suggestion.

Mr Heseltine was invited to address the Parliamentary Information Technology Committee on SDI in November, and subsequently to address a joint meeting of PITCOM and the Parliamentary and Scientific Committee, both chaired by Conservative MPs who are deeply concerned. No such meetings took place prior to Mr Heseltine's resignation. We must now expect the joint meeting to be addressed by both Mr Heseltine and his successor, Mr Younger, to whom the invitation has been extended.

It has been very hard for scientists and concerned industrialists and civil servants to obtain answers to key questions concerning SDI. The Computing and Social Responsibility group at Imperial College wrote to the Ministry of Defence in early December, asking to meet an MOD representative to discuss the technical feasibility of the SDI, a matter which was the subject of a special meeting of the British Computer Society on 13th December. Here is an excerpt from the reply from an MOD official, dated 19th December 1985:

I am afraid it will not be possible to meet your request. The extent to which public servants can publicly discuss matters bearing on Government policy is by long-standing practice severely circumscribed. Equally to the point, however, the SDI is a research programme addressing precisely the sort of questions which you yourselves are considering. It is not therefore the technical feasibility of the SDI which is at issue so much as the validity of the answers which may (or may not) emerge from it at some point in the future. Since they have however not yet emerged, it follows that there is little to discuss.

On the contrary, there is a great deal to discuss. It seems to me that decisions have been taken in secret and in defiance of scientific and administrative advice. There was no parliamentary debate prior to signature of the Memorandum of Understanding and none of the many civil service advisers known to me can be persuaded to speak in its favour. I have received correspondence from Members of Parliament of all parties expressing their grave concern at the threat to civil research, jobs and industry posed by British participation in SDI, apart from their varying views on strategic, moral and political issues. Democracy itself is threatened by the lack of discussion in Parliament and the media, and SDI is advertized as providing a "peace shield" for democracy. It is horrifying for those who had believed the Hollywood account to find that the emphasis at the Pentagon, as evidenced by statements by a spokesman at the Pugwash Conference on 6th December 1986, is on point defence of missile sites. For those who welcomed a non-nuclear defence system the details of the X-ray laser, tested in the Goldstone test in Nevada on 28th December, and preventing a Comprehensive Test Ban Treaty, are the realization of a nightmare.

It is incumbent on those opposing SDI to offer alternative policies. Opposition to SDI transcends all party, class, scientific and professional barriers. A consensus is emerging that SDI and the present mode of collaboration entered into by the British Government is offensive to a free country, and that the policy must be changed. If the established democratic institutions cannot accomplish that change and choose between alternatives, then their own future is thrown into doubt. There must be a free and open debate, not simply dominated by the lure of lucrative American contracts. Scientists have to participate in the democratic process if the process is to continue. I would hope that any prospective Parliamentary candidate from any party should be able to rely on assistance in presenting his or her case against British involvement in SDI, and that organizations such as the United Nations Association and Greenpeace will join in offering all-party discussion meetings. Democracy is at present imperilled by mistaken attempts at its "defence".

I close with some questions to be explored by politicians and journalists:

1. What restrictions will be imposed on academic freedom by parti-

cipation in SDI? What security conditions and rights of access to laboratories have been agreed by government on behalf of scientists in the Memorandum, which is to be "secret in perpetuity"?

2. What impact will SDI participation have on international research collaboration under ESPRIT, EUREKA, UNESCO, the British Council, the Royal Society? Will overseas academics be subjected to security screening?

3. Are government, through the University Grants Committee, already abandoning information technology as a lost cause and seeking to establish courses in optoelectronics to complement SDI-funded work?

4. Given the latest public expenditure figures, which show projected cuts in expenditure on education and support for industry, is it not the case that British civil funding is being replaced by American military funding, to the detriment of British industry and society?

5. What is to be the fate of fundamental scientific research, in the face of SDI and the new joint MOD/research council grants?

6. What research in British academic and research institutions is currently supported by American military funds? How and to what end are the results exploited?

7. Who is taking a long-term view of research, development and training in Britain at a time when short-term monetary targets and the reduction of public expenditure are pre-eminent?

8. Is there going to be a free democratic society in Britain in which my children can live at peace?

The policy of collaboration with SDI must and will be changed. A new Secretary of State for Defence could choose to suspend the Memorandum of Understanding and review the situation. It could require a change of government. If the issue is not addressed by Parliament, the political parties and the media the consequences will be grave. Scientists must realize that they have the power to affect the policy. They can withhold their labour from SDI. They can ask questions and organize. They can become politically aware and active. Silence at this time constitutes assent. If one works for a government department one is obliged to implement the policies determined by the government of the day, or to resign. There was no period of discussion when alternative approaches were explored prior to the signing of the secret Memorandum. Placed in this position, I resigned from the Government's Alvey Programme for research and development in advanced information technology, and thus from my position of Research Manager in artificial intelligence and parallel computing at Imperial College, the largest centre of Alvey research. I now hope to assist in changing the policy, and developing peaceful uses of the technology in education and training.

2.2

Star Wars: SDI and the Corruption of British Science

It is all too easy to dismiss Star Wars as a Hollywood fantasy, as a dream retold by an ageing "B movie" actor and dressed up as primary school science. It has become more than that, as the research phase of the Strategic Defence Initiative has a provisional budget of $26 billion, and the costs of full implementation of a system would be truly astronomical. It has been authenticated, not only by the interested parties of the American military-industrial complex, but by a secret Memorandum of Understanding between the British and American Governments that lasted from 6th December 1985 until 5th March 1986, when the Pentagon investigation team was sent packing from Britain through the collaborative activity of the British research, Civil Service and defence contracting communities, aided by courageous investigative journalism, debate led by the peace movement, and the parliamentary pressure of politicans of all parties. Government had the wisdom to think again, aware of the damage that the continuance of the secret agreement would cause to its civil programme, budget statement and electoral plans.

Paul Hopler is chief technology analyst responsible for updating the Pentagon Militarily Critical Technologies List. His brief is to classify those technologies which the American Administration, together with NATO allies, and Japan through COCOM, want to withhold from the

From a lecture given at Queen Mary College Computer Centre as their Annual Lecture, part of the Centenary Celebrations of the College, on 12th March 1986.

Warsaw Pact (and others). Paul Walton interviewed him for *Infomatics* (3rd March 1986). What follows are direct quotations from Hopler:

> The general programme is looking at the foreign capability for technology. I had close links with a portion of the SDI Office. My mission in life is to determine what are the technologies that are critical to defence that we would not want the Soviets to know about.

> We are trying to re-define what other items they might be interested in that we don't already have.
> There's a lot of judgement involved. We're not necessarily going to go into all companies in all countries, although I am sure that we will in Great Britain.
> Great Britain is in a very peculiar position. We already have a signed agreement on SDI. This is one of the political aspects of what I am doing: does it mean I have more freedom, or less?
> We are coming to Great Britain to talk about advanced technologies, the SDI type of thing's along with it.

Hopler thought that the British Government's approval would be required:

> I think so – but the situation is fluid, it changes every day. Whatever, we're coming.

Hopler did not object to publicity about the study:

> It wouldn't bother me, except that all the people I talk to here are very nervous about what I'm doing. People want to know what is happening. It may eventually cause some hassles, but I'm just going to have to deal with that.
> I guess the biggest concern is "am I really doing a study into SDI?" I am saying "Hey, I'm a technologist. I study all technologies, now including those in SDI". So I'm not doing an SDI study. I'm doing a study of the technologies associated with SDI. If it comes across as if I am doing a study into SDI people get very nervous.

One eminent spokesman in the computer industry Dr William Bardow, Director of Research for GEC-Marconi confided:

> If the Americans are really saying, "We've come to take a look at what you're capable of in case you want to take part in SDI," we'd tell them to piss off. No firm is going to work under those conditions.

He proved true to his word.
Hopler felt sure that his study would go ahead, meeting its April

deadline for the completed report, so long as Britain is signatory to the
Memorandum of Understanding. But he was cautious of avoiding the
political flak, particularly given the conflict over Westland and the BL
sale, and the apparent lack of interest in SDI contract work amongst
British firms. He described the kind of conversation he had been
having, on handling the politics of the affair, with the State Department:

> Thatcher is saying, "Why are you studying all this while we are dealing
> with you on the MoU . . . why are you doing this independently of us
> when we are supposed to be working together?"
>
> And I'm saying . . . "I don't think I'm doing anything directly in
> conflict with that." But some people worry that I might.
>
> If it comes across as if I'm doing a study for, and of, SDI, they may get
> very nervous. So I'm trying to abstract myself from the SDI pro-
> gramme and the SDI Office. I'm looking at any kind of technology, I
> just want to know what technologies might have a military use.

Paul Walton concluded his article by saying:

> Completion of the study, and the classification of British research, is by
> no means a foregone conclusion.

He was right. On the day after his article was published the Cabinet
met, already under attack from all parties including their own former
leader Edward Heath. Former industry minister Norman Tebbit
had fought an unsuccessful rearguard action on 3rd March. It was
time for wiser counsels to prevail. The Pentagon team was sent
home on Wednesday morning. Mr Ken Hambledon, head of the
Ministry of Defence SDI Participation Office had refused to give
Clarence Robinson clearance to discuss classification of research
with British companies.

The incident is excellently described in *The Financial Times* for 8th
March 1986, by Peter Marsh, in an article entitled "Mystery tour
leaves MOD in the dark". He found Clarence Robinson curiously
defensive when he contacted him at his home in Vienna, Virginia. Mr
Robinson said:

> I'm not going to talk to you. You talk to the Pentagon. Whatever I say,
> you're going to twist.

On talking to the Pentagon, reporters were referred to the State
Department, to the US Embassy in London, to the Ministry of
Defence. A rich variety of contradictory accounts of events was made
available. Even at this stage, the various parties to the Memorandum
of Understanding showed few signs of understanding either the
problem or each other. The Memorandum must be regarded as
defunct, and this is a contribution to its obituary: in the words of

ICL's advertizing slogan: "We should be talking to each other".

The SDI episode, already part of political history, can be seen as reflecting some of the strength of our democratic system, a system which goes far deeper than the periodic exercize of general elections. By the same token, it casts some stark light on British science. SDI cannot simply be regarded as a cause of the corruption of British science, but a symptom of its diseased state. It has been taken for granted that scientists are for sale, and that they should have no say in the applications of their work. The reasoned stand in recent months by computer scientists against involvement in a project which their discipline and experience tells them is infeasible was long overdue. British scientists have benefited from the lead taken by American scientific colleagues, and there is some cause for optimism if that spirit of social and political awareness can be maintained.

It is an indictment of British science and its influence in the political world that Star Wars was allowed to go so far. I am concerned here not so much with the undoubted corrupting effects of SDI on the future of British Science, and with the ill-advized antics of British political leaders, but with what the Star Wars question has revealed about the current corrupt state of British science. To quote Sir Ian Lloyd MP, Chairman of the Parliamentary Information Technology Committee and scientific critic of SDI in the House of Commons on 19th February 1986: "We have found the enemy, and he is us". (In *Intelligent Systems: the Unprecedented Opportunity*, ed. Jean & Donald Michie, Ellis Horwood 1983).

It is not my purpose to be anti-American. My family have been in Virginia since the eighteenth century and I was an English-Speaking Union scholar at Phillips Academy, Andover, many years after Vice-President Bush attended the school, and four years ahead of Dr David Schwartz of the Institute of Strategic Studies, until recently Director of Strategic Nuclear Defense Policy for the United States State Department.

Dr Schwartz and I were taught the same courses in American History, based on the American Constitution: we are both familiar with the 1868 14th Amendment to the Constitution which prevents the restrictions of the rights, liberty and property of the citizen without "due process of law". No state could "make any law which shall . . . deny to any person . . . equal protection of the law." This amendment, arising from concerns for civil rights in the post civil war reconstruction era, has a long history as a block to attempted legislation and state action in the economic and corporate sphere. Precedents include the cases of Munn v Illinois 1876, E.C. Knight and Co. v US 1895, Plessey v Ferguson 1896, Smith v Ames 1898, Lochner v

New York 1905, Muller v Oregon 1908, Loewe v Lawlor 1908, Standard Oil v US 1911, Hammer v Dagenhart 1918, Bailey v Drexel Furniture 1922, US Steel v US 1920, US v Butler *et al.* 1933, Schechter Poultry v US 1935, West Coast Hotel v Parrish 1937, Mitchell v US 1941, Sipruel v Board of Regents of University of Oklahoma *et al.* 1948, Brown v Topeka 1954. There are many other cases which Dr Schwartz and I both studied, as the backbone of a constitutional approach to American history. To the extent that American legislation is applied extraterritorially in the United Kingdom there appears to be a case for invoking such precedents and seeking guidance from the Supreme Court, concerning the rights of UK citizens, whose interests are not visibly represented and for whom there was no "due process of law" preceding the extra-Parliamentary Memorandum of Understanding.

In the United States, SDI has been subject to "due process of law". In the United Kingdom, a secret agreement was reached in private without public discussion. There are ample precedents, such as those cited above, for well-intentioned legislation being declared invalid by the US Supreme Court (this happened particularly during the presidencies of Woodrow Wilson and Franklin Roosevelt, disabling their attempts at social reforms). Our American legal colleagues would have been delighted to help us where the British legal system, in the absence of a constitution, has failed. If the threat returns we will seek their assistance.

I have discussed these issues at some length with General Abrahamson, Director of the SDI Programme, and Dr David Schwartz. They have been commendably open about their work. The same cannot be said for the British Government, which seems to have been struck down by "An Intelligence Deficiency Syndrome,"(AIDS) retreating into Trappist silence. Only when defence contractors such as GEC Marconi sought clarification of the position of the Ministry of Defence regarding jurisdiction over the classification of their high technology research was the courageous decision made to reconsider the British position.

Secrecy remains a cancer nibbling at the core of British intellectual life. This time it did not prove fatal, but it remains a suitable case for treatment. Should we not give up secrecy while we still have a choice?

Just as it would be mistaken to regard SDI as an excuse for anti-Americanism, it would be ill-advised for scientists to use SDI as a crude stick with which to beat the British Government and political leaders. The corruption, the cancer, is more widespread and deep-seated. He who pays the piper often calls the tune. Look in the mirror when you shave or apply your make-up in the morning: are there visible signs of corruption? If there is an increase in the number of bearded scientists we will draw our own conclusions: is this why Ross Perot, winner of the Winston Churchill Award for Anglo-American collaboration, and founding chairman of the General Motors subsidiary Electronic Data Services, employs only clean-shaven computer scientists? How many scientists could shave every day with a cut-throat razor? If not, how could they consider entrusting the defence of our planet to an automatic, untested system?

My involvement in recent years has been with computer science, at Imperial College, in the Alvey Programme, in the European ESPRIT Programme, and in international projects concerned with education and training. Just as physicists were placed under new pressures by the Manhattan project, my colleagues in computer science face new pressures from Fifth Generation Computer Programmes and from the Strategic Defence Initiative. I want to draw on the experience and wisdom of distinguished computer scientists before looking at the particular position of British science. Some of the issues that follow were raised at the British Computer Society meeting on 13th December 1985 to discuss the professional implications of participation in projects that are technically infeasible, with particular attention to cases such as SDI where such participation could cause a damaging distraction of effort and resources from collaborative civil research and development programmes. These issues will also be raised at the Pugwash conference on 14th April, and at meetings around the United Kingdom in the coming weeks, organized by bodies such as the United Nations Association, Greenpeace, European Nuclear Disarmament, Medical Campaign Against Nuclear Weapons, Computing and Social Responsibility, the Parliamentary Information Technology Committee, Campaign for Nuclear Disarmament, FREEZE, and the Parliamentary and Scientific Committee. Such questions transcend party politics, but address fundamental questions of democracy and science.

I wish to draw on the work of four courageous computer scientists: Professor Edsger Dijkstra, Professor David Parnas, Emeritus Professor Manny Lehman and Dr Henry Thompson. Each is concerned with the use of their work in the wider world.

Professor Edsger Dijkstra wrote "How do we tell truths that might hurt" in 1975, and it was reprinted in an issue of SIGPLAN in 1982. Some excerpts of this paper are worthy of our consideration today:

> Sometimes we discover unpleasant truths. Whenever we do so, we are in difficulties. Suppressing them is scientifically dishonest, so we must tell

them, but telling them, however, will fire back on us. If the truths are sufficiently unpalatable, our audience is psychically incapable of accepting them, and we will be written off as totally unrealistic, hopelessly idealistic, dangerously revolutionary, foolishly gullible, or what have you. (Besides that, telling such truths is a sure way of making oneself unpopular in many circles, and, as such, it is an act that, in general, is not without personal risks. Vide Galileo Galilei.) . . .

Is not our prolonged silence fretting away Computer Science's intellectual integrity? Are we decent by remaining silent? If not, how do we speak up? . . .

The tools we use have a profound (and devious) influence on our thinking habits, and therefore, on our thinking abilities . . .

We can found no scientific discipline, nor a healthy profession, on the technical mistakes of the Department of Defence, and mainly, one computer manufacturer . . .

In the good old days physicists repeated each other's experiments, just to be sure. Today they stick to FORTRAN, so that they can share each other's programs, bugs included . . .

About the use of language: it is impossible to sharpen a pencil with a blunt axe. It is equally vain to try to do it with ten blunt axes instead . . .

Projects promoting programming in "natural language" are intrinsically doomed to fail . . .

What are we going to do? Return to the order of the day, presumably.

On 28th June 1985 Professor David Parnas resigned from the SDIO Panel on Computing in Support of Battle Management. The technical arguments that he gave for regarding the SDI Programme as infeasible remain unanswered. His papers explained:

1. The fundamental technological differences between software engineering and other areas of engineering, and why software is unreliable.
2. The properties of the proposed SDI software that make it unattainable.
3. Why the techniques commonly used to build military software are inadequate for this job.
4. The nature of research in Software Engineering, and why the improvements that it can effect will not be sufficient to allow construction of a truly reliable strategic defence system.
5. The nature of research in Artificial Intelligence, and why I do not expect it to help in building reliable military software.
6. The history of research in Automatic programming, and why I do not expect it to bring about the substantial improvements that are needed.
7. Why Program Verification cannot give us a reliable strategic defence battle management software system.
8. Why the SDI Office is an inappropriate vehicle for funding research.

In March 1983 the President asked us, as members of the scientific community, to provide the means of rendering nuclear weapons impotent and obsolete. I believe that it is our duty, as scientists and engineers, to reply that we have no technological magic that will accomplish that. The short term applied research and focused development that SDI is now funding is not going to solve the problem; the President and the public should know that.

Emeritus Professor Manny Lehman accepted a personal consultancy to advise on software evolution, software maintenance, and the programming process with respect to SDI. In a memorandum to his colleagues at Imperial College on 5th November 1985 he set out the moral basis of his decision:

> In so far as morality is concerned there are three distinct issues to be considered:
> 1. *Involvement in any defence or government directed research programme*: I do not seek such activity but will, if asked, get involved provided that I am satisfied there is a significant defensive (as distinct from offensive) element to the programme, or if involvement is likely to produce significant side benefits outside the scope of the project.
> 2. *Working on a project whose objectives are unrealistic*: Provided one has clearly stated that project objectives, as stated, appear unachievable, and provided one can identify alternative goals for the work to be undertaken, for example clarifying what can and what cannot be done and why, there seems to be no moral problem of this type in involvement.
> 3. *Restrictions on intellectual property rights and/or publication rights*: I would not be prepared to accept limitation of this type other than on publication rights of material prepared at the behest of the contractor.
>
> Two significant benefits may accrue from my SDI involvement. Firstly, the problem of developing software technology that overcomes the threat of software pollution is an urgent one. SDI is an extreme example of the challenges that face system and software designers everywhere . . .
>
> Secondly, claims are being made and objectives set as to the benefit to be derived from SDI. We who know that the system is not feasible, that the claims are incorrect and that, therefore, any benefit stems from side-effects, have the duty to demonstrate scientific and technological reasons for our views: the intrinsic nature of the problem that makes it about as unrealistic as a project to build a projectile whose speed exceeds the speed of light. Only activity from within can develop a technically convincing case.

Dr Henry Thompson of Edinburgh University was one of the founders of the American Computing Professionals for Social Responsibility, and of the British Computing and Social Responsibility.

He wrote an article entitled "Why scientists are speaking out" in *New Scientist* for 21st November 1985:

> People are uncertain about the wider significance of their work and its relationship to social and political issues which concern them. Sharing their concern with others proves beneficial – talking about it helps clarify what one thinks and how one ought to act.
>
> Whatever the cause, the perception among scientists is clear: there is no one in Whitehall who is competent to understand technical arguments about issues of any significant complexity.
>
> As computer scientists, we know what computer systems are like, what they can and cannot do. Not one of us, or I am confident any other responsible computer scientist, could ever literally or figuratively turn the switch which placed the means for starting a nuclear war under fully automatic unsupervised control. From that it follows that it would be profoundly and morally dishonest to connive at the creation of any programme with that as its stated goal.
>
> We have moved from the purely private goal, of clarifying for ourselves why the system cannot be built, to the public goal of developing a sufficient popular awareness of this fact to make a political impact on the government.
>
> There is no value-free science, but, until recently, in disciplines other than nuclear physics at any rate, scientists have, by and large, been happy to allow their governments to make scientific policy decisions. We no longer believe the government capable of grasping the complexity of the issues involved, or of making sensible decisions in the absence of such understanding.

There has been vigorous scientific debate in the United States on the technical issues underlying SDI since President Reagan announced the programme in 1983, outstripping the imagination of even his closest advisers. In Britain, the public debate has only commenced after the Government has entered into secret agreements regarding British participation. This is a sorry reflection on British science, its insularity, its isolation from the world of politics and economic decision-making, its professional divisions and academic compartmentalization. How can we in all honesty blame our political masters for lacking knowledge of science when scientists show little knowledge of or interest in politics, even as it impinges on their area of professional expertise? C.P. Snow has been proved all too right in his account of the "Two Cultures". I too have now walked in some of the corridors of power. Little has changed. SDI is not simply a harbinger of a new era of corruption, but the tip of an existing iceberg.

We must as a matter of urgency try to analyse some of the signs and symptoms of what I pray may not be a terminal disease for science and humankind. Some of my concerns are expressed in Douglas Adams' analysis of the destruction of the earth to make way for an intergalactic by-pass in *Hitchhiker's Guide to the Galaxy*. He advises: "Don't Panic!", but at all times "remember where your towel is". If you are lucky, you might encounter a Babel-fish to stick in your ear, offering universal natural language understanding beyond the dreams of the Fifth Generation. On a bad day you may have to talk to a depressed android or an obsequious lift, possibly one of Professor Mike Brady's promised intelligent robots. "42" is the answer to the ultimate question. But what was the question that triggered science? As a nation of telephone sanitizers, advertizing sales executives, chartered accountants and other service industries we should be reminded before it is too late. Is the universe indeed an experiment controlled by white mice? How would we know? (Toothmarks in the cheese).

Scientists must address the big questions, seeking to understand but not replicate "Life, the Universe and Everything Else", before we meet up at the "Restaurant at the End of the Universe". The illusion of technological invincibility must be abandoned, as scientists recognize how little they know and understand. Humankind needs scientists to contribute to the solution of real human problems of hunger, ignorance and deprivation, rather than just offering technological solutions in search of a military problem. We need there to be a world in another hundred years. It should not be demolished to make way for an intergalactic by-pass.

2.3
Star Wars Super Sale: The Scramble Behind the Headlines

US witholds guarantees

From March 1985 Michael Heseltine, with the assistance of Geoffrey Pattie, was engaged in secret discussion with Casper Weinberger and the American Pentagon. These talks were described in the optimistic press releases from the Ministry of Defence that were intended to precede the autumn announcement of £1 billion of British SDI contracts, providing work for defence contractors in unemployment blackspots in marginal constituencies. Mrs Thatcher was concerned to strike a quick deal, possibly having been embarrassed by the failure of the Plessey PTARMIGAN system, with her support, to win a large US military communications contract, with heavy consequences in unemployment among defence contractors. A number of factors, including the fiasco of the GCHQ Cyprus secrets trial, and the reluctance of the US Congree to subsidize overseas companies, led the US to withold all of the requested guarantees regarding the scale of contracts and technology transfer.

Scientists' stance

In October 1985, US military contractors were visiting British research groups to assess the potential for SDI collaboration. At Imper-

From *Liberation*, March 1986

ial College I received a group from United Technologies on October 15th, as part of a visit which included discussions over the Sikorsky involvement in Westland. The delegation was led by a former senior Pentagon official, who described himself as having been:

> chief custodian of President Reagan's nuclear stockpile and principal architect of his SALT negotiating position.

The talk was of work at Imperial College in parallel computers, artificial intelligence and expert systems, of military contracts and the Strategic Defence Initiative. I was proud to be able to state that none of the computer scientists who I represented at the meeting were prepared to be involved in such work, and that we had written to the Prime Minister to that effect. (See Chapter 2.1). The visit led to considerable discussion at Imperial College, in the computing press, and at a special meeting of the British Computer Society on 13th December.

The FLAGSHIP project

Let us focus on events in early December 1985, contemporaneous with the events of the Westland affair, and with many of the same participants. On December 2nd the Alvey Board, in charge of Britain's collaborative research programme in advanced information technology, approved a national initiative, of which I was coordinator, in the field of logic programming, the core technology for fifth generation computer software. On 3rd December the Alvey Directorate launched FLAGSHIP, a world-leading project to build highly parallel computers, involving ICL, Plessey, Imperial College and Manchester University, and closely linked to the MAST (Machine Assisted Speech Transcription) Demonstrator Project, building a speech-driven desktop workstation.

Heseltine signs secret memorandum of understanding

On 6th December, without any public discussion, Michael Heseltine, in front of hastily assembled TV cameras, signed the Memorandum of Understanding (secret in perpetuity, but leaked to *Aviation Weekly* in January 1986).

Continuing uproar

We now switch our focus to the first week of February 1986. Heseltine and Brittan have gone. The news was leaked that the Government proposed to split British Leyland and sell most of the parts to General Motors and Ford (both of which have subsidiaries engaged in SDI work).

'After Alvey'

The instant Parliamentary outcry led to the heir to Guinness, Paul Channon, in a stroke of genius, cancelling the negotiations with Ford. The following morning came the unnoticed announcement from Geoffrey Pattie that some weeks previously Sir Austin Bide, Chairman of British Leyland, had agreed to chair the "After Alvey" Committee, to report by October 1986 on future support for British advanced information technology. Government suggested that little new public money would be forthcoming but that closer cooperation with Europe was envisaged.

Policy in shreds

The policy of collaboration with Europe is in shreds as it is feared that the technology would come under the control of the US. A first installment of $300 million is reported to have been lodged at the SDI Office in Whitehall, General Abrahamson is meeting British companies (including Westland whose work in composite technologies is valued for its potential for mounting mirrors in space), all British universities and colleges are being invited to bid for SDI funds, and a Pentagon team is drawing up a list of British research to be classified as falling under SDI. Still there has been no discussion.

Is the future of democracy and science in the United Kingdom being threatened for a fistful of dollars?

2.4
Star Wars: Goodbye to the Pie in the Sky

The last few months have been a painful learning experience for all those who have been concerned with advanced information technology as a component of national and international policy. Politicians, scientists, journalists and the general public have found themselves exploring unknown territory, trying to make sense of issues which they know to be important but in which they and their advisers have insufficient experience and expertise.

This dilemma is most clearly demonstrated in the case of "Star Wars", as even British Government ministers such as Lord Trefgarne have taken to calling President Reagan's Strategic Defence Initiative. The Parliamentary debate on 19th February 1986 was notable for the lack of knowledge exhibited, particularly by some supporters of the Government position, for whom ignorance was almost a prerequisite for loyal attendance. Those senior ministers and recent ex-ministers who knew what had been going on, who had read the secret Memorandum of Understanding, were conspicuous by their absence, and the Government majority in the division lobbies was reduced to 70. Subsequently, senior back-bench Parliamentarian of all parties have been disquieted by the fiascos of Westland, British Leyland and the Strategic Defence Initiative. Not a conspiracy, more a way of life paved with banana skins, which bodes ill for the future of British democracy and economic regeneration.

From the *Times Literary Supplement*, May 1986

President Reagan launched his Strategic Defence Initiative in March 1983, to the evident surprise of his advisers and NATO allies. He had a vision of developing a technological fix to make nuclear weapons obsolete, a technological advance which at times he has proposed sharing with other nations such as the Soviet Union, which came as a surprise to those who know that the Soviet Union are officially denied access to IBM personal computers and accompanying software on grounds of military security.

President Reagan is an unrivalled communicator, with an evident yearning for peace, and an imagination that can outstrip the potential of Twentieth Century science, taking him back to the days of Twentieth Century Fox. In a beguiling mixture of political fact and Hollywood fantasy, even General James Abrahamson, Director of the SDI Programme, has taken to saying that: "The Force is with US".

Other political leaders are placed in an awkward predicament: how can they tell the Emperor that he has no clothes, that his noble vision is "pie in the sky" (as Margaret Thatcher put it in an interview with *The Times* on Good Friday 1986)? Mrs Thatcher is a trained research scientist and a Fellow of the Royal Society. She must not be expected to suspend her critical faculties in the cause of some illusory presentation of unity between allies who enjoy a special, though secret, relationship. She laid down clear conditions for British participation in the "Camp David accords". The evidence is clear that they have been breached. Sir Geoffrey Howe made clear his reservations about the strategic aspects of SDI in his March 1985 speech, comparing it to the Maginot Line, for which apologies but not retractions were made. Michael Heseltine said in September 1985 that he was far from convinced of the technical feasibility of the peace shield, but that participation under the Secret Memorandum would be in the best interests of British industry, a view which he has yet to reconcile with his public stand over Westland. In both cases he faced opposition from the Department of Trade and Industry.

The underlying problem is surprisingly simple, given the astronomical cost, surface complexities and technical terminology of computing, space and laser technology. It derives from a fundamental philosophical mistake regarding the nature of Western science, which has its expression in many other grandiose scientific and technological schemes, including those with laudable objectives in fields such as health, education and business. The awareness of such problems arises afresh from research and development work in the field of artificial intelligence, on which the Strategic Defence Initiative and many other schemes place such conspicuous reliance, despite the youth and frailty of the field even in the view of its most experienced research leaders.

As recently as 1973 the British Government deemed the field of artificial intelligence not worthy of official research funding (in the Lighthill Report to the Science Research Council). Now the same field, with the same researchers and few if any major new break-throughs, is regarded as a secure basis for the unaided automatic defence of our planet. The truth lies somewhere in between: workers in artificial intelligence now have an emerging consensus view of the problems they can solve today, those which could be soluble given certain necessary scientific advances, and the problems that are not amenable to solution by a "technological fix". The problem of general strategic defence from incoming missiles falls into the latter category, as does the problem of universal protection from illness, or universal salvation of small businesses from economic problems. Such an awareness derives from work on problems of knowledge and preceded the explosive expansion of science, but had to be rediscovered before it is too late.

The philosophical argument revealing the fallacies of universal protective systems has a common structure, and holds irrespective of views regarding defence policies, geopolitics or political ideology.

1. If you as a human expert cannot give a complete and correct description of a problem, then you are not entitled to expect a computer system or another human expert to be able to solve it, except by chance. Computers can only solve problems where each of the component elements, and the nature of their interaction have been specified, and the computer system aids in dealing with the complexity and volume of those elements.

   In the case of SDI, we cannot give a complete description of the problem to be solved, the attack of tens of thousands of missiles of unknown ballistic and aerodynamic characteristics, all of which have to be stopped in a matter of minutes in an environment of nuclear radiation by a system which cannot be tested in the absence of a spare planet.

   We cannot even build a system to take the place of Mike Gatting in the MCC cricket team facing West Indian fast bowling, though we do have a static machine which can hurl cricket balls at journalists. After the Challenger disaster, it is harder to point to the space shuttle as an example of a complex smooth-running system, part of the efficient march of scientific progress.

2. Even if you have what you regard as a complete correct description of a problem, that is not sufficient to guarantee a practical, attainable solution.

Following the insights of academic research we are accustomed to the concept of a long period of research and development of practical methods and technology. The process of discovery, described since Averroes, is driven by trial and error, conjecture and refutation until we find or elicit a description that matches the underlying structure of a problem and available problem-solving mechanisms. The process of justification *post hoc* is usually more elegant, and is often what is published as an account of the knowledge area.

In knowledge areas where little attention has been given to rigorous development of theory that is accepted by the domain experts, it is absurd to expect that computer systems can succeed where humans have failed. There are remarkably few subject areas where theoretical structures are both universally accepted and applicable to the complexity of real world problems in real time. Nuclear warfare and politics is not a strong candidate for such status; there will be nobody left to pass judgement when our systems fail.

3. All that we can ever do with available technology is to augment or automate the incorrect and poorly understood systems of classification and expert procedure that underly current human practice.

If we choose the option of fully automatic systems, as are required for SDI, then we remove the human element of control, and abdicate responsibility for dealing with problems such as the protection of our planet. In other domains, such as management decision support, this abdication may be either to machines or to other expert decision-makers or consultants over whom we have no influence and whose operations are veiled by the secrecy of the "black box".

Note that this argument makes no assumptions about the nature of the technology in question, and the feasibility or advisability of component elements. It is an argument that addresses issues of knowledge, power, democracy and science in an age of complexity, where technology can be introduced to support a chosen ideology or social structure, as an instrument of policy rather than a determinant of policy.

John Biffen, Leader of the House of Commons, said on 25th March 1986, in an adjournment debate initiated by Tam Dalyell MP:

The hon Member for Linlithgow (Mr Dalyell) demonstrated a most formidable case on the Strategic Defence Initiative. I could not even begin to answer a fraction of his points. I hope, therefore, that he will excuse me if I merely say that, whatever our views about defence policy, is it not important to consider the fact that the defence system may become so important and dominant that the policy serves the defence system but really the defence system should serve the policy? I welcome the hon Gentleman's interest in this topic. I hope that he will remain the good, sound, radical, irritating Member of Parliament he has been these 20-odd years.

This enlightened view by an outstanding democrat and Parliamentarian may explain the response since my resignation from the Alvey Directorate over the implications of the Memorandum of Understanding on SDI for the British Alvey Programme of advanced research and development in which it was my privilege to serve. I have enjoyed the full support of my colleagues in the Civil Service, academia and industry (including defence contractors), and Members of both Houses of Parliament from all parties. Together with concerned scientists and investigative journalists we have been concerned to discover what is going on before misunderstandings prove irreversible, with international consequences.

There is no debate raging in the scientific community regarding the feasibility of SDI, as it has the status of fantasy and there is no attempt by the Pentagon or the British Government even to describe what a "peace shield" would be. Any working system, it has been conceded, would be partial and concerned with the point defence of missile sites, and working subsystems would have offensive capability in upgrading current deterrent systems.

Until December 1985, SDI was commended as being non-nuclear, but the reliance on the nuclear technology of X-ray lasers, themselves requiring an extensive programme of testing at the expense of current attempts by the Soviet Union at negotiations on the Comprehensive Test Ban Treaty, has made it clear that SDI involves a significant amplification of the Arms Race, with a technology much more easily and cheaply deployed for offensive rather than defensive purposes. It is easier to focus a laser beam on a static city than on a moving set of missiles, with consequences akin to nuclear winter.

The public may have the impression that there still exists a Memorandum of Understanding between Britain and the United States on SDI, and that this example is to be followed by West Germany, Japan, Israel, Argentina and other allies in supporting a defensive shield that owes more to ideology than geography. It was signed on 6th December 1985 but was in effect torn up on 5th March 1986 as Clarence Robinson left Britain after having expressed interest in British classified research. The British Government asked the US Government for a report on the role of Mr Robinson and the background and purpose of his visit. Caspar Weinberger subsequently expressed regret at the misunderstanding over the circumstances of the visit, as his Pentagon colleagues increased the inducements to 50 British companies, whose representatives were wined and dined at the Pentagon on March 25th.

Why has the atmosphere suddenly and privately changed, so that the only officially stated justification for British firms and research institutions participating in SDI, namely the prospect of lucrative contracts, is itself no longer mentioned?

The answer is startlingly simple. One purpose of the SDI Office in the Pentagon is to attract the participation of overseas companies and researchers to raise the technological level of the SDI Programme as stated, and of resulting products of the American military-industrial complex. Notably the Alvey Programme, with work at centres such as Imperial College, enjoys a lead in parallel computer architectures, sequential and parallel logic programming, and software technology, seen as central to SDI, and open offers of collaborative projects were met with firm refusals. On 15th October 1985 I received a delegation from United Technologies at Imperial College, led by former senior Pentagon nuclear policy officials, seeking access to such technologies. None of the research community which I managed at Imperial College or nationally will countenance involvement in SDI, as we explained in a letter to Mrs Thatcher in October, following the example set by thousands of American scientists across the United States. We have been joined in this position by numerous colleagues in Britain and Europe.

Another part of the Pentagon, led by Richard Perle, is concerned with technology transfer, and shares the public American concern that Europe and Japan lead the United States in key areas of advanced information technology hardware and software. Clarence Robinson was working in Perle's department for Paul Hopler, whose task is to assemble a Militarily Critical Technologies List, including technologies at present or in future relevant to SDI, of technologies which should be controlled unilaterally and extraterritorially by the State Department and administered through the COCOM regulations governing trade with Warsaw Pact countries. COCOM regulations have proved irksome to British and European companies and government in the past, as they have tended to work to the commercial advantage of American companies.

As reported by Paul Walton in *Infomatics* (3rd March 1986), (see Chapter 2.2) Hopler thought the Memorandum of Understanding might give him more freedom to classify technology from British industrial and academic laboratories, and there is no full public text of the MoU with which to disabuse him. The text leaked to *Aviation Week* of 27th January is likely to be a draft.

What do we learn from this mercifully brief excursion into the fairytale imperialist world of Strategic Defence?

1. The outside world regards British research and development work in advanced information technology as outstanding, even crucial to the defence of the planet (if you accept the Honeywell assessment, for example, of the parallel logic programming language PARLOG, developed at Imperial College as central to Command, Control, Communications and Intelligence for SDI – the glue to hold the system together). This work is British and European in origin, and should not necessarily be placed under American control and used for military purposes. It has great potential as a training tool on microcomputers today: nobody who knows PARLOG as I do would trust the fate of a company to it for some years, or would ever consider using it as the basis for the defence of civilization as we know it.

2. The key underlying enabling technology is that of human thinking aided by tools and techniques of artificial intelligence. If the hardware and software required is placed under COCOM control through the State Department, it will not be freely available for use in civil programmes in Britain and Europe as currently planned. I am, for example, lead consultant for expert systems on a number of large-scale imaginative initiatives yet to be announced by the Government and private industry in the areas of training and education, whose committed budgets greatly exceed the *Financial Times* estimates of likely British contracts under SDI. Is it worth sacrificing what we know we can do to human benefit in favour of a scheme which we know to be infeasible and devoid of significant civil spin-offs? IBM have characterized such benefits as "drip-offs": maybe the appointment of John Fairclough of IBM as Mrs Thatcher's principal scientific adviser will help to restore some equilibrium at the centre of policy making.

3. There is a debate which has yet to begin regarding the appropriate use of technology as an agent of policy, rather than policy being improvized in the wake of what is regarded as technological inevitability. SDI research will not continue if enough of the key people decide it is not in their interest. It can only now be seen as in the interest of the American military-industrial complex, and possibly their Soviet counterparts, in enhancing the military domination of society. There is a wealth of alternatives. There are real human needs to be met in solving problems of hunger, disease and illiteracy, thrown aside by the Governments of the United States and the United Kingdom in their shameful withdrawal from UNESCO and downgrading of the significance and influence of the United Nations. We have few expert technologists and a finite

budget – they must be used wisely.

It is a cruel irony that as British polytechnics are told that they have to reduce their student numbers, even in subjects like computing and engineering, to save a paltry £23m, heads of department in universities, polytechnics and colleges of higher and further education are receiving intellectually obscene letters following instructions from the Ministry of Defence. I quote from the letter circulated at Imperial College:

> The College has received from the SDI Participation Office at the Ministry of Defence details of that part of the Strategic Defence Initiative programme which is available for research in British universities. This area has been designated the Innovative Science and Technology programme (IST), which has a budget of $2.7 billion this year (some 3.5% of the overall SDI funding). The terms of reference of the IST programme are defined as providing full funding for high technology research programmes of a novel or advanced nature, or for programmes offering a new approach to, or involving innovative technology in, areas already funded by US Government agencies. The IST Office has supplied a detailed list of the areas in which it intends to sponsor research, a copy of which is attached. Research contracts awarded under the IST programme will not be classified and will allow the College to publish the results according to normal academic practice. The present round of applications is for research to start on 1st January 1987 . . . The college deadline for this year's round is Friday May 3rd.

You should recall that no government civil funds are currently available to support research in advanced information technology, as the Alvey budget is fully committed and the only other source of funding is a new scheme joint between the Ministry of Defence and Research Councils. Even more agonizing is the discovery for scientists such as astronomers that their life's work has been retrospectively and unilaterally classified as falling under SDI, a form of extra-terrestrial extra-territoriality.

Science is being sacrificed on the altar of technological hubris. We are no longer "the people of the book", but "the people of the machine", serving Mammon. No man can serve two masters, and I have made my personal choice.

I look forward to reading the contributions to this wider debate of the authors of a number of books on Star Wars. The consensus and cooperation that have arisen in face of the threat posed by SDI is a novel political form of precompetitive collaboration, as espoused in the research and commercial arena through the Alvey and ESPRIT Programmes. All stand to benefit from the sharing of information and the removal of barriers of secrecy.

Alan Chalfont **Star Wars: Suicide or survival** *Weidenfeld & Nicolson London 1985*

Lord Chalfont is placed in an embarrassing position, not unlike some members of the American State Department and the British Cabinet, who endorsed President Reagan's vision of peace and honestly, though in light of current knowledge erroneously, thought the SDI offered a road to peace. As a former distinguished journalist and Minister for Disarmament, Lord Chalfont will be able to reassess his position, following the noble example of John Selwyn Gummer, a current government minister, when faced with new uncomfortable evidence.

Christopher Lee **War in Space** *Hamish Hamilton London 1986*

Christopher Lee's account holds up very well. As a concerned journalist in the best traditions of the BBC, he was sounding notes of caution from the beginning, seeing several levels of significance behind the changing official story as presented in press briefings. It is a sad indictment of the British media that the debate has been so subdued, that SDI has been policy for three years without awkward questions being asked by many informed journalists. *The Financial Times, Guardian* and *New Scientist* deserve honourable mention, as does the courageous investigative work of Paul Walton, who originally became a freelance journalist when he founded "Online Aid", a contribution of the British computer industry to the problems of Third World hunger.

Edward Thompson (editor) **Star Wars** *Penguin London 1985*

Edward Thompson edited this collection with a feeling of weary outrage. After all the years of campaigning against Cruise missiles and Pershing here was another scaling up of the Arms Race, with the novel twist that President Reagan was advocating the withdrawal of Cruise and Pershing missiles in return for the continuation of SDI. Thompson's polemic, based on incisive research, awakened the dormant political awareness of many scientists, and paved the way for the current broad coalition of concerned groups who are seeking to complete the process of policy reversal and open up a debate on respectable alternative uses of technology, turning swords into ploughshares and addressing social needs.

Thompson is bitterly critical of the *Economist:*

Any historian of ideas could tell the *Economist* that "new ideas" beneficial to humankind have not normally been announced by politicians and then instantly been supported by the armed forces and by industrialists and incarnated in budgetary appropriations. It is more usual for new ideas to survive on bread-and-cheese on the margins of respectable society for several decades before they are noticed by the editors of respectable weeklies. Nor is it clear how a strategy which, the *Economist* concedes, is designed to improve a nuclear umbrella and to protect the nuclear missile sites of one party is "an anti-nuclear idea".

EIU Regional Review: Eastern Europe and the USSR 'Economist Intelligence Unit 1986

The new *EIU Regional Review of Eastern Europe and the USSR* is on a much higher intellectual plane, as one would expect from distinguished economic historians such as Alec Nove. The analysis is informed and sophisticated, with John Kiser nailing the lie of universal Soviet technological inferiority in advanced research, and Philip Hanson offering an incisive account of Strategic Trade Controls, COCOM and extraterritoriality. Let me end by quoting from the last paragraph of Hanson's analysis:

> The whole subject remains a rich source of mutual misunderstanding within the Western world. The fashionable West European view, that the US administration is either exaggerating the problem (of the leakage of high technology) for purely domestic political reasons, or exploiting it to gain unfair competitive advantages for US industry, is frivolous. Richard Perle's inclination to embargo anything that Moscow wishes to buy (except grain) distorts the original rationale of Strategic Trade Controls and makes for an overextension of both the resources and the political will to monitor them. Between these two positions there is room for a more sensible view.

For the sake of our planet, we need more sensible views, and informed discussion. I would not claim to offer hard and fast solutions, though I have firmly held views, but I have asked a number of questions to which I and fellow concerned citizens of a democratic Britain and Europe would appreciate answers.

2.5
SDI: The Secret Agenda Item at the Tokyo Economic Summit

There have been long preparations for the Tokyo Economic Summit of Western leaders, to be held, terrorists permitting, on 2nd–4th May 1986. International agreements will be reached on the problem of terrorism, intended to paper over the cracks in the Western Alliance caused by the bombing of Tripoli. Portentous announcements will be made regarding the "Human Frontier Programme" to be launched by the Japanese as a context for the application of their Fifth Generation Computer Project, which has changed the face of international research and development in advanced information technology in the last five years.

Less will be said in public regarding the Strategic Defence Initiative, though a great deal is likely to be discussed behind closed doors following a series of bilateral negotiations and visits in recent months.

So far the United States has signed Memoranda Of Understanding with the United Kingdom and West Germany, the general terms of which are now clear from the text of the German Memorandum reprinted in the *Cologne Express*, translated in *The Financial Times*, *The Guardian* and *Le Monde*. Terms have been agreed with Israel. Technical approval has been given by a Japanese delegation, though the response of Japanese companies has been ambivalent, and Mr Nakasone, following his humiliation over Tripoli and American pressure for changes in his domestic economic policy, is unlikely to announce

From a lecture given at Queens Hall, Edinburgh on 29th April 1986 agreement on a Memorandum of Understanding on SDI before his general election in Japan in June. He has not been encouraged by the turmoil SDI has caused in West Germany, where the Coalition Government also faces imminent elections. Terms have been negotiated through the visit of Mr Watanabe of MITI to the Pentagon, whereby American protectionist pressure on Japanese chip companies will be reduced in return for participation in, and political endorsement of, SDI.

To what is a government committed by signing such a Memorandum? In this paper I want to focus on the issues of economics and research management. The issues which I will describe are faced by my colleagues in each of the countries represented in Tokyo, many of whom share my concern. Indeed, it was at the request of my senior colleagues in the British Civil Service that I began last summer to share our professional concerns with a wider circle of friends, including the Members of Parliament who so ably assisted Clive Ponting in airing his concerns over the sinking of the Belgrano. My work has not depended on leaking of or access to classified documents. My letters to ministers, civil servants and the media have been on my own note paper, and signed. I and colleagues operate a "reverse leaking" service, seeking to inform government, with financial support from consultancy for industry and for other government departments concerning the application of artificial intelligence to industry and training.

The British Government, and the others represented in Tokyo, have to decide whether their advanced research is to be controlled by the United States and regulated under COCOM rules as a condition of participation in SDI, or whether they can continue with civil programmes using the same technology following their own political and commercial judgement. For the British Government the choice is simple. They can continue with SDI or with Alvey, ESPRIT, EUREKA, and new programmes for artificial intelligence now running and yet to be announced by the Manpower Services Commission and the Department of Education and Science. They cannot do both: this presents a cruel dilemma for a government which is soon to face a general election.

I would advise the British Government to withdraw gracefully from SDI. The alternative is to be ejected noisily by the democratic means which have been cast aside in the rush for the fools' gold of SDI.

Let me outline the facts, known to the Government and not denied by them even when stated in Parliament and recorded in Hansard. They are known to many of our overseas colleagues meeting in Tokyo, and in the view of many provide ample justification for the continued suspension of the British Memorandum of Understanding which has been filed in the waste paper basket since 5th March 1986.

We must introduce another side of the Pentagon. We must meet Richard Perle.

Richard Perle is Assistant Secretary for Defence with responsibility for technology transfer. To quote the recent *Economist* Intelligence Unit Study of Eastern Europe and the USSR 1986, and the article by Philip Hanson on Strategic Trade Controls:

> The Perle-Weinberger approach is close to a strategy of economic warfare against the USSR. The tendency of US policy since 1981 has been to push both foreign policy sanctions and national security controls to the point where their implicit intention seems to be to impede Soviet economic development . . .

> It has been hard to reach a stable consensus on the coverage of the strategic embargo when the most powerful country in the NATO alliance is striving to extend that coverage beyond those items which can make a direct and near term contribution to Warsaw Pact military capabilities . . .

> The USA continues to maintain its own list of militarily critical technologies, which is more wide ranging than the agreed COCOM list and reportedly some 700 pages long. This extra coverage, plus the more zealous US approach to enforcing the controls, continues to cause friction within the alliance . . .

> The agreed COCOM control system can be breached in one of three main ways. First, a member government may license on its own authority an application to export an item which should have been subjected to multilateral consideration by COCOM. Secondly, a member government may license an application which it is within its agreed competence to approve but which would in fact have given grounds for rejection if properly considered according to the agreed guidelines. Third, a sale may go through without a license having been applied for. In the last case, the relevant Western government might perhaps be open to charges of negligence or it might in fact be trying strenuously to stop the smuggling of militarily sensitive technology and just not catching all the smugglers . . .

> The result . . . is that investigating US officials are now more of a threat than invading Soviet armies. Where a machine, or a technology embodied in it, are subject to US strategic controls, are of US proprietary origin, and have been transferred to a West European country, the US Government seeks assurances that they will not be passed on to a Communist country. To enforce these assurances it seeks evidence, and has sought to impose commercial penalties on West European firms which have sold such items on (directly or indirectly) to Soviet or East European customers . . .

One way or another, the US economy matters more to most potential suppliers of high technology than the Soviet and East European economies . . .

The Western analysts who argue that the USA lacks the market power to make such embargoes stick (for more than a few narrowly defined technologies) are probably wrong . . .

The whole subject remains a rich source of mutual misunderstanding within the Western world.

It was in connection with the British MCTL entry that Richard Perle's subordinate Paul Hopler sent a team to Britain in March 1986 (see Chapter 2.2).

Dr Andrew Walker is a member of the research team at Heriot-Watt University Department of Physics, which won the first UK SDI contract, and as yet the only UK SDI contract involving British university research groups. The Heriot-Watt team is part of a consortium, based on the SDI contract held by the University of Dayton, Ohio, to build an ultra-fast optical computer. When approached by Paul Walton in February 1986 he did not know about the MCTL study, or the terms of the MoU on SDI:

We have not been notified as yet, but there may be something in the pipeline. Alternatively, it may be because we are treated as a subcontractor.

Walker added that while there was no contractual obligation to:

speak to those sort of people, we would be sensible about it, and see exactly what they wanted to do.

Asked whether Heriot-Watt would allow Pentagon researchers to look over its work, with the provision that US money accounted for a small part of their work, Dr Walker replied:

We cannot fail to respond to whatever that collaboration requires.

In practice, that would mean the classification of more work than could be considered useful to SDI. Such a classification could slow the introduction of optical computers, Walker felt.

The former Head of the Department of Computing at Imperial College, now Emeritus Professor, was concerned to hear of the proposed visit. Manny Lehman, who accepted an SDI consultancy from SAIC in order to demonstrate the ludicrosity of SDI from within, said:

If the Americans were to do this in the present atmosphere it would raise hackles. The suggestion that without signing a contract to the effect, the Americans could discover what research was being continued and even prevent publication of findings (in some cases) would cause an uproar . . .

If the Americans want to prevent the publication of research, by classifying it, it would infringe basic freedoms. Academics and industrial employees would not accept such classifications. I would certainly not accept it.

Clarence Robinson, a former correspondent for *Aviation Week and Space Technology*, and a consultant to American defence contractors such as BK Dynamics, was recruited to head Hopler's team. In 1976 he had been one of the California-based group who, with Edward Teller, had formed the High Frontier lobby group which developed the concept of SDI and X-ray lasers. Tam Dalyell MP kindly placed his work and home telephone numbers on the record in Hansard for 14th March 1986, if you wish to use Mr Robinson's expertise.

On 16th February 1986 I discussed SDI with General James Abrahamson on the BBC television programme *This Week Next Week*, and raised the question of Robinson's proposed visit. Abrahamson was pressed further on the point by British defence companies on 17th and 18th February and confirmed that the visit would occur. He gave no details. On 19th February the House of Commons debated SDI, and James Wallace MP quoted from that week's article by Paul Walton in Janes' *Defence Weekly*. On 21st February I raised the issue in debate with John Selwyn Gummer MP, a junior government minister and former Conservative Party Chairman, in a debate at Birmingham University where he spoke together with Dr David Schwartz of the American State Department in favour of SDI. Dr Schwartz has accepted the truth of my account of events, and indeed shares much of my concern. Numerous Parliamentary questions on the matter asked.

Paul Walton's article for *Infomatics* for March 1986 was widely circulated in draft prior to publication on 3rd March, with copies provided in advance for the SDI Participation Office in the Ministry of Defence. On 3rd March, the day of publication of the *Infomatics* article, Peter Marsh of *The Financial Times* asked pointed questions to the Ministry of Defence and the Prime Minister's office.

On 4th March Clarence Robinson arrived at the US Embassy in London as planned; it appears that he contacted the research director of GEC Marconi and asked to discuss research that turned out to be classified. MOD clearance was sought but refused. On 5th March Robinson left the United Kingdom.

It has not been generally reported that on 17th March Casper

Weinberger when in London apologized for the misunderstanding over the circumstances of the visit. Weinberger's apology must have been accepted, because on 25th March the representatives of 50 British companies were the guests of the Pentagon at a secret briefing on the Memorandum of Understanding, held in Washington. Tam Dalyell MP was considerate enough to summarize the business of the meeting for Hansard on the same evening.

The *Guardian* Parliamentary sketch-writer described Tam Dalyell as building up his case: "with the craftsman-like care which others might devote, say, to building a model Belgrano out of matchsticks."

So what can we say of Mr George Gallagher-Daggitt, representative of the Department of Education and Science in the SDIPO at MOD, beloved of the *Guardian* columnists, and known to his former colleagues in SERC as "bullet head"? At a recent Pugwash conference on SDI he praised the accuracy of research which had provided Pugwash members with a copy of the letter to Imperial College academics (quoted in Chapter 2.4 and also printed in *New Scientist*) inviting their participation in SDI, he noted a minor error. The letter should not, he said, have offered $2.7 billion for the year beginning January 1987, to be applied for by 3rd May 1986. The figure he had in mind was more like $7 million at the outside. He did not in fact question *The Financial Times* estimate of total British contracts of £45 million. He asserted that no academic research would be classified, but international lawyers and Stanford physics professors clarified the problem, citing precedents. He was greeted with amazement and helpless laughter when he assured his audience that no approaches would be made to British academics, and that the initiative would always be theirs.

Helpless laughter is not an adequate response, but it is a start. We should listen to the laughs from Tokyo, and decide that we can no longer act as if we are helpless. If information is not enough to enable government to change its policy, it is clearly time to change the government. British and European democracy and science are not for sale: they are not ours to sell.

Questions following the above speech concerned:
1. The legal position on classification.
2. The computer science elements of the Innovative Science and Technology Programme of SDI.
3. The significance of the 1972 Anti-Ballistic Missile Treaty.

My answers are printed below:

1. Classification

The first amendment to the US Constitution guarantees freedom of speech, and thus prevents classification in advance. However, contracts with the Department of Defence assign it rights of ownership over research products, which can be exercized at any time. Classification can be applied retrospectively on the unilateral decision of DOD, to whom papers have to be submitted prior to publication. Publication can be restricted, delayed or prevented in areas deemed to be militarily sensitive. The Pentagon MCTL list, which operates in addition to the standard, though controversial, COCOM list of restricted technologies, is appealed to as an authority analogous to the Bible. US researchers are accustomed to such a DOD regime as the norm. It has produced benefits such as DARPA and generous funding for work that appeared devoid of application to military purposes, such as logic programming and artificial intelligence. Compliance with COCOM rules is sought from COCOM signatories (NATO members and Japan), but there is provision for enforcement by the Pentagon, the US Department of Commerce and their agents through the exercize of extraterritoriality. Recent events concerning the closure of Systime with the assistance of CIA agents provide vivid demonstration of the system.

In the United Kingdom secrecy is all-pervasive. The Memorandum of Understanding governing British participation in SDI is classified, and intended to remain secret in perpetuity. Section 2 of the Official Secrets Act is universal in its application, and does not depend on the individual having signed the Act. Signature merely constitutes evidence of the awareness on the part of the individual of the existence of the Act and its provisions. Since the cases of Sarah Tisdall and Clive Ponting, Section 2 has fallen into disrepute. Section 1 concerns more serious cases where a threat to security is involved, and penalties can be severe. The German MoU included assurances that German security provisions would be strengthened, and trade with Eastern Europe curtailed, and there is strong evidence that the British MoU, produced from the same draft as released to *Aviation Week and Space Technology* for 27th January 1986, assumes a stronger regime. Security includes vetting of individuals, restrictions on the involvement of researchers from Eastern Europe, and clearance on publications. British universities have traditionally resisted involvement in research projects that were known in advance to be subject to classification. These problems are illustrated by the current disputes over the conditions restricting the use of American supercomputers in British universities.

Agreements under MoUs to participate in SDI appear to be governed by the strongest of available security regimes, which can, following precedent, be applied retrospectively, unilaterally, extra-territorially, and lead to the cessation of work by research groups in their own long-standing projects.

2. Computing aspects of the IST

The letter to Imperial College scientists, based on a letter from George Gallagher-Daggitt of the MOD SDIPO, is a covering letter to the IST prospectus, which includes contact telephone numbers of the senior American military scientists and managers.

The financial basis, confused in the letter, is now clear. Some 3.5% of the current financial year assigned budget of $2.7 billion is available to the IST programme in universities worldwide. Of the rough total of $100 million for universities, British universities might anticipate some possible total such as $7 million, though the process of submitting bids and tenders is expensive and competitive. The most realistic ambition is to cover the costs of application, according to John Pike of the American Federation of Concerned Scientists.

The computing requirements of IST are to an extent generic, which would mean drastic consequences if the technology was restricted to military use for SDI under Pentagon control following classification. SDI requires for its success, whatever one's assessment of its level of feasibility, certain commonly desired features of computer systems, which are not available but on the common international research agenda. These would include:

parallel architecture;
high performance;
reliability;
fault tolerance;
artificial intelligence;
real time sensor and expert system capability;
speech input;
modularity;
built-in correctness characteristics;
automatic operability;
very large databases;
non-monotonic reasoning;
security;
telecommunications;
networking;
distributed processing.

The support of such a project under IST would be likely in practice to preclude its availability for development for civil or European purposes under Alvey, ESPRIT, EUREKA etc.

It is hard to see what benefits are offered to non-US participants, other than possible finance. Non-Americans are barred from many conferences, must accept a security "minder", and should be aware that their work can be compulsorily terminated.

3. The 1972 ABM Treaty

SDI breaches the treaty in a number of ways, both immediately and in the foreseeable future, and could lead to the unilateral abrogation of the treaty by the USA in the near future, despite assurances.

One particular example is the provision, under Article 9 of the treaty, preventing the proliferation of ABM technology to non-signatory powers.

Architecture studies for the Strategic Defence Initiative, or the newly mentioned European Defence Initiative, even at the level of feasibility studies, are in breach if they involve the exchange of blueprints. A case in point is the Ford EDI project involving GEC–Marconi, and with approaches made to Ferranti, Logica, SD, and the Universities of York and Newcastle. It is likely that the implementation of a credible "testbed" system as proposed would imply a breach of the treaty.

One ingenious but unfortunate solution to this problem in the short or longer term would be to ensure that technology transfer was one-way, from the UK to the USA. This would clearly, while complying with international law, be to the commercial disadvantage of the UK and other non-US participants.

It should be noted that the above arguments do not depend on a particular view on the technical, strategic, defence, moral or party political aspects of SDI, but focus instead on issues of finance and management. It would appear that they are of relevance to any nation contemplating involvement in SDI as currently constituted.

2.6
The Last Days of SDI

The funeral arrangements for President Reagan's Star Wars Programme are now being made. SDI has very few close friends, but doubtless messages of condolence will be sent from relieved NATO allies, and from those State Department officials whose lives have been a living lie since President Reagan made his visionary speech in March 1983, to the surprise of his policy advisers. It will be a quiet funeral, as the victim will die through lack of financial support, probably without the administration of a single coup de grace. As long as President Reagan is reigning supreme in the White House, his allies feel unable to oppose him. They can, however, fail to support him, and turn off the life support system for SDI in September 1986, denying it further financial sustenance after 1st October. The monstrosity was not aborted during the gestation period, it was not strangled at birth; it was even given formal godparents through the Memoranda of Understanding, signed with Casper Weinberger by Michael Heseltine of the United Kingdom and Herr Bangemann of West Germany. However, when the celebration party was held, nobody from Europe came; nobody offered to sign binding contracts. Instead, those who were invited to join made polite but embarrassed noises, and refrained from practical commitment.

The Peace Movement should send a wreath to the funeral of the Strategic Defence Initiative, with the message of condolence:

> Here lies an attempt to make nuclear weapons obsolete: we who also seek a nuclear-free world and an alternative to the obscenity of Mutually

From a lecture given at Oulu, Finland on 14th June 1986

Assured Destruction hope and pray that the process of arms reduction can be resumed. SDI has revealed the folly of the human race depending for its salvation on man-made technology. We should be talking to each other, not arming for war.

President Reagan, in his mistaken zeal for SDI, offered to remove Cruise and Pershing missiles from Western Europe. We share his view that they stand in the way of the peace process. He offered to share the results of American advanced research with other nations. We also prefer a collaborative approach. He prefers the company of ordinary people to that of generals and highly qualified military advisers. We praise his attempts to communicate his hopes and fears in simple terms: it would indeed be pleasant if life could be seen in black and white, if the bad guys always wore black hats.

SDI was the computer implementation of a flawed ideology. Driven by the naive certainties of the Moral Majority and the California arms industry, brought together by the magic of American technological superiority, it offered the security that "The Force is with US". Whatever happened, the chosen people in the United States would be safe, while still being able to attack and disable their enemies with high technology rapid deployment strikes at will. As an automatic knowledge-based complex system of diverse and esoteric technologies operating in real time without the possibility of testing, it succeeded in removing human beings from the process of decision-making about the future of our planet. As the Pentagon spokesman put it: "We have the technology to make sure that the President does not make a mistake."

No doubt President Reagan believed in the concept of a peace shield. Nobody else who has examined the issue believes that such a system is technically feasible, and indeed the SDI Office is not attempting to coordinate the building of such a system. They are working instead on enhancing the anti-ballistic defence of missile sites. Few in the NATO alliance believe that SDI is strategically sensible, as in its official form it is in direct conflict with the MAD approach to deterrence. Few outside the American military-industrial complex believe that it makes economic sense for them to participate, as it can be seen as a thinly-veiled extension of American Strategic Trade Controls which is intended not only to deny critical technologies to the Soviet Union and its allies, but also is intended to strengthen American high-technology industry at the expense of its European and Japanese rivals. No respectable scientist can believe that his work should be exclusively devoted to unattainable military objectives at the expense of attainable and socially beneficial civil objectives.

The assumption was that our support could be bought. It was a fatally flawed assumption. Science and democracy are not for sale: they are not ours to sell. We must not allow ourselves to be placed in such a position again. NATO politicians and defence contractors will have won the war against Star Wars. The Peace Movement must win the peace that can follow.

Let me outline the simple logic of the fallacy underlying SDI. The argument does not depend on detailed technical knowledge, and it applies to all automatic knowledge-based systems which are used in place of individual human judgements. SDI is, after all, the computer implementation of an ideology, the ideology of the military-industrial complex, within which all problems can be solved by technology given resources and determination (see also Chapter 2.4).

1. If we cannot give a full description of our problem, we cannot expect another human, or a computer system, to solve it. We cannot give a full description of the problem of an attack by many thousands of intercontinental ballistic missiles, of unknown origin, ballistic characteristics, and destinations.
2. Even if we believe that we have a full description of our problem, it does not follow that it provides a solution.
3. If we automate the partial understanding of a human expert, building an expert system, we have a flawed system without the restraint of human control.
4. SDI is simply a clear case of the more general problem of reliance on man-made technology.

At each stage of the technology of SDI the system makes requirements that go beyond what is possible. There has been no rebuttal of Professor Parnas' analysis of the technical infeasibility of the computing aspects of SDI, and indeed the Pentagon has publicly acknowledged major problems. Some months ago the Shuttle programme was used as an example of a complex but dependable system. Since the Challenger disaster, and the failure of American Titan and Delta disposable rockets, they have no dependable launch capability. The moon landing in 1969 was a success, but there were no decoy moons, and no defensive systems to defeat.

SDI was described as non-nuclear, but in fact depends on nuclear explosions in space from the X-ray laser. Since the Chernobyl disaster, there is distrust even of civil nuclear power, and there are now reports of radiation leaks from the Nevada nuclear tests in April. No laser physicist or particle physicist believes that an overall SDI system is feasible, though advances could be made in component technologies. We have no spare planet on which to test.

How was SDI allowed to become part of NATO policy, supported by the British and West German Governments with Memoranda of Understanding? Both Memoranda were supposed to be secret, but are now in the hands of the Peace Movement. SDI follows previous American military programmes which have involved European agreements, and has similar terms. Although it was a unilateral American policy decision, and the European allies expressed great reservations, imposing public demands as Mrs Thatcher did at Camp David, they went ahead rather than risking damaging relations with the USA and within NATO. In December 1985 Leon Brittan, the Secretary of State for Trade and Industry expressed reservations about the contractual implications of the involvement of the British researchers in SDI. The position was similar in West Germany, where Mr Bangemann only wished to agree to open civil research, and did not wish to be prevented from trading with Eastern Europe. In Britain only £1.2 million of contracts were agreed before the signing, and none have been signed since. There is no real collaboration.

American defence policy is now seen as threatening the stability of a number of Western countries. SDI, the attack on Libya and the suspension of SALT-2 are all deeply unpopular. The Craxi Government in Italy fell over the *Achille Lauro* affair, the Kohl Coalition in West Germany and the Nakasone Government in Japan are under threat. Mrs Thatcher's position in the United Kingdom is far from secure. All of them are secretly praying for Reagan to abandon his crazy plans before his allies are removed from office in disgrace for complicity in his actions.

The Peace Movement has a new popularity, with a new breadth of support from a wide diversity of groups, uniting in a common cause. New members are joining, and public meetings are well attended. The British Government is going through "political meltdown" and needs SDI to be terminated if it is to recover independence and a place in Europe. It is our responsibility to raise the level of awareness and debate, and following the defeat of SDI, to make sure that the American military-industrial complex do not succeed with subsequent obscene plans.

We have to offer government a choice. Either they proceed with civil programmes in education, training, health and industry using the best of our technology in our hands, or they continue with the sordid charade of SDI. They cannot do both. They have covertly chosen to proceed with civil programmes, recognizing what that implies for SDI. Until they publicly withdraw from SDI they will be attacked vigorously by the Peace Movement in meetings, books, television programmes, international academic and commercial conference, and lobbies of Parliament.

We must provide a link between the different issues that worry our people. People must see the link between military research and civil decline, between the civil and military nuclear power programmes, between military and civil uses of computers. They must be encouraged to participate in the choice of society that we want to build with our technology.

EUREKA offers a novel example of a practical collaborative project in a wider Europe. It deserves the attention of scientists and peace workers as a possible vehicle for constructive programmes and easing of tensions. At present it lacks support from the European Parliament pending the death of SDI, which casts a blight on European projects. We should be involved in planning now.

We must not allow American unilateral actions, as with SDI, to jeopardize the whole fabric of international arms agreements. Pentagon vultures do not want arms control, but Europe does. Europe has to begin to assert itself as a wider cultural community, even at the risk of adjusting the balance within NATO. It must not rely on technology, but on human contacts.

We must take note of the new field of computational politics, concerned both with the politics of computer policy and applications, and with the use of computer technology in policy modelling and implementation. We can look at both computers and politics afresh, and begin to build a survivable world for our children.

2.7
The Strategic Research Initiative

This is a proud time for Britain. Our institutions of government, industry, education and science have been put to the test by the American Strategic Defence Initiative, and have proved that democracy is not just a matter of elections. An agreement was negotiated by government on our behalf. Since the Memorandum of Understanding to participate in SDI was signed no new contracts have been concluded. The sum total of actual British involvement remains at $1.2 million, as it was in the autumn of 1985, in contrast to the $1.5 billion which was promised. General James Abrahamson, Director of the SDI Office in Washington, omitted all reference to British collaboration in his testimony to Congress on 6th June 1986, while noting the contributions from West Germany and Israel.

The story is becoming well known, a story of fairy-tale imperialism. Scientists deal in complexity, so despite the total lack of scientific credibility for the Hollywood-style peace shield, a general public, press and business community whose scientific understanding has been shown to be lacking were content with statements of faith in American technology from political and military leaders.

SDI is in essence a game of celestial snooker. Although it would be a long-term project to teach a robot to play snooker, as is proposed by Professor Richard Gregory at Bristol University, we have been expected to believe that the power of technology could enable us to safely "pot" thousands of incoming nuclear missiles, using the nuc-

From a lecture given at the Strategic Research Initiative Seminar on 25th June 1986

lear "cues" of Edward Teller's X-ray lasers, without fail and without practice, within seconds, and without even, in the words of Jeffrey Archer, "telling the President". SDI is nothing but a load of intercontinental balls, designed to fill Californian pockets. We would be better off with a "Quiver Full of Arrows", and we may rather find the explanation of the conduct of the British Government in terms of the ambitious bankrupt depicted in "Not a Penny More Not a Penny Less", published by the Vice-chairman of the Conservative Party and based on his own experiences.

SDI should be seen as the computer realization of an ideology. The project was to build an automatic knowledge-based system to operate in real time, without the benefit of the luxury of human intervention or control, to be launched on warning. The creationist funda-mentalism of the Moral Majority was united with the technological whizz-bang wizardry of the High Frontier, giving us "The Word Made Flash", a horrendous blasphemy, the reduction of science to inhuman technological obscenity. Whatever the question may turn out to be at the time of a nuclear attack, the system was to be relied on to know the answer and save our planet.

There was laughter in the Pentagon and the scientific community when the Star Wars concept was first announced, taking Edward Teller's technology beyond even his wildest imaginings; this rapidly turned to terror when the President announced it as his policy in March 1983, and clung to it through thick and thin, forsaking all other policies and priorities if they stood in the way. Apart from breaking international law, it was seen, even in the Pentagon, as breaking the laws of nature, or at the very least requiring a battery of research breakthroughs each worthy of a Nobel prize. The young Alice had the habit of believing in six impossible things before breakfast, but she was a character in a children's story rather than President of the United States. President Reagan may yet enter legend as Ronald Duck, the lame duck president who should be encouraged to take more interest in bread, and less in circuses.

Possibly the British Government have felt obliged to humour their transatlantic ally, going through the motions of collaboration while praying for a change of wind that might blow his policy off course. The wind has indeed changed following the disasters of Challenger and Chernobyl, exposing the undue reliance of both East and West on man-made technology. At last the people and the media have begun to question what is going on, and the predicament of the British Government has become plain. How can the Government or their muzzled critics tell the electorate that their official policy of participation in the Strategic Defence Initiative is a polite mask behind which is intense disquiet and disarray made agonizing by the attack on Libya from British bases? How can they explain, as Geoffrey Pattie has conceded, that the real purpose of the SDI Participation Office in the Ministry of Defence has been to ensure that no disadvantageous contracts are signed, and that therefore no contracts have been agreed that result in real work and transfer of technology?

The masks can be taken off now, and it can be revealed that few in the United Kingdom ever seriously considered that SDI was technically feasible, strategically wise, intellectually honest or commercially attractive. The Ministry of Defence continue a token activity, organized from the chaos of their SDI Participation Office. The hapless representative of the Department of Education and Science in the SDI Participation Office, George Gallagher-Daggitt, has continued to argue that academic participants in SDI will not be subject to classification and restriction but the case of Dr Andrew Sessler of the Lawrence Livermore Laboratory shows that civil research on nuclear fusion was halted for 13 months by the SDI Office on security grounds, confirmed as accurate by the US Department of Energy.

Members of all political parties, in both Houses of Parliament, including chairmen of the relevant Parliamentary Committees and Select Committees, across the Civil Service, in universities and across British industry, have sought to disassociate themselves from the Government's policy in this matter. They have been assisted by colleagues in the United States State Department, Department of Energy, Senate Armed Services Committee, and in the House of Representatives, as well as in the scientific community, and further collaboration in the common task of restoring honesty to government has come from scientists, academics and the peace and environmental movements internationally. In Britain, the same collaborative approach which was the basis of the Alvey Programme has been used in its defence against the threat from SDI and the American military-industrial complex. The concept of precompetitive collaboration which has applied in research and development in advanced information technology has been extended to the sphere of politics. Having removed SDI, the unacceptable face of modern technocratic militarist capitalism, there is a diversity of choices to be made.

Twentieth Century science has to be considered in the context of social, political and economic choices. The same technology of intelligent computing that was required to underpin the flawed SDI, under the control of the Pentagon through their planned extension of

COCOM and other Strategic Trade Controls, has now been freed again to deploy as we choose. There is a wealth of choice, and no shortage of financial resources, though these are currently in the wrong pockets and devoted to many of the wrong objectives. We should be talking of Strategic Initiatives in Health, Education and Training, of the regeneration of British industry and economic conditions. We should be strengthening our ties with our European partners through programmes such as ESPRIT and EUREKA, which have been thrown into disarray during the confused and turbulent life of SDI.

Archimedes is reported to have shouted "EUREKA"!" (loosely translated as "screw it!") when he climbed into his bath and the water overflowed across the floor. The Archimedes screw is a notable example of intermediate technology deployed in the Third World to assist in irrigation, transferring water, without which life cannot be sustained. I would like to think that we can derive similar practical results from the overflowing of the nonsense that has been SDI. Let us perhaps launch a new international collaborative programme, known as UNSCREWIT: the United Nations Scientific and Cultural Research and Education programme With Informed Technology. We have been screwing things up for quite long enough.

2.8
"No" to Star Wars

In a sensible world where policy issues were discussed openly and honestly we would not be considering Star Wars. It has not proved possible to debate the subject in Britain as nobody has been prepared to argue a coherent case in favour of President Reagan's Strategic Defence Initiative. Even Mr George Gallagher-Daggitt, whose role in the MOD SDI Participation Office is to deal with relations with universities, refuses to be drawn on issues of defence or economic policy, and clings to the myth of academic propriety for participation in the Innovative Science and Technology Programme.

A surprising number of people have said "No" to Star Wars, though in many cases their position has not been made public. In the campaign over the recent months led by the Coalition Against Star Wars, our platforms have been filled by politicians from the Labour, Liberal and Social Democratic Parties, by scientists from the full range of disciplines in which the SDI Office have shown an interest, and by members of a wide range of peace and environmental groups. Our campaign has been highly collaborative, with free exchange of information, and it has enabled us to use advanced technology and human intelligence rather more effectively than has been possible for the Pentagon.

There have recently been a number of new recruits to the campaign against Star Wars, and I would like to summarize their reasons for opposing British involvement in the Strategic Defence Initiative.

Dr Bill Bardow, Director of Research for GEC Marconi, was

From a speech given at Central Hall, Westminster on 8th July 1986 alarmed when Clarence Robinson asked to discuss research that was classified.

Sir Ian Lloyd, MP, Chairman of the Parliamentary Information Technology Committee, has been trying in vain since the autumn of 1985 to hold a discussion on the technical and scientific aspects of SDI, which would be addressed by the Secretary of State for Defence and would provide an opportunity for Dr Henry Thompson of Edinburgh University and myself to raise our concerns. In the House of Commons on 19th February 1986 Sir Ian raised the technical problems identified by Professor David Parnas, to which the Ministry of Defence have provided no answers. He has remained in contact with our Strategic Research Initiative.

Ken Warren MP is Chairman of the House of Commons Select Committee on Trade and Industry, which was given evidence in closed sessions on the impact of SDI on current British and European research and development programmes in advanced information technology. My former colleagues in the Alvey, ESPRIT and EUR-EKA Programmes have shared their concerns with Members of Parliament, and with the scientific, academic and commercial community who have been collaborating in developing civil programmes of great importance for the future of our country. Our concern has been echoed from IBM, who have described the likely outcomes of SDI as 'drip off ' rather than 'spin off '. John Fairclough of IBM is currently seconded to government as Chief Scientific Adviser, and has voiced his concern for valid commercial outcomes of research and development. Ken Warren has voiced his concerns over SDI in public, and has remained in contact with our Strategic Research Initiative.

Geoffrey Pattie MP, formerly Minister of State for Defence Recruitment and now Minister of State for Information Technology, has been involved in all the critical stages of negotiation for British participation in SDI, as well as the Westland affair and the attempted sale of part of British Leyland. At the Alvey conference held in Sussex on 1st July 1986, Geoffrey Pattie outlined his hopes for the development of British and European advanced information technology. He was asked by Paul Walton of the Strategic Research Initiative what would happen if the Americans offered large amounts of money to British companies and researchers under SDI. His reply was fascinating

> Mr George Chantry of the Department of Trade and Industry is working in the SDI Participation Office to make sure that the Americans do not gain control of our technology.

In other words it could be said that the secret purpose of the SDI Participation Office is to make sure that no contracts are signed by British companies and academics to participate in SDI. In this they have been completely successful – nobody outside MOD research establishments is currently working on SDI in Britain. Mr Pattie has received insufficient praise for this achievement.

Dr David Schwartz was formerly in charge of Strategic Nuclear Defence Policy in the US State Department and is now at the Institute of Strategic Studies. He and his colleagues in the State Department have a long-standing concern for arms control and the reduction of the threat of nuclear war. SDI, manipulated by the vultures in the Pentagon, poses a fundamental threat to arms control and the peace of our planet. The State Department and the Senate Armed Services Committee, chaired by Barry Goldwater, have asked us in Europe to provide two things. Firstly they wanted the technical infeasibility of the SDI project to be demonstrated by the scientific community. Secondly, they wanted political opposition to SDI to be stated by all opposition parties in Britain and Europe, making it clear that new governments to be elected in the coming months would not be bound by so-called Memoranda of Understanding. In return they would cut the budget for SDI requested by President Reagan. Both sides have kept their word, and the objective continues to be the withdrawal of the financial means of support for SDI, even if President Reagan continues to be devoted to it as policy.

John Selwyn Gummer MP, Minister of State for Agriculture, spoke with David Schwartz against Rip Bulkeley and myself at Birmingham University in February 1986 on the subject of SDI. Both have reconsidered their position since, and have remained in contact with our Strategic Research Initiative. It is now accepted by Mr Gummer and his colleagues, such as Chris Patten MP, Minister of State for Education and Science, that continuation with SDI participation would preclude the free use of our own advanced technology for government civil programmes in education, training and industry.

The position of Michael Heseltine, former Secretary of State for Defence, is insufficiently understood. In a fascinating interview for the Radio 4 *Today Programme* Michael Heseltine described the Memorandum of Understanding, still officially secret in perpetuity as a "private agreement". This has been interpreted by Tam Dalyell MP as meaning that it only bound the Prime Minister of the day, and did not even bind subsequent Secretaries of State for Defence, such as George Younger. Michael Heseltine himself, as a potential future Prime Minister, could therefore not see himself as bound by the

Memorandum which he himself negotiated and signed.

So who says "Yes" to Star Wars? It only appears to be in the interest of the California Defence Establishment, whose ideology it embodies. SDI is an automatic knowledge-based system intended to operate in real time without human control. The SDI system will know the answer, whatever the question turns out to be.

SECTION 3

CONSTRUCTIVE ALTERNATIVES

3.1
Fifth Generation Computers: Their Implications for Further Education

The United Kingdom has set a lead in the introduction of micro-computers into schools. It has also set a lead in advanced computing research, and in particular in logic programming, that has contributed to the current development of a new fifth generation of computers. These new computers are very different from those being introduced into schools, and require a very different style of programming and use. As it becomes clearer what form the new computers are to take, this chapter seeks to examine the implications of fifth generation computers for further education.

Fifth generation computers

The Japanese proposal

Since the first computers were produced following the Second World War, computer power has increased enormously but their size and cost have dramatically fallen. However, their design has remained fundamentally unchanged.

Written with Arthur Cotterell, and first published by the *Further Education Unit*, 1985.

The first computers resulted from considerable research activity in cryptography and numerical analysis, with the earliest computer languages at binary and machine code level, reflecting the mode of operation of the machine. Successive languages have been progressively "higher level", reflecting more the way humans think and use languages, such as English. Computer applications, formerly dominated by "number crunching" in mathematics and science, have extended to a wide range of subject areas, particularly with the developing use of databases.

The computer world has been dominated by American companies, and in particular IBM. However, the Japanese Ministry for International Trade and Industry (MITI) decided to coordinate a Japanese challenge, and commissioned an extensive study of research and development prospects. The results were announced in 1981, with the revelation of the plan to produce "fifth generation computers". The concept of generation derives from the hardware, successively built of vacuum tubes, transistors, integrated circuits and large-scale integrated circuits, stages shown in Figure 3.1.1. The new machines will be based on very large scale integration (VLSI) and involve several radical departures from conventional computer design.

Computers have always operated sequentially, with one central processing unit dealing with a sequence of instructions, known as a program. But fifth generation machines are highly parallel, with numerous processors working together. Traditional sequential programming languages will no longer be adequate, together with the concepts of computing which they embody. Accordingly, a new family of languages will be used, based on logic programming and running on the parallel machines.

At the user level these new machines will be very different from present day machines, where we "input" data using a "QWERTY" keyboard, and are normally obliged to use a particular computer language or notation. But it is proposed that in future we should be able to address the computer in our own natural language, or with graphics. Indeed, some microcomputers already accept some spoken commands, with others offering graphical features directed by a hand-held "mouse".

The user will be able to perform what the Japanese call "knowledge information processing", allowing computers to give advice on tasks such as repairing a car, making management decisions, translating from a foreign language. In fact, expert systems in America, from which many of the Japanese ideas were taken, have dealt with problems such as medical diagnosis and mineral exploration.

Figure 3.1.1 Five generations of computer technology

Generation	Electronic component	Advantages	Disadvantages .
1st generation 1940–52	Vacuum tubes	Vacuum tubes were the only electronic components available.	Large size; Generated heat; Air-conditioning needed; Unreliable; Constant maintenance.
2nd generation 1952–64	Transistors	Smaller size; Less heat generated; More reliable; Faster.	Air-conditioning required maintenance.
3rd generation 1964–71	Integrated circuits	Even smaller size; Even lower heat generated; Less power required; Even more reliable; Faster still.	Initially, problems with manufacture.
4th generation 1971–	Large-scale integrated circuits	No air-conditioning; Minimal maintenance; High component density; Cheapest.	In 1981 less powerful than mainframe computers.
5th generation		Currently under development.	

The expert systems are to be written in logic programming languages, for which the basis is PROLOG, with added facilities for knowledge representation. This represents both a departure from conventional computer science and software engineering where languages such as PASCAL, BASIC, etc. are used, as well as the dominant American artificial intelligence language LISP.

At the Fifth Generation Computer Systems Conference in Tokyo in November 1984, it was demonstrated that the ambitious research project is on schedule. PROLOG machines are running at ICOT (The Institute for New Generation Computing Research) with a new knowledge representation language, Mandala, and Concurrent PROLOG. Work continues in developing both the parallel machines and expert systems application, some of which were demonstrated. There is particular work on natural language understanding, using PROLOG, and on translation from spoken English to Japanese.

The international response

The Japanese initiative has prompted research and development programmes around the world. In particular, it was the Japanese invitation to collaborate that led in Britain to the setting up of the Alvey Committee by the then Minister of Information Technology, Kenneth Baker. In the United States, DARPA (Defence Advanced Research Project Agency) have an ambitious programme; IBM have greatly increased their activity in logic programming, and a number of major companies have combined their efforts in the MCC consortium. In Eastern Europe there is a Soviet-led Fifth Generation programme, building on logic programming expertize in Hungary. New research centres are being established in Australia, Israel, France, Germany and Canada, as well as in China.

The Alvey Programme for advanced information technology

In March 1983 government approval was announced for the main recommendations of the Alvey Report, a £350 million national prog-ramme of research and development involving collaboration between the Department of Education and Science, the Department of Trade and Industry, the Ministry of Defence, academic research groups and British industrial and commercial companies, with companies paying half the costs of their involvement. The Alvey Directorate was set up to direct this programme.

The Alvey Programme is less focused than the Japanese Fifth Generation Programme, but the Alvey Directorate has identified the enabling technologies of (see also Chapter 1.1):

Man-machine interface, (MMI) dealing with the ways in which humans interact with computers;
Intelligent knowledge-based systems (IKBS), the artificial intelli-gence part of the programme;
Software engineering, including the development of languages and techniques of software;
Very large scale integration (VLSI), the physics of small devices, their design and manufacture.

A further initiative in 1984 has addressed declarative systems architectures, supporting work on parallel computer architectures, logic programming and large databases. Declarative systems place emphasis on enabling the user to describe his problem, rather than being concerned with how to solve it.

The scope of the Alvey Programme can be illustrated by describing selected projects. These projects (termed demonstrator projects) have been chosen to exhibit and explore the potential of the enabling technologies:

1. A desktop voice-driven computer is being developed on a large demonstrator project led by Plessey. Using the new FLAGSHIP parallel computer under development at Imperial College and Manchester University with ICL and Plessey, and work in phonetics and linguistics at Edinburgh University, the company intend to produce a computer workstation that will, for example, take dictation for word processing.
2. ICL lead a large demonstrator project with the Department of Health and Social Security and the Universities of Surrey and Lancaster, together with Imperial College. Expert systems are being developed to aid claimants and DHSS staff, and to aid in the interpretation of legislation and regulations.
3. Numerical Algorithms Group Ltd. and the Departments of Computing and Mathematics at Imperial College are developing an "intelligent front end" to the GLIM statistical system, enabling wider range of users to make sure of its specialist facilities.

There is an increasing awareness that high-technology manpower is the key to the effective use of advanced information technology, and that failure to recognize this manpower need could be fatal for our national competitiveness. Alvey has responded with funds for supporting new information technology lectureships in universities, as well as research projects in numerous universities and companies. New distance learning courses are under development with the Open University, and the new IKBS Journeyman Scheme supports the secondment of experienced people from industry to work for six-month spells in selected research centres, initially Imperial College, London and the Turing Institute, Glasgow.

The research community remains small, and urgent measures are needed both to train researchers and to equip the wider community for the intelligent use of the new generation of technology. This is also an international problem, requiring new kinds of collaboration and institutional structures.

The problem regarding fifth generation computers and further education

A first reaction to fifth generation computing is to view this development as an extension of present day computing. However, fifth generation computers are not simply a development of present technology. They cannot be treated in the same way, nor introduced with the same courses, languages, hardware and attitudes. We are obliged to explore new approaches for the following reasons:

1. The speed of technological changes has exceeded the capacity of academic computer scientists to keep up. The problem is all the greater for college lecturers.
2. Until recently there has not been available literature on which further education lecturers can draw for considered views on fifth generation computers.
3. The research community in the UK, particularly in Intelligent Knowledge-Based Systems, although distinguished, is small in numbers.
4. To date, government plans in fifth generation computing or advanced information technology have given little place to education and to non-advanced further education, in particular.
5. Government has not regarded further education as its preferred instrument of technology transfer, and control is being increasingly passed to other agencies, such as Youth Training Schemes run by the Manpower Services Commission.

The problems posed by fifth generation computers for education and training

The manpower crisis in the information technology industries

The Alvey Report on advanced information technology makes frequent mention of the manpower implications of work in advanced information technology, and of the need for an extensive programme of education and training at all levels. The Alvey Report and the Government regard British success in advanced information technology as essential for a sound economic future. However, government cuts in education provision have reduced the number of computer science and other technology graduates since 1981. Indeed a succession of reports, including the Butcher Report and the NEDO Report, have identified a shortfall of several thousand high technology graduates per year. A group of high technology companies have responded by proposing the funding of a new information technology university at Milton Keynes, and possibly a further institution at Salford, using former university buildings.

Further, the need for high technology education applies at non-advanced and technician level if British industry is to have skilled manpower. Numbers employed in information technology in Britain have, in fact, fallen in recent years while the rival industries overseas have expanded. Whereas 152,000 jobs existed in 1970, by 1983 the number had dropped to 123,000. Many traditional apprenticeship schemes have closed and at the same time Britain has many more unqualified school-leavers than her industrial rivals with less provision for vocational training for all. Many industrial training boards have ceased activity, while few high technology companies have accepted responsibility for the training of their employees, preferring to attract trained personnel from their rivals through the offer of higher salaries. They, in turn, lose many staff in the face of better financial offers from overseas and, in particular, the USA. This syndrome is persistent and increasingly powerful. Thus, there is a resulting manpower crisis in the information technology industries.

The inappropriateness of traditional solutions

Traditional solutions for training problems in this new fifth generation computing field are inappropriate, for the provision of limited computer hardware without a coherent education or training methodology or strategy is placing considerable strains on the institutions concerned. Present provision also gives undue emphasis to hardware and to programming in BASIC, offering the student a limited and limiting impression of the power of the new technology. Indeed, the Alvey Report expressed concern about the spread of a low-level understanding of BASIC due essentially to the wide availability of microcomputers; the report stated that the provision of hardware was not enough, for "teachers must be properly trained, and the languages taught chosen with an eye for the future" and college courses in computer science have of necessity been limited by the degree of understanding and experience of the lecturer. Indeed unversity departments of computer science prefer their undergraduates not to have taken such courses, seeking instead evidence of sound studies in traditional subjects, especially mathematics.

There has been an increasing divergence in the emphases of university computer science courses and the stated requirements in industry for short-term recruitment. Data processing departments still advertize for FORTRAN and COBOL programmers, while university courses emphasize languages such as PASCAL, ADA LISP and PROLOG.

Such divergence is a manifestation of a software crisis in computer science, where the main cost of a large computer application is software development and maintenance. With large complex systems in defence or commerce, it is essential that systems should be reliable and comprehensible. For example, the recent problems in launching satellites from the American space shuttle have been attributed to a simple syntax error in a FORTRAN program, and the panic at the Three Mile Island nuclear power station was exacerbated by the computer system being unable to explain what was going wrong and resorting to cause lights to flash. So conventional programming has not proved adequate to the task, and the new approaches that are being developed represent a radical departure from standard practice. New techniques of software engineering, of formal methods, of the use of fourth generation languages such as PASCAL etc. have so far had limited impact in college courses, where syllabuses can be slow to change. A similar situation exists in industrial training courses.

New techniques of fifth generation computing may have a limited impact in an educational and training environment that preserves an approach to the problem from previous decades. Experience suggests that the introduction of new ideas and techniques through traditional computer science courses may be less effective than adopting a "knowledge-based" approach, where the emphasis is on thinking about particular problems with the aid of the computer, enriching the teaching and learning of other subjects rather than perceiving computing as a separate, unrelated study.

Further education and fifth generation computers

The possible impact of fifth generation computers in further education and, in particular, of expert systems can be described for each of the three areas: the curriculum, education technology and the management of learning, and the organisation and management of colleges. Expert systems, as developed in the last decade in American research laboratories, and now becoming increasingly widespread on microcomputers, have a number of distinguishing characteristics. They contain:

1. Knowledge concerning a particular subject.
2. Rules of inference so that the knowledge can be organized and manipulated.
3. The means of users having a dialogue with the system using a form close to natural language.
4. The means of explaining the reasoning used in arriving at conclusions.

Early examples, concerned medical diagnosis and mineral exploration. A great variety of areas, from the curriculum, through educational technology to college administration, are amenable to the application of such systems, as the example concerning legislation indicates.

It will be evident that the actual impact of the use of new computer technology in further education will be partly consequent on policy decisions yet to be taken, so we illustrate the possible impact with a series of examples, trying to make reference to areas of current FEU concern, as evidenced by sponsored projects.

Curriculum issues

We envisage that, rather than computer studies being a separate curriculum area, the use of the technology should increasingly underlie the teaching and learning of each subject area, offering a knowledge-based approach to computer literacy. We draw the parallel with the initial stages of learning to read and write in primary school, where the activities of reading and writing increasingly occur in the context of different subjects. Experience suggests that the initial familiarization using advanced computing can be brief, if it is well presented. Furthermore, new microcomputers that are entering use in colleges assume no past technical knowledge from the user, and present fewer obstacles to intelligent use than the previous generation of microcomputers whose use is now prevalent. Some examples are given below.

Car maintenance

Students need to gain familiarity with different vehicles and their maintenance problems. We are familiar with diagnostic checking equipment which gives a numerical and visual display of the results of electrical and mechanical tests. Students will use diagnostic fault-finding expert systems to help them identify the causes of vehicle malfunctioning. A conversational interaction will occur, using a keyboard, "mouse" device or voice communication, with the system providing advice and guidance to the student. The system can also simulate problems for the student to solve, including those that could be dangerous in workshop conditions, and monitor his or her progress.

Plumbing

Plumbing can be taught as a knowledge-based skill, enhanced with the assistance of advanced computing. We can envisage handheld powerful computers used on the job, giving access to the databases of local suppliers, and to the records and plans of the local council and water board. Complex planning and design problems may be resolved by describing them to the computer. "How can I design this kitchen so that it contains a washing machine, a dishwasher and a sink, as well as radiators and a central heating boiler?" "Can the heating system that has been ordered support all those appliances?" "What modifications can be made to satisfy different constraints?"

We can envisage the plumber seeking the advice of an expert system, possibly based in the site hut. His problem might be the choice of appropriate pipes to meet the needs of the kitchen, and he may be restricted to a certain number of suppliers. The dialogue in the site hut could take the form:

Plumber: What pipes should I choose?
Computer: What appliances do you have and what do they take in?
Plumber: The sink, washing machine and dishwasher each take in cold and hot water. The boiler takes in cold water. The cooker takes in gas.
Computer: What sources do you have and what do they give out?
Plumber: The water main gives out cold water. The boiler gives out hot water. The sink, washing machine and dishwasher give out waste water.
Computer: What does the sink work with?
Plumber: The water main and the boiler.
Computer: What dimension is the sink input?
Plumber: 1 inch.
Computer: What dimension is the water main output?
Plumber: 2 inches.
Computer: 1 inch pipe and 2 inch pipe are available from Store B. 1 inch to 2 inch converter is available from Store B.

Using a simple programme, the computer has solved some problems by obtaining information from the plumber, and others by checking the database of stock listed by local suppliers, from whom it could place an order at the end of the interaction. It can explain how it arrives at a conclusion. For example:

Plumber: Why do I need a 1 inch to 2 inch converter?
Computer: You need a 1 inch to 2 inch converter because you said that the sink takes in water and the water main

gives out water. In order to connect the sink with a dimension of 1 inch and the water main with a dimension of 2 inches I have suggested a 1 inch to 2 inch converter, which I know is available at Store B.

The plumber is not likely to want to type text on a keyboard. Rather, he should have the option of using a touch-sensitive screen, where he might touch the picture, or "icon" of a sink, washing machine or other familiar part of the plumber's world instead of spelling it out. Such facilities are becoming available for microcomputers, and can be used for practical purposes, especially for problems where the likely components to be fitted are known in advance. The computer is coming closer to the plumber's world, and could become as familiar a tool as a wrench. This has implications for further education as students can easily develop, modify and use systems to help with such problems and they will expect to see such techniques as part of their further education course.

Financial modelling

Financial modelling is a concept with far broader applications than economics and business studies. Current research is developing "intelligent front end" interfaces to complex modelling systems, giving the non-specialist student access to economic and financial models, and the means of receiving explanations of answers given. A student may be asked to explore the impact of a change in the level of rates in the financial planning of the local authority, using a computer model of the borough finance department. He might want to ask what level of wage increase would produce the lowest rate of increase in unemployment according to the Treasury model of the economy, already open for public use in computers. Courses on developing a small business could use models taking account of cash flow problems, changes in personal and indirect taxation, as well as non-numerical factors such as employment legislation.

Design

New computer systems are making increasing use of graphics, and graphically-based operating systems. Using the hand-held "mouse", the designer can select from different "icons" displayed on the screen, and can develop complex designs. Different "windows" can be opened on the screen to give "painting" or "editing" facilities, and the final design can be printed out. Photographs and maps can be displayed and incorporated. If a tool or system is being designed, the computer can be so programmed that the design can be used as a model of the system, performing some of the functions in simulation.

History, humanities and social science

Computer usage needs no longer to be based on a numerically-oriented view of computers. Historians and social scientists need to ask questions, to explore complex bodies of knowledge and to understand the actions and belief systems of others. Local and national records are increasingly available in computer form. Understanding a complex situation is often made easier by developing a model or simulation. Historical and social scientific research projects can be enhanced by the classroom use of the computer. For example, students of nineteenth century history may make use of the local trade directories and census returns in the form of databases, enabling them to explore historical issues in greater depth. Progressively, computer use will not require knowledge of computer languages but the ability to express oneself clearly in natural language.

Languages

Considerable research has been devoted to natural language understanding and translation using the computer. Systems available to colleges will cope with defined subject areas where the vocabulary is known and sentence structures are not too complex. Such systems are also likely to be powerful teaching tools, showing how grammatical rules work in practice, and de-mystifying some linguistic concepts that are not explained in courses today. Language systems could be used in both written and oral work, and could be developed by the student.

Electronic office

We are approaching the time when issues of the electronic office, as of computer studies/literacy, may be subsumed in the teaching of other subjects. Already many American colleges require their students to have a computer, which is used for word processing and electronic mail as well as for programming and the running of applications. Such courses may initially become more "experience-centred", allowing the working of an office to be explored in more depth. Changing hierarchies in modern electronic offices must be reflected in courses in further education.

Science

Considerable use has already been made of computers in some science courses and we can here explore the enhancements to be expected from fifth generation computers. Non-numerical knowledge will have greater attention, with students manipulating, experimenting with and interrogating knowledge structures. For each rule or connection there will be a corresponding explanation available to the student. A complex piece of reasoning can be traced and examined. Models can be tested. Large databases can be consulted, and pilot expert systems constructed to organize and explain problems in science. What conclusions can be drawn from the periodic table of the elements? How is chemical nomenclature arrived at? How do we measure the age of archaeological finds? How can we develop our own taxonomy for plants or insects? What threats to the environment could be posed by fertilizers, chemical plants, or conversion of marshes to agricultural use?

Engineering

It is likely that engineering courses will pay increasing attention to formal thinking. Clear descriptions will lead to a design for a product or a programme for a robot or control device. Ideas of expert systems will be used in application areas such as water control and vehicle monitoring. Already the discipline of software engineering is influential, with a corresponding growth of engineering software. Further, the distinction between hardware and software is likely to become less significant with students building devices incorporating microprocessors with software or VLSI programmes. For example, robots and robot arms will be used with other more conventional machine tools providing a significant extension of current college work in CNC and CAD/CAM. The new field of Computer Integrated Manufacture (CIM) is developing the use of advanced information technology throughout manufacturing industry.

Information technology

Information technology in itself affects the nature of what is taught, as well as methods of teaching. We have yet to see the educational effects of college-wide networks with electronic mail, bulletin boards for interest groups, and communication with computer systems around the world. Just as styles of writing have been affected by the advent of word processors, styles of research and communication will change with computer networks. Electronic reference sources will take over some of the current roles of the books in the college library, and may enable students to pursue their studies in greater depth. There is a growing case for courses in the implications of information technology, possibly as an extension to current courses in communication and media studies.

Overall issues

There is likely to be a challenge to conventional curriculum subjects, in that teaching will have to reflect technological advances with emphasis on clear logical thinking, and on personal study skills. The computer may facilitate a more individual approach to learning by the student, and a more knowledge-based approach to teaching by the lecturer with a greater and more thorough use of library facilities, where material will be stored on magnetic media and videodisc as well as in books.

Educational technology

As computing becomes an increasingly universal technology, it will also change its role in educational technology. The computer will lead to more flexibility in educational technology and the result will be a system more responsive to the needs of the individual.

This analysis draws on the work of Pickup and Cameron on the FEU Project "Computer-based Educational Consultancy"*, at Garnett College. The work was concerned with applying artificial intelligence techniques in creating microcomputer software to assist teachers in course planning. Traditionally the methodologies and expertise employed tended to be informal or *ad hoc*, and therefore not readily specifiable as a "knowledge base".

Current requirements, however, are reversing this pattern and an increasing burden is being placed on course planners to specify their intentions in detail, often in the terms of complex schemes. Computer software, which assists openly and intelligently in this activity, should not only serve as a productivity aid but also enhance the lecturer's own conception of the task in hand. Indeed, an important additional application for such software will be in context of teacher training.

Pickup and Cameron have developed a programme for:

* "Computer-based Educational Consultancy", FEU Research Project 141, formerly at Garnett now at Kingston College of Further Education.

1. Categorizing educational objectives;
2. Checking a course against complex requirements and recommendations;
3. Selecting teaching strategies using decision-making principles described in three different forms.

However, a particular problem identified by Pickup and Cameron, in common with other researchers, is that of knowledge acquisition – the problem of transferring expertise from the human expert to the machine. The work at Garnett College has explored the use of decision nets and, using specific examples, demonstrates the selection of appropriate methods for teaching a particular subject. More advanced techniques are being investigated at the Turing Institute in Glasgow, where expert systems are designed to inductively learn new rules for classification or for chess-playing, with some impressive results.

The same technology that is being used to advise lecturers could, of course, advise students on what courses to take, on which teaching method (given a choice of learning) they will find must useful and on how to plan their work.

Similarly, "education consultants" could offer careers guidance and welfare rights information. In each case the text of the knowledge base should be accessible and comprehensible, and explanations should be provided for information given.

In general, educational technology is presented here as helping to make knowledge openly available. Elsewhere we are likely to see the use of the technology for purposes of persuasion, with the user denied free access and explanations. It may be, in a manner reminiscent of Vance Packard's *The Hidden Persuaders*, that by making open use of the technology in education we can help expose its dishonest and partial use elsewhere. There has been a tradition of work in "intelligent computer-assisted instruction" and "intelligent tutoring systems". More powerful low-cost computers and programming techniques are bringing such systems within reach of college budgets, and should increasingly incorporate the results of artificial intelligence research.

Organization and management

For many years organizations have been described in "systems" terms, and methods of management have been applied that derived from past generations computing research. We have the example today of the organization of ICOT in Tokyo, adapted to the management of the problem areas and methods of advanced technology. The

British Alvey Programme is likewise forcing new methods of organization and management to meet the needs of collaboration between academia and industry.

In further education there are likely to be changes in organization and management as a result of fifth generation computing that extend beyond the computer as a management tool. The very existence of the colleges may be called into question with the spread of powerful computing facilities in the home. There may be a radical reassessment of the role and form of face-to-face teaching, and institutional amalgamations may be necessary to meet the new perceived needs. Further, companies may decide to massively increase their own computer-aided training in-house, and place correspondingly fewer demands on the college.

Within colleges, some new concepts may have an impact on organization and management. Discussion of problem solving by "top down" and "bottom up" strategies, emphasis on clear description and specification, development of explanation facilities and "user friendly" interfaces, concern for structure, modular development and methods of debugging – all directly relate to organization and management. The presence of students and lecturers with expertise in the "electronic office" should motivate administrators to apply the new techniques to their own institutions, drawing on the experience of participative democratic systems design in Scandinavia and the work of Professor Enid Mumford in Britain.

Staff development

Of central importance is the provision of staff development that responds to differing staff reactions to new technology. Our experience to date indicates that the staff who take most willingly to expert systems are those with a clear perception of their own specialist area, a scepticism of conventional computing and a reluctance to compromise academic principles for a machine. On the other hand, the greatest resistance has been shown by those with the involvement with conventional computing, often at the expense of a concern for traditional subjects.

Colleges will have to assign significant periods of time for ongoing staff development, both in-house and in consultation with local companies and research centres, which could involve exchanges and secondments. Staff development should be based on the core areas of IT and expert systems where the aim is to familiarize the learner with concepts of knowledge, and information leading to procedural and declarative thinking. LOGO and conventional programming languages would be involved in the area dealing with procedural thinking, with PROLOG involved in declarative thinking. Important applications areas such as information handling (databases and spreadsheets) and word processing would be included. An introduction to expert systems would demonstrate how the knowledge structures of the "expert" are held in the computer and how such systems are put to use. Finally, the social implications (i.e. the effects on leisure and working activities) for all these areas would be taken into account.

The basic elements of a formal staff development programme should therefore include areas such as:

concepts of knowledge and information;
procedural thinking in LOGO and conventional programming;
declarative thinking with logic and PROLOG;
information handling: databases and spreadsheets;
word processing;
introduction to expert systems;
social implications.

An important dimension for staff training would be the applications of each of these IT areas in the subject areas of individual members of staff. In addition to the specialist skills and knowledge associated with each of these areas, staff would have to analyse their subject area to prepare a curriculum showing how these areas of IT relate to topics within their subject. More specifically, the participants should be able to:

1. Describe and model some of the learning problems of their students.
2. Describe in general terms how such descriptions or models can be handled by a computer.
3. Identify different approaches to knowledge representation related to particular learning problems.
4. Evaluate the possibilities of artificial intelligence ideas and tools as a possible solution to given learning problems.
5. Plan in cooperation with appropriate colleagues, the implementation of a learning activity incorporating artificial intelligence techniques.
6. Construct an effective learning activity incorporating artificial intelligence ideas and tools.

Resources must be provided to allow for individual study with a computer. These teacher-centred activities should be supported by lectures and wider presentations, but successful staff development is as much based upon participative learning, appraisal, visits and real curriculum development – as it is on formal sessions.

Staff development must relate to a number of organizational and management tasks that can now be performed (although taking into account the Data Protection legislation). Some examples of these tasks are:

1. The use of large rational databases used for records and profiles, with retrieval – using writing packages if desired.
2. Timetable construction, with its reasoning in terms of rules made clear, is a classic example for potential application of the computer, although at present heads of departments unaided can outdo the computer; increasingly complex tasks of budgeting and costing external courses can be done.
3. With an intelligent spreadsheet system, allowing automatic preparation of reports for governing bodies and local education authorities, policy models can be developed, refined and tested before implementation.

A central problem of organization and management in colleges is identifying the people for whom the computer can be used to solve rather than exacerbate problems, in management and interpersonal relations. The computer is a tool and not an end in itself. A college principal may want an "intelligent workstation" on his desk, to increase communications with colleagues and sources of information, but the management of the college will not necessarily be improved by linking all lecturers to a network.

Policy recommendations for further education

Further education should not be seen in isolation from more general problems and from the activities of other education and training bodies.

Consideration should be given at ministry level to policy initiatives in further education, in consultation with the Department of Trade and Industry and the Department of Employment.

The following policy recommendations are made:

1. There should be a DES national conference on implications of fifth generation computers for further education.
2. There should be an IKBS Education and Training Journeyman

Scheme whereby lecturers are seconded from further education to work in advanced research centres for periods of six months.

3. Video and text materials should be prepared for use in staff awareness courses in colleges, together with software.
4. Colleges should be encouraged to establish Information Technology Development Units.
5. College units should collaborate with each other and with subject specialists in developing applications courseware.
6. Company involvement should be encouraged in collaborative projects.
7. FEU and further education colleges should seek involvement in ESRC and Alvey Programme initiatives in the educational implications of fifth generation computers.

The role of an Information Technology Development Unit

An Information Technology Unit in a college of further education should be the focus of a number of interrelated activities in staff development:

1. The development and teaching of a core course in concepts of advanced information technology and expert systems to be offered to all students.
2. The development of modules incorporating applications of advanced information technology as components of the range of college courses.
3. Introducing artificial intelligence to teachers.
4. Collaborating with subject specialist teachers in the introduction of applications of advanced information technology into the teaching of their courses.

The central purpose of the unit should be technology transfer, from the few with specialist expertise to the many who can make use of it. It will require computer hardware with sufficient power to run small expert systems; the same microcomputers that are now in commercial use. The management structure and system of accountability will vary between colleges, but the Information Technology Development Unit should not be identified with mathematics, science, or even computing, but involve representatives of each college department.

A college-based unit should enjoy the support of the Further Education Unit New Technology Working Group at a national level, and should establish connections with research groups and centres in

their geographical vicinity, whether based in universities, polytechnics or industry.

Extending the core

There is considerable potential for building on the core course for
students and the introductory course for lecturers by progressively
developing modules incorporating applications of advanced information technology as components of specialist courses.

Some materials will have to be developed by the college unit with
staff from the appropriate departments, some may become available
from outside sources including other colleges, and some may be
produced by adapting existing software systems for tutorial use. For
example, intelligent front end programmes can be developed for large
software systems making them more accessible to the non-specialist
user.

The expertise of the subject specialist lecturer is of central importance in the educational developments of expert systems and other
forms of advanced information technology. Systems that are developed must meet the criteria of the expert, and should involve him
in the development where possible. Staff of the Information Technology Development Unit take on the role of "knowledge engineer",
seeking to represent the knowledge of the subject area in a way that
satisfies the expert and provides appropriate answers and explanations in response to questions.

The lesson of previous collaborative research projects in this field is
that this is the crucial stage in "technology transfer", where the new
technology is taken on by the expert teacher or lecturer without
sacrificing his view of his subject. The resulting programmes and
educational activity will vary greatly according to the background and
educational approaches of the lecturers. The same programme should
be capable of use in a variety of ways.

3.2
Progress in Education and Training Applications: "Son of Alvey" Programme (SOAP)

Introduction

In this article we examine lessons that can be learnt from the "Alvey Experience" which can be of use to us as we seek to establish new programmes in education and training on a national scale. Particularly in the area of intelligent knowledge-based systems (IKBS), we find the same hardware and software in increasing use in industrial applications, education and training. It is an area of the Alvey Programme where the lead has been taken by university and polytechnic research groups, for whom education and training have been a long-standing research interest, and where training has had to be provided for industrial collaborators before they can make a viable technical contribution.

It is worthy of note that, in the absence of significant funding in the United Kingdom for research in education and training with advanced information technology, many researchers in the field in the Alvey period have been diverted into work on industrial applications. Others, have moved to the better-funded research environment of the United States. During the Alvey period some have returned, but the Alvey Programme is now closed to commitment, and no further significant civil funds are on offer up to or after 1988–1989.

First published in *Newsletter of the British Computer Society Expert Systems Group*, Summer 1986.

The active research and development community in IKBS in Britain is small: one meets many of the same people in both the Alvey Programme and in education and training. They are a scarce resource: the country cannot afford any diminution in their numbers. On the contrary, apart from the general needs of industry, frequently emphasized by the Government in Industry Year, to enhance the quality of and commitment to training in general, taking advantage of advanced techniques and technology, there is a critical need to train more experts in advanced information technology, and in particular in IKBS. The line between training with and in artificial intelligence can at times be a fine one, as is appropriate for an area where thinking is the subject matter. My experience, and that of others involved in the new profession of research management, is that technical issues are by no means our only concern in developing and transfering knowledge and expertise.

The Alvey Programme is itself an experiment in research management on a national scale, and has involved considerable reflection, evaluation, and modifications in the light of experience. Formal evaluations are at present being undertaken by the Science Policy Research Unit at Sussex University, the Centre for Business Strategy at the London Business School, together with Templeton College Oxford, and the Manchester Business School. Interim reports are now becoming available. There has been some study of technology transfer in areas such as software engineering (where companies seem reluctant to modify long-established obsolete practices) but there has been little attention given to training *per se*. This is despite the Alvey Director, Brian Oakley, and the IKBS Director, David Thomas, placing an increasing emphasis on training, and the fact that there are many current unfilled research posts as either the qualified people do not exist, or they are not attracted by the university research salaries which are dwarfed by what is on offer in industry or overseas.

All too often we hear sweeping criticism from the Department of Employment, the Manpower Services Commission, the Department of Trade and Industry, the Confederation of British Industry with their new Skills Shortage Agency, the major information technology firms that have survived since IT Year (overall employment in information technology industries in the United Kingdom has fallen in the last five years, and the trend shows few signs of changing), and from highly paid firms of consultants who state the obvious in stark, well-illustrated terms. Government says that industry is not spending enough on training by comparison with our rivals. Industry says that government is not spending enough on education. Neither visibly plans to spend more themselves, and will doubtless continue to blame the other as they collapse into bankruptcy and "fourth division" status.

The argument of this paper is that there is an alternative: that the means exist to mount a national programme for education and training with expert systems technology, and that there is no excuse for not starting right away. "Son of Alvey" must start now, learning lessons from its parent, and perhaps benefiting from some initial pocket money and seedcorn. We should not waste time looking for a pot of gold: the key resource on which we have to draw is between our ears.

At some stage an official report will doubtless be commissioned. Here are some interim conclusions, based on three years experience of the "Alvey Experience".

EXECUTIVE SUMMARY OF THE "SON OF ALVEY" REPORT

It is possible to set up and run a national collaborative programme of research and development involving three government ministries, numerous companies, and almost all universities.

For "Son of Alvey" the ministries concerned would be the Department of Employment, the Department of Trade and Industry, and the Department of Education and Science, with their associated "Quangos" such as the Manpower Services Commission, the Council for Educational Technology, the Further Education Unit, the Economic and Social Research Council, the Microelectronics Education Programme, the Microelectronics Support Unit, the British Library, Open Tech, and the Open University. All other government departments would be obliged to participate at the planning and implementation stages, in order to set a lead as models of good practice in training and industrial relations.

Companies would be drawn from the fields of computer hardware, software and services, publishing, exhibitions, video and communications, together with industry sectors reorganized in an approximation of the former structure of the Industrial Training Boards, of which a few, such as the Engineering Industry Training Board, are active today. They might also be represented through employers organizations, the Confederation of British Industry, the Trade Unions and the Trades Union Congress. City companies, financial institutions and regulatory bodies would be involved, to give added insights into the market consequences of increased investment in training, and to put their own houses in order.

Universities would have a less significant role, except inasmuch as they are centres of excellence in particular enabling technologies or applications domains. A larger role would be played by polytechnics and colleges of higher and further education, where there is a close acquaintance with the requirements of industry.

Support for fundamental research and teaching must be maintained in addition to collaborative industrial applications work.
It is noticeable that Japan, taken as a model for commitment to industrial development, is placing an increasing emphasis on pure, fundamental work, seen as providing the source for future generations of applications.

In Britain whole research groups are obliged to emigrate, and departments are closed. It is not surprising that there is a campaign to "Save British Science". A first step must be for government to regard education, and for industry to regard training, as an investment to be increased and not a cost to be cut.

In Japan companies run their own in-house technical universities, and are concerned with the lifetime employment and development of their employees.

In Britain short-term economic thinking leads to the closure of skills centres and company reluctance to release staff for in-service training. Government is among the worst offenders, with a high proportion of in-service activities for teachers still being funded by teachers in their own time. Computer companies are notorious for preferring to "head-hunt" skilled staff than to train them in-house. On that basis the stock of skilled professionals stays roughly constant, but the number of companies falls through bankruptcy.

More attention must be given to the underlying rules and infrastructure, which should be in place before the programme starts. Different ministries, departments and companies have different bureaucratic procedures and financial regimes, which have to be reconciled if any collaborative project is to obtain its full complement of paperwork. In education and training this will include attention to the varying local, regional and industrial sector structures, together with the attendant regulations of sponsoring ministries.

A system of intellectual property rights and royalty payments should be drawn up consistent with overall government policy.
The Alvey Experience has shown that collaborative projects require legal collaboration agreements, which will vary greatly, though conforming to one of a limited number of general models. Where public and private sectors are working together, or where a process of privatization or merger is under way, there can be problems which are best addressed early on. Increasingly the Treasury assumes that state-supported educational institutions will attract outside funds. Universities can regard themselves as having suffered under Alvey financial terms, as they receive no overheads payments and are often not even provided with the physical premises in which to do the work for which they are contracted. Royalties should reflect this.

University and college administrators should be involved in the running of the programme as it affects their institutions, and encouraged to gain an insight into the way "the other side" lives in industry.
This was a major omission from the Alvey Programme, due to be remedied if there is an "Alvey 2", following recommendations of the "After Alvey" Committee and the Committee of Vice-Chancellors and Principals. To a significant extent, existing programmes in further education and training with industry have provided experience in this critical area of institutional interfaces, though there is clearly room for improvement, which could be facilitated by a new collaborative programme.

Collaborative projects and training should involve full participation of trades unions and staff associations.
This has again been a defect of the Alvey Programme, which has diminished the effectiveness of particular applications projects. The very structure of the Manpower Services Commission with its trade union commissioners, and the tripartite involvement on NEDC should be built on in a new programme. Research in Scandinavia and in Britain funded by ESRC suggests that the introduction of new technology and practices is enormously more effective if it is accomplished through a process of consultation. Research managers themselves need training in personnel management and industrial relations.

There should be discussion of, and consideration given to, the social implications of the new technology in the workplace, possibly through the participation of ESRC.
Again this was a notable omission from the Alvey Programme, and from many conferences on intelligent knowledge-based systems.

Training makes no sense without an awareness of the social context in which it is to be acquired and deployed. We must not fall into the easy trap of talking about instructional delivery systems. Authoritarian instruction can be delivered. Learning is an interactive process of mixed initiatives in an appropriate environment, of which the computer or expert system is only a part.

There should be provision for the administrative, legal and employment aspects of bankruptcy or take-over of participating companies and government agencies.

This is particularly in light of the continuing process of privatization and of restructuring in the information technology industry. The implications of British firms falling into foreign control (as is increasingly the case) have to be considered.

Research and development funding for the academic institutions involved should be assured over the long term, with rolling grants for centres of excellence.

It takes many years to build up a strong team in an educational research group, and a lapse in funding can destroy it beyond repair in days.

Key research centres should be encouraged to build associations with training agencies, enterprise boards and trades councils to aid the transfer and dissemination of the technology.

There are a number of emerging models for this, ranging from science parks such as in Cambridge, Aston and South Bank Polytechnic, to associations between Imperial College and Kingston College of Further Education, Turing Institute and Glasgow College of Technology, the London New Technology Network and the Greater London Enterprise Board. Teaching companies, joint studentships, secondments and consultancies offer further routes to technology transfer.

Demonstrations and exhibitions should be organized in London and the regions to raise awareness of practical industrial training with and in new technology. These should be organized by collaborative teams including user companies in each industrial sector.

The Alvey Programme is now encouraging the establishment of demonstration facilities administered by the National Computing Centre and the Edinburgh Artificial Intelligence Applications Institute. Companies should be encouraged to host exemplar projects for their industrial sector.

Government departments should take a lead in the innovative use of intelligent training, and in procurement of appropriately generic systems.

Further encouragement should be given to the ethos of "precompetitive collaboration" which distinguishes successful projects under Alvey, ESPRIT and ICOT.

Close relationships should be maintained with professional associations, such as the British Computer Society, the Institution of Electrical Engineers, the Society for Artificial Intelligence and Simulation of Behaviour, the Society of Education Officers, the British Association for Commercial and Industrial Education, the Historical Association, the Mathematical Association, the National Association for the Teaching of English, the Geographical Association, the Institute for Training Development and the Institute of Personnel Management.

Useful Alvey structures to be adapted for "Son of Alvey"

1. The Alvey IKBS Journeyman Scheme, running at Imperial College and Turing Institute, whereby professionals are seconded to work in a leading research group for a period of months, has been adapted in a secondment scheme for industrial trainers financed by MSC at Kingston College of Further Education. This can lead to a long-term association between the research centre and a group or club of companies.
2. The Alvey Expert Systems Starter Pack, produced with the National Computing Centre, is being emulated in a Further Education Unit/MSC project at Kingston College of Further Education, building on previous work at Exeter University School of Education, Imperial College and Logic Programming Associates. Different "toolkits" and "shells" are being developed to aid in teaching and training in different subject domains.
3. Alvey IKBS Community Clubs, addressing different industrial sectors such as banking and finance, water, process control, transport and planning now involve about 200 companies. They should be extended and augmented to incorporate training, from their present role in co-sponsoring an exemplar project of their own specification.

4. Alvey Category Clubs, now being formed, bring together workers on related projects in the national programme to exchange experiences and formulate new proposals. In the IKBS Directorate, for example, clubs address knowledge-based systems, logic-based environments, vision, speech and declarative systems. A joint club is likely to be established with the Man-Machine Interface Directorate concerning intelligent computer-aided instruction.

5. Demonstrator projects, whether run on a large scale and embracing all enabling technologies or on a smaller scale in IKBS, can be a powerful way of "pulling through" the technology to the industrial workplace. A national training programme should have a firm basis of geographically and industrially distributed practical demonstrators, with successive levels of sophistication over time.

6. Directed programmes, such as the Alvey Logic Programming Initiative, can be an effective way of deriving the maximum benefit from scarce manpower that is spread around the country. Effort can be dissipated if a plethora of unsolicited and unrelated projects are supported. Often an effective project will be designed by the contractors with the programme research manager.

7. The Alvey IKBS and MMI Advisory Groups should be called on to offer technical advice regarding the application of IKBS technology to training.

8. Project steering committees should include representatives of project participants together with civil servants from sponsoring ministries, and professional monitoring officers.

9. Theme managers should be appointed, on a part-time consulting basis, at a national level, to provide an overview of a particular aspect of the technology or its application. This provides an additional opportunity for strengthening "human networks" in a national programme.

10. There should not be a large bureaucracy, but a small group of managers with the power to take decisions, drawing on a variety of advice. Members of this group, or directorate, should be drawn from the sponsoring ministries, together with collaborating companies and academic institutions.

11. Independent evaluation teams should be commissioned to make regular reports on the management of the programme and the extent of dissemination of good practice. Some research will be required to establish appropriate methodologies.

12. Close links should be established with equivalent programmes elsewhere in Europe.

The ingredients for such a programme exist today. Government and industry have resources which can be deployed in training, but lack experience and expertise in new technologies and techniques deriving from work in artificial intelligence. Experience and expertise can be found in the education system. As the people concerned get to know each other better, traditional barriers can be broken down, and progress can be made in education and training applications. We now have encouraging examples of small-scale projects: as with software it is not always easy to scale up to national systems running in real time. It will be harder if we are not prepared to learn from relevant experimental results.

3.3
A Way Forward for Advanced Information Technology: SHI — a Strategic Health Initiative

As the Alvey Programme for advanced information technology moves into its third year, the writer suggests one way forward after 1988, a Strategic Health Initiative (SHI). After an analysis of current collaboration in the applications of artificial intelligence, an overview is given of the potential in the field of health, and of current work with expert systems. A number of research questions are raised for the SHI, including implications for the patient and for social provision. Practical suggestions are made for initial moves, and the issue is placed in an economic and moral context, in addition to technical considerations.

The context
UK current strength in advanced computing research

The United Kingdom has a considerable reputation internationally in the field of advanced computing and, in particular, in the area known as "intelligent knowledge-based systems". This strength lies largely in the area of academic research, as British companies have not to date

---

First published in *Artificial Intelligence for Society*, ed. Karamjit Gill, Wiley, 1986.

led in exploitation. Funding for this research has been erratic. British companies have invested little in research, development and training by comparison with their overseas competitors, in particular the United States and Japan.

British government research expenditure has been heavily weighted towards military applications. Fundamental research in artificial intelligence has rarely been in favour, and the 1973 Lighthill Report to the Science Research Council led to the withdrawal of a large proportion of the support for current projects and departure overseas of many outstanding research leaders.

The Alvey Programme of research in advanced information technology is a brave attempt to recover, with an innovative basis of collaboration between government, industry and academics. An extensive set of projects is now in place, developing the enabling technologies of intelligent knowledge-based systems, man-machine interface, software engineering and very large scale integration, as well as demonstrating their practical application. In particular, in the area of intelligent knowledge-based systems (IKBS), funds are now fully committed for the Alvey Programme up to 1988.

Thoughts have begun to turn to the issue of what happens next. Is there to be continued research after Alvey? What will be the emphases? Which application areas will be given special emphasis? Who will do the work? Who will pay?

UK National Health Service under threat

One significant area for the application of advanced technology is the Health Service. At the time of its establishment in 1948, the National Health Service was a model for international health care provision and a central part of the policy of a government concerned to strengthen its people after suffering and war, seeing such provision as an essential investment. It has since suffered from government neglect, with funding failing to match needs and hospitals not being equipped with the same level of technology that is standard in other advanced countries. It has become regarded all too often as an optional expense, increasingly to be devolved to the individual or the "community", where the financial resources required for work with advanced technology are not available.

Collaboration in the current Alvey Research Programme

The present Alvey Programme involves a degree of collaboration which has no British peacetime precedent. Within government three separate ministries (Trade and Industry, Education and Science, and Defence) are learning to coexist, progressively resolving inconsistencies between their bureaucratic methods. Companies were unfamiliar with "precompetitive collaboration", and the last two years have been very much of a learning process. Many universities are participating in their first collaborative research with industry, as opposed to contract research. There have been exchanges and secondments of personnel, and new working relationships have been forged. Through a variety of schemes understanding has increased between industrialists and academics. In the strategic projects real collaboration has meant parity of esteem and mutual respect between the sides. The Alvey Programme has had to pioneer new forms of collaboration that could form the basis of research and development in other scientific fields, going beyond conventional funding through government research councils and commercial contract research.

Broadening government involvement

There is considerable potential for the involvement of further government departments. The Manpower Services Commission, part of the Department of Employment, is concerned with training of the young unemployed and with increasing the quality of training provision for clients in industry of all ages. The same technology that is being developed in the Alvey Programme can be deployed in training. For example, an expert system that knows about maintaining robots can be adapted to provide training in robot maintenance. A system that knows about regulations or legislation can explain them to trainee civil servants. There is considerable scope in the Department of Energy for the adoption of expert systems for oil and mineral exploration, whose potential has been demonstrated in the United States with PROSPECTOR and Dipmeter-Advisor. The Department of Education and Science could make considerable use of intelligent knowledge-based systems in education, building on work using micro-PROLOG and LOGO, and on broader work in intelligent computer-assisted instruction and expert tutorial systems. The morass of university entrance procedures and careers options could be made more penetrable with intelligent advice systems.

Perhaps the Department of Health and Social Services is the most likely candidate for involvement in research and development. Within the current Alvey Programme there are a number of relevant projects on which to build; for example:

1. A large demonstrator project led by ICL with the Department of

Health and Social Services, Logica, Imperial College, Universities of Surrey and Lancaster. This is concerned with providing intelligent decision support for DHSS officers and claimants, who are faced with complex rules and regulations which they have to apply to their own circumstances.

2. A large knowledge-based project in molecular biology led by the Imperial Cancer Research Fund, GEC and Reading University. Work in cancer research has resulted in a significant body of knowledge of molecular biology, which needs to be made available to the doctor or researcher in response to a wide variety of possible questions.

What happens next?

The Alvey Programme does not end its current phase until 1988, but discussions and planning for what is to follow have already begun. Those within the Alvey Programme hope the collaborative process will continue, building on the successes and learning from the setbacks of this, the first British programme of its kind, in what is known as Alvey 2. Those who look for certain demonstrations of the efficacy of work in artificial intelligence after the first two years of a five-year initial programme may fail to find them, and advocate the redeployment of scarce resources to a different problem area, in a manner reminiscent of Sir James Lighthill's report in 1973 to the Science and Engineering Research Council, with an outcome known as Lighthill 2. More discriminating commentators may accept the power of the technology, but may wish to have activity less directed by research ideas, favouring "applications pull" as well as "technology push".

In the United Kingdom the applications which pull are all too often military, with the subsequent civilian spin-off being ill defined. Defence research is justified, by its proponents, in terms of the scientific benefits of its wider application. This chapter seeks to maintain that a stronger case can be made for the field of health care. Arguments have been presented elsewhere for a greater emphasis on applications in education and training. In both cases the argument is for investment in human resources, with a justification that is not merely expressed in economically quantified terms, but which has a strong moral, social and economic rationale.

Many leading researchers in artificial intelligence in the United Kingdom are not prepared to engage in defence-related work, and have been prepared to state their position in public. In the United States a large proportion of AI research is defence funded, and this position seems unlikely to change. The American Strategic

Defence Initiative is intended to provide financial support for a broad area of basic scientific research, further increasing the percentage of researchers with military support. The invitation is at present being extended to European companies and researchers. With the drying up of funds from the Alvey Programme in Britain, there will be un-doubted pressure to participate in "Star Wars" and perhaps a dimin-ishing number of organized alternatives. Among those alternatives may be the European EUREKA initiative, exploring non-military applications of advanced technology with an emphasis on the needs of the civilian market, in collaboration with the more advanced members of the European Economic Community.

Researchers prefer to work on projects they believe in. Their brains cannot simply be hired for whatever purpose. At present skilled researchers are in short supply: they are well known for being able to command astronomical salaries overseas and for being transferred between research centres like football stars. Their choice of where to work need not be determined by money: after years of neglect and maltreatment they are suddenly in a new position of power where they can refuse work they find ethically unacceptable. They can choose instead to focus fundamental research effort on attempting to solve human problems.

In this spirit there follows a suggestion of a new initiative to tap this supply of idealism. We need a strategic focus for the next stage of development of an infant generation of technology, to the benefit of society in general – a "Strategic Health Initiative".

An overview of the Strategic Health Initiative (SHI)

UK need to catch up in health defences

The United Kingdom has been falling behind. While our competitors have been raising their defences against illness and poverty, in Britain illnesses that had previously been eradicated are making their pre-sence felt once more as a growing "Fifth Column". The conscription process for the First World War showed up the decrepitude of a large proportion of the population, meaning that they were unfit to fight. Many of the subsequent precautionary measures such as school milk and balanced school meals have been abandoned on short-term cost grounds, and the present population is physically becoming neither leaner nor fitter despite economic exhortations. Unhealthy foods are being marketed to the many for the commercial interests of the few. Officially commissioned scientific reports on the nation's diet are withheld from publication to avoid offending vested interests. National programmes of vaccination and preventive medicine are given little emphasis: prevention may be better than cure but the system of financial incentives is biased towards cure.

Where known enemy diseases threaten, our detection equipment is out of order. Straightforward tests are available for many forms of cancer, yet general scanning is not carried out on grounds of cost, and where intelligence of invasive disease has been acquired, all too often it is not transmitted to the individual concerned. The computer systems capable of managing the information exist but the funds are not provided to pay for them. We have the necessary technology for much of this work but have lacked the political will to apply it. To quote Sir Ian Lloyd MP "We have found the enemy, and he is us."

Our front line medical troops are pitifully resourced and are made to work inordinate hours in the medical trenches with substandard weapons. Patients have to be turned away from high-technology treatment in the cause of economy. Casualty wards servicing the M1 motorway are closed through lack of funds. Intensive care facilities are kept in mothballs. With changes in cleaning and catering arrangements, hospitals may not be healthy places to be if you are ill.

The non-commissioned medical ranks need expert advice, as they are all too often left in charge of a "MASH" unit, providing intensive care without intensive training. They need access to the best technology where the medical expert is unavailable, and such technology needs to form part of their training.

Patients would rather not be ill and, if ill, would rather not trouble the doctor. Civil defence advice is needed for the patient in his home, aid in diagnosing the source of attacks of headache or nausea, preventitive measures to enable him to take evasive action, getting out of the line of fire of heart disease, cancer, or cirrhosis of the liver. "Protect and survive" should be the watchword for the citizen in the blasted wasteland of community medicine.

Better coordination of resources

Often we have the resources available to repel an attack from outside, but they are not sufficiently organized. Doctors need decision support as they seek to define a strategy with a particular patient, and crisis management tools as numerous complaints emerge or as competing demands are made for finite resources. Increasingly they need a mastery of the official rules and regulations (on, for example, the prescription of certain drugs and their generic substitutes) and an encyclopaedic knowledge of drugs and their interactions. They need to be able to explain their diagnoses and treatment in appropriate language, based on a model of the level of knowledge of the patient and his family, and to draw on the experience of others. In the community medicine field, whether of barefoot doctors or a team of mobile professionals, information needs to be assembled, available and explicable. Advanced medical teamwork requires advanced information technology if the varied knowledge of the interdisciplinary team is to be brought to bear on shared problems.

Aids to independent health

Medical research has developed numerous aids for the disabled, some of which have not been made widely available for economic reasons. Many disabled people have been enabled to lead a normal life, including employment, with the aid of some prosthetic device. Artificial limbs and specially adapted keyboard input devices are well known, enabling people to make use of any controlled movement. Life for the blind or deaf, or even the deaf blind, is made more possible by language and communication systems. A current mathematics student at Imperial College is both deaf and blind and works with the aid of a computer with braille input and output, also using electronic mail.

With the advent of artificial intelligence techniques, further advances are made possible. Artificial intelligence is concerned with the study of human thinking and its modelling in computer programmes. We can learn about particular problems by attempting to model them, and the consequent programmes can be of use in helping people to solve such problems themselves. Early work has been done in psychiatry and psychotherapy, and in problems of vision and speech, which shows the potential for further work. Military funding has gone into systems for voice and speech recognition and for message understanding. An application focus in the field of intensive medical care or care of the multiple handicapped could be extremely beneficial, using, for example, speech-driven workstations as are being developed on an Alvey large demonstrator project.

Artificial intelligence in medicine today

American medical expert systems

For twenty years research in the United States, where the majority of work in artificial intelligence to date has been done, has been undertaken into medical "expert systems", systems embodying knowledge about a particular specialist aspect of medicine. The names of some of the best known are given below, together with their area of specialist application:

MYCIN   bacterial infections
CASNET   glaucoma
INTERNIST   internal medicine
VM   intensive care
PUFF   respiratory conditions
ONCOCIN   cancer

These systems have each taken many person-years to produce and have relied on access to highly expensive computer hardware. In recent years the cost and size of the necessary hardware has fallen dramatically and advances in software technology have made it much easier to develop systems for new specialist areas. Techniques have become more modular and transferable, and advances have been made in eliciting the knowledge of the expert which forms the basis of the system.

Artificial intelligence and medicine in the United Kingdom

In the United Kingdom, partly for reasons of economic necessity, there has been an emphasis on what can be achieved with affordable hardware, regarding systems that are developed as tools to aid the practising doctor or nurse rather than as any kind of replacement. Dr John Fox of the Imperial Cancer Research Fund has developed an expert system shell called PROPS, which supports aids for the diagnosis of a number of cancers and related ailments, as well as being used in education and training. Current demonstration systems deal with ischaemic heart disease and cystitis. Dr Peter Hammond and Marek Sergot of Imperial College have extended PROLOG (the language used to write PROPS) to provide a flexible system called APES in which expert systems can be built. APES is one of the components of the diabetes management system under development by the London New Technology Network. These systems offer explanations of their diagnoses in terms of the facts and rules with which they had been provided and are available for commonly used personal computers. It is envisaged that within two or three years general practitioners and hospital doctors should all be offered the use of such systems.

Research questions to be tackled on the SHI

Can a system be comprehensible, affordable and useful?

Given that the potential applications of medical expert systems have already been demonstrated, is it possible to develop systems that are at the same time comprehensible, affordable and useful? Can the same systems be useful for medical use and for medical education? (This had happened for MYCIN.) Can the same system be comprehensible to doctors with different approaches, and to the patient? What kinds of explanation are medically useful? How many doctors have chosen to use such systems? Do patients sometimes prefer their original consultation to be with a computer? (Professor Joseph Weizenbaum of MIT found that his secretary preferred to talk to his ELIZA system rather than to him.)

How much involvement can the patient have in his or her treatment?

Does the technology offer opportunities to improve the relationship between doctor and patient? Can the patient take the initiative and take a more active role in both diagnosis and treatment? Is there some information to which the patient should not have access? Can the system be made sufficiently "friendly" for use by the patient? Is medicine less effective if it loses its mystique? We have evolved the heuristic "principle of symmetry" in collaborative problem solving with the computer. Can there be a symmetry between the doctor and the patient (with the computer potentially standing in for either)? Do concepts of object-level and meta-level knowledge cast light on this problem? To what extent do we know how to represent the knowledge of the medical expert?

What are the implications of computer access for the disabled?

Can we revise our concepts of disability when new forms of communication and functionality are opened up? Can we provide voice input, touch-sensitive screens and hand-held devices like "mice" to satisfy all needs?

Would we be offering an outlet for abilities that have not previously had a mode of expression? The experience with the use of Bliss symbolics to aid the communication of non-talking handicapped students and early experience with word processors for the disabled suggests that considerable abilities have been wasted. Are there implications for the provision of housing and training for the disabled? How will governments and officials be affected when the disabled are enabled to answer back?

What is the appropriate means of offering computer access?

Should computer access, like telephone facilities, be provided as a facility through local authorities? In France an attempt is being made to provide computerized enquiry facilities for all telephone subscribers. Could something similar be provided for the disabled and housebound? Should there be some kind of "prescription system" for computer consultations? What precautions can be taken against the inappropriate use of computers in medicine? Will we have computerized medical malpractice cases?

What can current robotics offer the disabled?

Artificial intelligence offers the prospect of considerable enhancements to current prosthetic limbs, which can take on progressively more programmed tasks. Current commercially-available domestic robots suggest that a similar process will happen to the revolution in personal computers, as prices drop with rising sales and simpler design. Will this remain subject to the private market or can we expect robots on prescription? We should take full advantage of increasingly intelligent machinery, but many aspects of care for the sick and disabled are more a matter of human contact, communication and response. In that sense the "caring professions" should not be threatened by the new technology, but should find themselves more concerned with the human needs of the patient.

Are disease levels lowered by effective computer-aided screening?

The evidence overseas suggests that computer-aided screening can be highly effective, while equivalent work remains to be done in the United Kingdom. On a broader scale, epidemiology aided by medical signal processing has already brought results, predicting the geographical pattern of movement of diseases such as rabies and identifying the source of outbreaks of cholera. Work is beginning in the application of artificial intelligence techniques in this area. The implications are considerable for the relief of suffering (and consequent budgetary savings) both in the United Kingdom and, in particular, in Third World countries.

What are the implications of medical expert systems with hypothetical reasoning for preventative medicine?

If a patient can be confronted with the choices that face him/her at a given stage in an illness, this may affect his/her later behaviour and prognosis. An expert system may offer a richer and more acceptable environment for such issues to be explored. It may also help produce an improved relationship between doctor and patient. Current disputes about the association of tobacco smoking and lung cancer, or of excess fat consumption and heart disease, would be advanced if the evidence were more open to scrutiny and explanation. The fear associated with the possible side-effects of vaccinations could be alleviated by a system that could assign and explain the weightings of different factors. It is possible that many prescriptions for tranquillizers and anti-depressants could be rendered unnecessary given the means of exploring the problems faced by the individual and choices open to him. In this sense the expert system could serve as an extension of medical counselling in the hands of an experienced counsellor.

What systems should be standardly provided for the GP?

The General Practitioner cannot be expected to have a complete knowledge of all specialisms, but needs to identify signs and symptoms and to know how to proceed. Is it possible to develop an affordable system that would actually be used? Should such a system be standard, or would doctors be better advised to make a free choice? Early experience with PROPS suggests that doctors may find such systems to be of considerable practical benefit. We need extensive pilot studies.

How can medical education be enhanced by expert systems?

There has been some relevant experience in medical schools in the United States and Japan, and development work is clearly required, as in other areas of education and training. In the case of MYCIN, an expert diagnostic system, with the addition of a tutorial component GUIDON, is used for medical education. Doctors can gain vicarious experience in diagnostics without using real patients, with monitoring assistance and advice from the computer. Increasingly advanced technology systems are appearing in hospitals; with work in artificial intelligence we should expect the systems to be made comprehensible to the user, possibly through the addition of an "intelligent front end". This intelligent front-end programme should incorporate expert knowledge of the specialist subject and should offer tutorial explanations of its working.

What can be done in occupational health?

Advisory systems could be envisaged for a number of occupational contexts, which could reduce accidents and illnesses related to working conditions. Considerable economic savings could be made through the strategic location of low-cost personal computers, which could both provide advice and monitor the information provided by workers. Fire, safety and building regulations are obvious candidates for representation as programmes, as are official standard procedures. Professional bodies, trade unions and employers' organizations could all see the value of supporting such developments, and government should gain through paying less sick pay.

Launching a Strategic Health Initiative

A Strategic Health Initiative would seek to draw on and advance progress in medical science, advanced computing and social administration. Its success would have enormous potential benefits, not only for the health of the nation but also for the economy, through the export of software, hardware and medical technology and know-how developed on such a national programme. Improved health and medical services would provide considerable financial benefits, as would the development of a better trained workforce. It would have direct effects on the whole population, bringing them into contact with computer technology in a benevolent context, reducing the division into two nations of "haves" and "have nots" with respect to health and computer literacy.

To start the programme would require the kind of emphasis on collaboration that we have seen in wartime, and which has been developing in the Alvey Programme. It would require the political will to identify the priority and allocate the level of resources required. Alvey is costing a total of 350 million pounds over five years (200 million from government). This is, of course, as nothing against defence budgets, from which less tangible gains for the lives of civilians emerge. If we lack that will, then we become "the enemy within", the "cancer in the body politick".

Richard Titmuss analysed societies in terms of how blood was transmitted in his book *The Gift Relationship*. In the National Health Service blood is donated without charge. A similar analysis could be given in terms of the transmission of knowledge and lies behind the campaign for a strong system of state education, free at the point of need. The proposal for a Strategic Health Initiative concerns the amalgamation of the two. The health of individuals is seen as integral to the health of the nation. Illness is not a crime to be punished by financial penalties, and information concerning the restoration of health should be freely available in accessible terms.

A Strategic Health Initiative would need to start on a pilot basis before it could expect to be adopted as government policy. The Alvey Programme teaches us, by its own omissions, that it is worth planning beforehand and establishing the groundrules for collaboration. Many existing voluntary bodies might see fit to collaborate in activity in the field, and organizations such as the Imperial Cancer Research Fund and the London New Technology Network have experience in uniting academics with medical and industrial needs. We might expect to elicit a response in terms of practical involvement from Community Health Councils, Citizens' Advice Bureaux, single-illness charities such as those concerned with multiple sclerosis, heart and lung disease, cancer, leukaemia, medical pressure groups such as MIND, SENSE and MENCAP, and the medical royal colleges and professional associations and unions. Paramedical professions such as speech therapists, occupational therapists and physiotherapists would be essential allies, and are already commencing their involvement with computer technology on a somewhat *ad hoc* basis. Funding should be attainable for a pilot phase through charitable foundations and pharmaceutical companies, as well as from the Medical Research Council, the Science and Engineering Research Council, the Economic and Social Research Council, the Manpower Services Commission and the Department of Health and Social Services.

If such an application of advanced computing technology to health is to take place, initial moves need to be made without delay. A committee should be established, drawn from some of the bodies above and from the various professional associations in the Health Service, including appropriate representation from industry. It should be asked to produce a report within a period of months, outlining a programme of action. Pilot studies should commence immediately in the relevant practical areas in advance of general government funding, and a nucleus organization should be established on the premises of a contributing body.

If such a programme were successful, the strategic results for the country could be spectacular. We could expect an improvement in the health of the population, with a cost-effective change of emphasis to prevention rather than cure, and a fall in the number of working days lost each year through illness. Industry could benefit from export sales of the resulting systems and the applications that followed in other sectors. The research community could benefit from the motivation of a continuation of work in "advanced technology with a human face".

Intelligent computer technology places a new burden on us to determine the kind of society in which we choose to live. It assumes the form laid down by its masters. If we abdicate from participation in the decision as to how the technology is to be used, we must accept responsibility for what follows. I close with the words of Lord Beveridge, whose work laid the foundations of the British Welfare State, including the National Health Service:

> The object of government in peace and in war is not the glory of rulers or of races, but the happiness of the common man.

Suggestions for Further Reading

Foot, M. *Aneurin Bevan 1945–1960*. Davis-Poynter. London 1973.

Gregory, R.L. (1984). *Mind in Science*. Harmondsworth; Penguin.

Hayes, J.E., Michie, D. (eds.) (1983). *Intelligent Systems: The Unprecedented Opportunity*. Chichester, Ellis Horwood.

Michie, D. Johnston, R. (1985). *The Creative Computer: Machine Intelligence and Human Knowledge*. Harmondsworth; Penguin.

Titmuss, R. (1972). *The Gift Relationship*. Harmondsworth; Penguin.

Weizenbaum, J. (1966). ELIZA – A Computer Program for the study of natural language communication between man and machine. Comm ACM 9, (1) 39–45.

Weizenbaum, J. (1979). *Computer Power and Human Reason*. Harmondsworth; Penguin.

Yazdani, M., Narayaran, A. (eds.) (1984). *Artificial Intelligence: Human Effects*. Chichester; Ellis Horwood.

SECTION 4

TECHNICAL ISSUES

4.1
Logic Programming in Education and Training

Logic programming was in regular use in the education of the younger generation before it was given new prominence in advanced research through the Japanese Fifth Generation Programme. Of necessity, use has been made of present-day microcomputer technology, and more emphasis has been given to clarity of thinking than to polished sophistication of software. The young user has become accustomed to making up for the deficiencies of syntax or interface in a manner that many computer professionals seem unable to match. The Fifth Generation Programme is seeking to develop powerful low-cost computers that are accessible to the naive user; work using logic programming in education and training has started with the knowledge area and the user, and has developed a range of systems that have proven to be accessible.

In this paper we provide an account of the motivation of the original use of logic programming in education, a survey of current diverse projects in the field internationally and a partial agenda for future activities. The wide availability of logic programming software for personal computers means that our survey is of necessity incomplete; often the first that is heard from an individual researcher is the publication of a book or the sale of a software package.

Commissioned by Hitachi, January, 1986.

Motivation

The initial proposal

The first research project concerned with the use of logic programming in education was directed by Professor Robert Kowalski at Imperial College, starting in September 1980. In his original draft proposal in November 1979, Kowalski wrote (Kowalski, 1979a):

> The object of this proposal is to develop and test materials for teaching logic as a computer language for children.
>
> The teaching materials will initially be based on ones developed by the applicant for teaching children at a middle school in Wimbledon . . .
>
> The project will also aim to produce a child-orientated microcomputer version of PROLOG to support the teaching materials . . .
>
> The teaching of logic as a computer formalism fits in well with the teaching of other subjects in school. Logic is the single academic discipline which is common to such diverse subjects as mathematics, language, natural science and social science. Indeed the teaching of such subjects as geometry and Latin has often been justified in terms of their intended contribution to the development of logical thought.
>
> The microcomputer implementation of PROLOG will be higher-level than existing PROLOG implementations and will include features of traditional logic, such as quantifiers, also found in certain programming languages such as SETL and HOPE . . .
>
> The proposal for teaching logic as a computer language can be justified by its contribution to the teaching of four otherwise independent subjects: logic, mathematics, language and computing.

The original source of funding for work on "Logic as a Computer Language for Children" was the Science and Engineering Research Council, who had previously supported work by Kowalski and Keith Clark on "Logic as a Computer Language", on which Frank McCabe was employed as research assistant. Accordingly, Kowalski's proposal emphasizes the advantages of the project for computing:

> Children and programmers in general need to learn the importance of producing correct programs. The work on programming methodology, program transformation and abstract data types demonstrates that correctness can be reconciled with efficiency if programmers begin with clear logical specifications as the starting point for the development of efficient programs. It follows that children should learn logic to specify problems before they learn conventional programming languages . . .
>
> Recent developments in the field of databases lead to similar conclusions. Because databases may be used for a variety of different applications, it is important that they can be viewed abstractly in terms

of the way they are implemented. Queries to a database, like program specifications, should describe the problem to be solved instead of implementation-dependent details about the solution. Many user-oriented query languages such as relational calculus make covert use of symbolic logic. Others such as query-by-example use logic disguised by syntactic sugar. As a computer language, logic has the advantage that it can be introduced as a database query language and later extended with minor additions to a full-scale programming language . . .

The use of logic as both problem description language and programming language simplifies the task of developing correct programs. Program verification and the derivation of programs from specifications reduces to the same discipline of logical argument as that involved in deriving geometry theorems from axioms or in constructing correct Latin sentences from the rules of Latin grammars. The passage from problem description to effective program requires only axioms about the problem domain and dispenses with the additional axioms or rules of inference which are needed when different languages are used for programs and their specifications.

It should be clear from the above that Kowalski had a broad vision of the significance of logic and logic programming, and that his interest was not confined to children. This is made explicit at the end of the draft proposal:

Applications:
It is anticipated that a logic programming system suitable for children will also be congenial to adults. It should also be possible to adapt the children's teaching materials for adults.

Exploitation:
A child-orientated microcomputer PROLOG system with its associated documentation should be able to compete with conventional language systems for many applications.

Initial classroom experience

Detailed accounts of the "Logic as a Computer Language for Children" project 1980–1983 have been published (Kowalski, 1984; Ennals, 1983, 1984, 1985). The intention here is simply to compare the motivation of this original project with experience in practice. We can identify some respects in which results were up to expectation, and others where the work fell far short of what had been hoped, leaving a clear need for further research projects. The original manpower was extremely limited: a secondary school teacher of history, Richard Ennals; an experienced PROLOG implementor, Frank

McCabe; and a part-time secretary, Diane Reeve. The project also enjoyed the support of the growing Logic Programming Group at Imperial College, in particular Derek Brough, Keith Clark, Marek Sergot, Peter Hammond and Chris Moss, and the interest of John Darlington's Functional Programming and Parallel Architectures Group.

The first objective was achieved, in that teaching materials were developed in the first year with a class of 26 ten-year old pupils at Park House Middle School, and retried in the two subsequent years. The database examples were based initially on Kowalski's experimental lesson materials (the family of Greek Gods was replaced by the Tudor royal family) with further examples developed with the pupils and relating to their own experience. Further use was not made of Kowalski's problem-solving examples (Kowalski, 1979b) to which Tom Conlon has returned with older students (Conlon, 1985).

A child-orientated microcomputer version of PROLOG was produced. Frank McCabe implemented micro-PROLOG on an Exidy Sorcerer in the summer of 1980, and this was used on the project from November 1980 using North Star and Research Machines PROLOG or IC-PROLOG as originally envisaged.

In the initial project, "Logic as a Computer Language" was a timetabled course in its own right, taught in collaboration with Ken Della Rocca, Head of Mathematics at Park House School, whose teaching methods had attracted Kowalski's interest. Teachers at the school perceived that logic could contribute to their separate subjects of history, French, science, mathematics, social studies and craft, which gave rise to support from the Nuffield Foundation for the applications of logic and logic programming across the curriculum, starting in 1981.

Micro-PROLOG is higher-level than previous PROLOG implementations, supporting the declarative use of logic by the user. In particular, it offers negation as failure, sets, conditionals and a powerful programming environment with a number of toolkits as modules. It offers a choice of interfaces and surface syntaxes, allowing progress to deeper issues. Links with languages such as HOPE can be seen in the continued emphasis on declarative programming, the offering of functional relations, and the aspiration to run programs developed in micro-PROLOG on new parallel declarative architectures such as ALICE, now running in prototype.

The case for the use of logic as a computer language for teaching logic, mathematics, language and computing is borne out by the fact that new projects with these emphases were set up during the initial project, to be described later. In each case, pilot materials were developed and tested at Park House Middle School and on courses for teachers funded by the Nuffield Foundation.

There have been more problems in the research objectives concerning computer science, doubtless relating to the lack of familiarity with school education on the part of academic computer scientists. Kowalski's vision was a radical one, involving a revision of many aspects of established computer science. Instead of education trailing behind, picking up chance side-effects of advances in research, he wanted to force research advances to meet needs described in the context of an education project. In this sense we see analogies with the Japanese fifth generation computer proposals.

In the original project, micro-PROLOG was used entirely declaratively, with no attempt to teach PROLOG as a programming language, and the original pilot pupils had no previous experience of a conventional programming language. By the third year of the project the situation was complicated by the proliferation of low-cost home computers running only BASIC, meaning that ten-year-old pupils were likely to have some previous experience of a Sinclair ZX 81 or BBC micro. From early 1983 micro-PROLOG was widely available for Sinclair Spectrum.

There has been no classroom work as such on programming methodology, program transformation and abstract data types, but advances in research projects at Imperial College and elsewhere (Hogger, 1985) have confirmed the appropriateness of a classroom emphasis on correctness rather than efficiency. Brough's work (Brough 1982, 1984) on looptrapping suggests that the obvious pitfalls of left recursion and mutually defining relations can be overcome. In class, attention has been drawn to the patterns which cause problems, and in small scale problems that has been adequate.

Databases have been extremely important in initial classroom work. Whereas we do not expect all pupils to become programmers, all are likely to need information from databases. Accordingly, the pupils start by asking simple queries in micro-PROLOG, and adding new facts in the same notation. They move on to complex queries, which are used to introduce rules. There is an arbitrary dividing line between querying a database and programming.

There is more to programming than database querying. The next step has proved elusive in work in middle schools, but has received attention in later projects. Programming must involve both declarative and procedural components, but the original classroom work was entirely declarative. The "cut" symbol was never used in the classroom as it could not be given a declarative reading. Instead a set of extensions to standard PROLOG were provided for the user which enable him or her to work declaratively, while behind the scenes procedural micro-PROLOG programmes contrived the appropriate machine behaviour. As the teacher was able to give a clear description of the interface and syntax required, the systems programmer was able to provide it. Increasingly this work was performed by Imperial College BSc and MSc students, many of whom now work in the field professionally. Many operations can now be performed "cleanly" that would previously, and in other PROLOGs, require "dirty" programming at the user level.

Kowalski, in his draft proposal, lays stress on the appropriateness of logic for expressing algorithms. He argues:

> It is a common fallacy to assume that, although logic may be suitable for problem description, it is useless for expressing algorithms. On the contrary, logic programs resemble algorithm descriptions as they were formulated for use by human beings before the existence of computers. Moreover, when used by computers, they give rise to algorithmic behavior which is similar to that obtained by programs expressed in more conventional machine-oriented programming languages.

This issue was not addressed in the original project, but is the subject of later projects using logic programming in education and training. Current work at Imperial College on PARLOG (Gregory, 1985) and HOPE with unification (Darlington et al., 1986) is also highly relevant, as we begin to consider execution of algorithms by non-Von Neumann machines.

Kowalski's view of logic as both problem description language and programming language has been sometimes described by critics as oversimplifying the task of developing correct programmes. Not all domains of knowledge can be seen as following the model of geometry or Latin. From the educational point of view it may be a helpful oversimplication, as it motivates ideas of interactive knowledge exploration. The "query-the-user" facility (Sergot, 1984) arose from the need of pupils to gain familiarity with the forms of complex queries, but has been extended, through amalgamation with augmented PROLOG for expert systems (APES) (Hammond, 1982), developed for work on expert sytems, to provide a tool which enables the student interactively to develop a running prototype system. This is used in later projects.

Applications of logic programming have developed as Kowalski anticipated. Micro-PROLOG now has thousands of users internationally. The original teaching materials were adapted to form the opening section of a tutorial book (Clark & McCabe, 1984), and numerous courses have been given for teachers, colleges, companies and national research programmes. A wider literature has developed to cater for different needs (Conlon, 1985; de Saram, 1985; Briggs, 1984; Berk, 1985; Hogger, 1985).

The field has expanded enormously since 1979, and many new projects have started to build on the early experience. As is typical in the early stages of a new research activity, researchers have often had limited communication, as their work has fallen between the two stools of advanced logic programming research and research in educational computing. Since 1983 there have been attempts to remedy this deficiency and to assemble a "critical mass" to support further advances in the use of logic programming in education and training. Conferences have been held on artificial intelligence and education and in September 1985 a PROLOG Education Group (PEG) was established, run from the University of Exeter, involving groups in Britain and overseas. An active community now exists.

Survey of current projects

Some common features can be identified in the "second generation" of projects concerned with logical programming in education and training. All have made use of powerful implementations of PRO-LOG on what is affordable hardware in their particular circumstances. They have involved a team approach, using the skills of experienced logic programmers, subject specialists and teachers. Problems of knowledge elicitation and representation have formed an essential part of their research. Each project has been motivated by an educational focus in addition to concerns of logic programming research. There has been a close liaison between many of the projects; as has often been the case in artificial intelligence research groups, there has been a concern to develop and transfer particular techniques and approaches, sometimes by means of key individuals who have worked on many different projects, under the aegis of different institutions and funding agencies.

With the support of the Nuffield Foundation, Richard Ennals and Jonathan Briggs explored application of logic and logic programming across the curriculum, using example programmes to excite the interest and involvement of diverse subject teachers and specialists. This has given rise to a number of projects described below, each influenced by the particular educational perspective of the principal investigator, for whom logic and logic programming were means to educational ends. This is in marked contrast with Kowalski's initial motivation, where the development of logic programming was and remains the central objective.

Concepts of logic programming in information technology in schools

Robert Hurst at Richards Lodge High School in Wimbledon wanted to develop a new course in information technology for girls aged 14–16, an increasing number of whom had encountered micro-PROLOG at the adjacent Park House Middle School. He designed and introduced a syllabus (Hurst, 1984) introducing simple concepts of logic programming: querying a database and writing programs on subjects of interest to his students, who were intending to enter secretarial and commercial employment. In addition, the course introduced concepts of information, and gave an introduction to word processing and data processing, reinforced by visits to data processing installations.

Jonathan Briggs, with support from Sinclair Research, took such ideas further, developing a new interface to micro-PROLOG to replace SIMPLE which had been in classroom use since 1980. His work at Park House and on numerous courses for teachers and students indicated that unnecessary difficulty was being faced at the level of syntax. In particular, the LISP-like internal syntax of micro-PROLOG gave rise to a proliferation of parentheses that could confuse the unwary. Working with Chris Tompsett at Queen Elizabeth School in Crediton he developed MITSI, an interface that was free of parentheses and driven by punctuation (Briggs, 1984). Intended for the novice user only, it offered less facilities than SIMPLE, but a friendlier environment in which to learn. After the introductory use of MITSI, learners are offered a choice of alternative interfaces with which to work, and programs are transferable. MITSI has proved popular internationally, and the documentation in translation is widely used.

Hurst and Briggs had shown up some of the limitations of Ennals' original course materials (Ennals, 1983). Ennals had used syntax and environment available at the time of the initial project, and research advances at Imperial College could now offer greater flexibility, allowing, for example, a choice of surface syntaxes as modules on the distribution disk for micro-PROLOG. Similarly, the examples were derived from his work in middle schools, and required considerable improvement for courses with older secondary pupils. Philip Hepburn (Hepburn, 1986) developed further examples for use in a data processing course in Further Education in Wales.

The field has been greatly enriched by the work of Tom Conlon (Conlon, 1985), whose work is consistent with the initial motivation of Robert Kowalski, acknowledged with George Polya as a particular influence. He sees logic programming very much in the context of problem-solving:

> a PROLOG computer system happens to be a marvellous tool for problem-solving, an activity which most human beings (given half a chance) find compelling. Problem-solving is both useful and educational too, but I think the reason why people choose to spend so much time solving problems (with Rubic cubes and adventure games, bridge matches and crosswords, dominoes and chess, crime stories and Logic puzzles . . .) is that problem-solving is great fun in its own right.

Conlon is based at Moray House College of Education in Edinburgh, working with school students and in teacher training. He is working with Edinburgh and Lancaster Universities with support from the Economic and Social Research Council.

Hugh de Saram of Marlborough College has taken a different tutorial approach, and emphasized procedural aspects of PROLOG in his book (de Saram,1985). His experience of working with students and primary school teachers was that the limited memories of affordable microcomputers meant that after loading micro-PROLOG and either SIMPLE or MITSI little space was left in which to develop an interesting programme. His concern was to make powerful ideas from computing and artificial intelligence accessible to more people, and micro-PROLOG was taken as a step towards that goal:

> Its structure is very simple, yet it can be made to do things that by computer standards are highly intelligent. It is well suited, for example, to natural language interpretation, to intelligent querying of large quantities of data, and to building expert systems that can learn from experience and act like a consultant in a particular field of knowledge. It is also designed to be easy to learn.

Yazdani (Yazdani, 1984) has argued in favour of presenting the procedural interpretation of PROLOG alongside its declarative interpretation to beginners, but to date his alternative materials for school use are unpublished.

PROLOG was first implemented in Marseilles in 1972, where there has been considerable recent activity with logic programming in education led by Marc Bergman (Ennals et al., 1984). Teaching materials from the initial Imperial College project have been adapted and translated for use with the French teachers and students on French microcomputers, using micro-PROLOG and the Marseilles PROLOG II, which is implemented for Apple microcomputers. The materials are being used in a number of projects in France and, since July 1984, on a project supported by the European Economic Community in France, Italy, Belgium and Greece. In a recent paper (Bottino *et al.*, 1985) the group in Genoa outlined their approach to "teaching with PROLOG":

> Our experience in computer applications to education tells us that a programming language such as PROLOG, besides helping in the acquisition of a cause-effect way of thinking when solving problems, offers advantages, both if you make the students themselves write the programs, or simply use them in the classroom.
>
> Firstly, logic programming breaks the privileged link between mathematics and computer sciences that was strengthened by the use of traditional algorithmic programming languages and numerical applications of computers.
>
> And this is a positive fact, because in this way all the teachers start on the same footing before the problem of introducing the new technologies. In this way teachers of different subjects are encouraged to collaborate with one another: they are stimulated into facing this topic as an interdisciplinary problem.
>
> Finally, using such a language as PROLOG lets us focus our attention on one of the main aspects of teaching because, independently from the specific contexts of each single discipline, it allows us to deal, clearly and explicitly, with the problem of the organization and structure of knowledge.

At a conference in November 1985 researchers from other parts of Italy, together with invited researchers from Britain and France, considered the role of PROLOG in education.

In a further extension of the work with PROLOG and micro-PROLOG in Marseilles, Claude Vogel in 1983 established a project in la Reunion, in collaboration with the Universities of Paris, Aix-Marseilles and Corsica (Vogel, 1983). Entitled "Language and Creativity", the project is concerned with building a computer system which is bilingual in French and Creole with which students can describe their world in their own language. This builds on the work of Colmerauer's group in PROLOG implementation and teaching (Colmerauer, 1982, Kanoui, 1982;) and in the approach of logic programming in the classroom developed at Imperial College and introduced by Ennals in Marseilles. The project has the support of the International Board of Creole Studies.

In the United States, where logic programming is still regarded as a European import and "not invented here", applications in education and training tend to be linked to research centres. There have been frequent academic visits between Imperial College and Syracuse University, and indeed the early plans for work in schools in England were discussed with Ken Bowen of Syracuse, who has conducted lessons with small groups of gifted students since 1981. In 1983 introductory lectures attracted interest from a number of university departments including Education and Political Science, and a pilot school project was established in the Syracuse School District, led by a history teacher, Mike Riposo, with support from the Logic Programming Research Group at Syracuse. In Syracuse, Alan Robinson and Ernie Sibert (Robinson, 1983; Robinson & Sibert, 1982) have developed LOGLISP, an implementation of logic programming embedded in a LISP environment, and there is considerable educational potential in a system which shows the same commitment to declarative style but lacks the extra-logical control features of PROLOG such as the cut. The work at Imperial College has tried to address the use of logic programming, and not simply the use of PROLOG, or of a particular implementation.

In Sweden, Kenneth Kahn has worked with children at Uppsala University using LM-PROLOG (Kahn, 1984). Although his environment was built on PROLOG, the methodology and philosophy are closer to that of SmallTalk (Goldberg & Ross, 1981) and LOGO (Papert, 1980). Kahn explicitly contrasts his work with the early Imperial College work, based on his belief that children should understand how PROLOG works in order to use it:

> The pragmatic reason for this is so that the children can cope with programs that don't behave properly. To some extent this problem is a consequence of the fact that PROLOG does not live up to the ideal of logic programming very well. The order of clauses and goals matters. Shortcomings of the language are filled by extralogical primitives. It may be the case that the most important thing that a child can get from using a computer is an understanding of process. A powerful and clearer logic programming language which comes closer to declarative programming than PROLOG may actually be inferior from this point of view.

He describes a grammar kit in PROLOG for use with children which, at the time of writing, had been developed on an expensive LISP machine and required a large address space for the entire system, so had not been tested with children. His arguments were summarized as follows:

1. That much of the work being done on natural language processing within the PROLOG community is both very powerful and well-suited for children.
2. That the dynamic graphics is very valuable as a tool for observing and debugging complex process
3. That one should provide kits for children, so that they can do exciting large-scale projects without having to start from scratch.

Kenneth Kahn has worked at ICOT, the Japanese fifth generation computing research centre in Tokyo, with Ehud Shapiro, of the Weizmann Institute in Israel. Shapiro has an active interest in education, and collaborates on research with Zahava Scherz and her colleagues in the Science Teaching Department at the Weizmann Institute, which has an exchange scheme with Imperial College. Shapiro is a specialist in logic programming implementation, working on concurrent PROLOG and flat concurrent PROLOG in collaboration with ICOT and in consultation with Keith Clark and Steve Gregory at Imperial College. He has also developed WISDOM PRO-LOG, an implementation in C which runs under Unix and on the IBM-PC. For education purposes they have developed a Hebrew interface, and are considering an Arabic version. They also use micro-PROLOG and APES for applications work, as will be described subsequently. Shapiro and Leon Sterling are preparing a tutorial text for students on PROLOG programming, while Shapiro and Scherz are preparing a book to accompany their work with schools. Shapiro's doctoral dissertation on algorithmic programme debugging (Shapiro, 1982) contains many powerful suggestions for educational research, some of which will be considered later.

Mathematics and science teaching in schools

Early examples of PROLOG programmes to assist in mathematics teaching were developed by Ennals with Ken Della Rocca, and used in mathematics classes at Park House Middle School (Ennals, 1984). Briggs (Briggs, 1982) developed micro-PROLOG modules to assist in mathematics, and continued to experiment with interfaces and approaches to graphics.

Derek Ball of Leicester University was involved in the educational use of PROLOG from 1981, and in 1982 discovered the power of micro-PROLOG as a tool for teaching geometry (Ball, 1982). At that time the performance of LOGO on British educational microcomputers was very slow, and Ball's implementation of turtle graphics was considerably faster and more flexible. This constituted the use of micro-PROLOG as a systems programming tool, with no concern for logic programming or the declarative use of logic, but with considerable educational effect. Similarly, Ball added machine code routines to micro-PROLOG on the Research Machines 380Z to enable it to drive robot arms and other control equipment. He had developed a powerful tool for the graphical and physical demonstration of spatial and dynamic concepts. His interests were broader (Tallon *et al.*, 1982) and extended to biology teaching, where he argued that concepts such as food chains were better communicated in PROLOG than in BASIC, and economics teaching, where his key example concerned Keynesian models of deflation and unemployment. With Barry Galpin, he now has support from the British Library in developing intelligent information retrieval facilities for schools (the SPIRAL Project).

Bergman in Marseilles has had an interest in mathematical applications of PROLOG for many years (Bergman & Kanoui, 1973) and has been Director of IREM in Marseilles, concerned with research in mathematics education. The French view of mathematics gives more emphasis to logic than is the case in Britain, and logic is not regarded as a discipline apart, but as the theoretical underpinning for different domains of discourse. Furthermore, in Marseilles logic has been taken as the source of the notation for PROLOG, which was primarily developed as a tool for natural language processing. Another laboratory in Marseilles with relationships with Colmerauer's GIA (Groupe Intelligence Artificielle) is LISH (Laboratoires pour l'Informatique dans les Sciences de l'Homme). In theory the flow of ideas between the disciplines should be easy. The problem has been to make the links between advanced research and classroom practices which by comparison with Britain are traditional, centralized and conservative. There is evidence from the work of groups in Marseilles, Nice, Toulouse, Rouen and Paris that progress is being made, and the French mathematicians are showing interest. There are prospects of Anglo-French collaboration in artificial intelligence and education through a number of initiatives involving the French embassy in London and the Economic and Social Research Council, and a number of French visitors have come to Britain through the British Council.

Zahava Scherz and her colleagues at the Weizmann Institute have a particular interest in science education, and have been developing prototype systems making use of micro-PROLOG and APES. Great attention is given to pedagogy, and to modelling approaches to scientific explanation in education. In building PROLOG-based systems they are concerned to develop a model of the student and a model of the subject domain. As opposed to the design principle of APES whereby there is a symmetry between the system and the user, they are concerned to develop a meta-level facility whereby the system's model of a subject domain can be compared with the student's model, and "bugs" can be identified. This is one mode of application of the research results of Shapiro's work in algorithmic debugging, which can be viewed as a conceptual extension of Sergot's query-the-user facility in extending the interactive relationship of the user with the system.

Jon Ogborn of the Department of Science Education at the London University Institute of Education has a distinguished record in exploring scientific thinking. At Chelsea College he had a long involvement with the Nuffield Science Project and, with his wife Joan Bliss, with psychological research into children's thinking. He has collaborated with computer scientists at Brunel University in work on knowledge elicitation and conversation theory. At the Institute of Education he is concerned with children's concepts of science and with scientific explanations by teachers and children. PROLOG is a powerful tool in this work, for which he has support from the Economic and Social Research Council.

Steve Jones of the SEAKE Centre (Social and Economic Applications of Knowledge Engineering) at Brighton Polytechnic has been using micro-PROLOG and APES in developing expert systems to teach about diet and nutrition to ethnic minority groups. Related work is being undertaken at the South Bank Polytechnic with teachers on part-time secondment on a project led by Peter Chalk.

John Fox and his group at the Imperial Cancer Research Fund Biomedical Computing Unit have developed knowledge engineering tools in PROLOG which they are recommending for educational use. The first version of their expert systems shell, PROPS, is being productized and marketed by Expertech as *xi*, but the successor system, PROPS-2, is seen as much more powerful and flexible, helping at least to de-mystify a number of terms and concepts of knowledge engineering on low-cost microcomputers. *xi* turned out to require more memory than is typically provided on educational microcomputers, and to suffer from a lack of educational expertise among the software development team. Software tools must not only be powerful but easy to use with little preparation by the motivated teacher.

Alex Goodall and his colleagues at Expert Systems International are beginning to address schools users, as appropriate microcomputers become more widespread and as the company product range develops. In addition to two PROLOG implementations for microcomputers they offer ESP-Advisor, an expert system applications shell which is being used for scientific applications in education and training. A reduced version is provided as part of the "Expert Systems Starter Pack" produced by the Alvey Directorate through the National Computing Centre.

Mike Coombs formerly of the University of Strathclyde (now at New Mexico State University) has provided a number of accessible introductions to expert systems with an emphasis on PROLOG (Coombs, 1984; Alty & Coombs 1984). His own research has included the development of MINDPAD, a prototype guidance system which both draws heavily on the work of Pask in conversation theory (Pask, 1975) and has many elements of commonality with Shapiro's work on algorithmic debugging.

Many of the largest PROLOG programmes have been developed at the Department of Artificial Intelligence in Edinburgh, and have been educational in motivation, though developed on equipment that is beyond the budget of secondary schools. Alan Bundy has directed projects such as MECHO (Bundy *et al.*, 1979), concerned with solving school mechanics problems, PRESS (Bundy *et al.*, 1982), concerned with solving equations, and ECO (Bundy, 1984), concerned with ecological modelling. Together with colleagues Helen Pain and Paul Brna, he is increasingly concerned with understanding students' learning problems, with improving the programming environment, and with developing intelligent front ends to complex software systems. The last interest relates particularly to education, as one tries to introduce the young learner to progressively more complex knowledge structures. Jim Howe and Peter Ross, formerly leading researchers in LOGO, are concerned with building user models in PROLOG, without which an expert system cannot, in their view, be considered intelligent, and is unlikely to be of great educational use.

At the other extreme, and at the other side of the world, work is going on in New Zealand using micro-PROLOG in primary school science classes (Cole, 1985). Carole Cole draws explicitly on the Imperial College Work, and on the critical framework provided by Tim O'Shea and John Self (O'Shea & Self, 1983):

According to O'Shea and Self the questions for research in PROLOG are:

1. To what degree do pupils have questions they want answered?

2. To what degree are pupils able to express their questions in micro-PROLOG?

My project was formulated to investigate these questions as well as to allow children to study data processing and for them to use a logic programming language which will assume increasing importance within their future.

Pupils collected data in a concrete way from environmental observations, film, pictures, diagrams. The information collected was organized as a database, using an Apple microcomputer. Example programmes concerned with the Beaufort wind scale and ocean food chains, with a leading role played by an 11-year-old competent programmer, Simon Mount, whose project diary contains some interesting insights:

> There was very little interference from people more accustomed to using computers . . .
>
> Those involved learnt much from the activity, in two ways:
> Firstly, about the topic – The Sea and the different types of fish, and what they eat and rely on and secondly, about the use of the computer as more than just a games machine, or something for balding scientists, working out pi to a billion decimal places. So I guess now, when they come across a data base in future life, they will not have to go through the period of getting to grips with the whole concept, which was so necessary in todays effort.

Accompanying traditional research included an historical study of guano, and an analysis of the "guano cycle", involving both the fishing and agricultural industries. We should recall that high on the list of social objectives of the Japanese Fifth Generation Programme is the improvement of productivity areas such as agriculture and fishing.

History and humanities teaching in schools

Ennals came to Imperial College having previously been Head of History at Rayleigh Sweyne Comprehensive School in Essex for students aged 11 to 16, where he had developed a number of historical simulation games and role-play activities. There are published accounts of the introduction of PROLOG into this work (Ennals, 1983, 1985).

A major expansion of activity in the field came in 1982 with the involvement of Jon Nichol and Jackie Dean of Exeter University (Nichol and Dean, 1984a, 1984b; Nichol *et al.*, 1984, 1985). Nichol had been a leading figure in historical simulation and evidence-based classroom teaching of history since 1970, and had not previously found the computer to be useful. He wrote that published example of computerized historical stimulations:

> tend towards trivialization and the under-identification of the assumed model of the historical situation.

Nichol saw micro-PROLOG as holding considerable potential for computer-assisted learning in history, but felt that considerable improvements were required for the user interface, which he regarded as "user hostile". He was excited by the potential of the database as a "surrogate memory" to be prodded and processed according to the interrogative skills of the pupil:

> micro-PROLOG allows the representation of historical information as a database which pupils can explore and manipulate. In doing this the pupils can become involved in simulation in two ways: either through role play, by representing some historical character or character; or by engaging in the activities of an historian. This requires carrying out the same activities as historians, by thinking like an historian in certain ways, or by working as an historian through to the resolution of an historical problem.

Their first program, BOGBOD, concerned the historical mystery of a body found in a Danish bog, where the students have to arrive at an explanation of the death. Further programs concern the Sutton Hoo burial ship, a Viking grave, the Peloponnesian War, Viking trading, the Russian Revolution, Saxon place names, the classification of remains of early man, the Domesday Book and the Battle of Jutland. By 1985 there was considerable experience of using the programs in the classroom and on courses for teachers, and a clearer perception of the problem:

> Potentially, using PROLOG, we have a reasoning machine which we can apply widely to problem solving in education. What is required is for the subject experts within a knowledge domain, and its sub-domains, to specify the structures of the logical reasoning involved to enable the logic programmer to produce the domain-specific authoring programs . . .
>
> Logical reasoning is only a small subset of the complex and mysterious process of thinking involved in children's intellectual development.

The Exeter Project is concerned with the teaching of humanities subjects, the teaching of computing to both normal and dyslexic pupils, the training of student teachers, and support for related groups internationally. The series of Exeter software toolkits are in trial use in schools around the United Kingdom, the United States, Australia, New Zealand, Bulgaria, Chile, Denmark and Norway. Each toolkit is intended to allow pupils to write their own programs without any formal knowledge of computing. All they have to do is to pose an historical question, research the historical topic it relates to, and organize and structure their information into an appropriate form for entering into the computer. The programming is the pupil's representation of their knowledge. The work has been supported by the Nuffield Foundation, Devon Local Authority and the MEP Programme.

There have been related smaller-scale activities in the humanities field. John Latham (Latham, 1984), an English teacher concerned with curriculum development at Bishop Wand School in Sunbury, has developed some programs in micro-PROLOG to stimulate creative writing in the English classroom. The computer serves as a catalyst to thinking and writing by the student, as it does when modelling aspects of a plot and relationships between characters in drama, or when using list-processing facilities to examine literary devices in poetry. Latham adds another perspective to the use of PROLOG:

> the computer, in the hands of the individual, can be a valuable tool in helping people to make sense of their world and therefore to have some control of it.

This is in direct opposition to the inappropriate introduction of technology into education, as criticized by Jonathan Swift in his account of the Academy of Lagado, where professors:

> invent simplified languages, write books by machinery, educate their pupils by inscribing the lessons on a wafer and causing them to swallow it, or propose to abolish individuality altogether by cutting off part of the brain of one man and grafting it onto the head of another.

Swift's account and philosophy were attacked by Orwell (Orwell, 1957), who saw the conservative aim of:

> a static incurious civilisation – The world of his own day, a little cleaner a little saner, with no radical change and no poking into the unknowable.

Latham's curriculum work was supported by BP and the Leverhulme Trust. Related activities have been undertaken by Graham Hawkins, Head of Humanities at Helenswood School in Hastings and then at Bath University. Frustrated by the approach to computer and education epitomized by the Schools Council "Computers in the Curriculum Project" 1951 Census, he turned to micro-PROLOG when it was first implemented, and has developed bibliographic programs for geographers. Such teachers are increasingly establishing links with the Exeter Project and exchanging software for trial use.

In Australia there is an active group in Sydney, involving the Department of Education at Sydney University at the initiative of Yvonne Larssen, the Department of Education of the State of New South Wales coordinated by Bryan Cowling, the Australian and New South Wales History Teachers' Associations, and Paul Fennell of the Federal Education Commission, formerly of the Curriculum Development Commission in Canberra. This serves as a reminder that the implementation of PROLOG in education in a radical thoroughgoing manner requires the approval and enthusiasm of the appropriate institutions and organization in the particular country. If there is a mismatch between the institutional requirements and the perceived applicability of the educational innovation, the institution is likely to prevail. Garth Boomer, formerly of Wattle Park Teachers Centre in South Australia and now at the Curriculum Development Commission, had addressed this question (Boomer, 1983)

> Before one can deal with computer education constructively, one must deal with the "machine", the institution, within which computing will be taught. The art of educating must come of age before the art of computing has a chance.

In Australia, matters are eased by the close relationships between universities, examination boards and syllabus content, school inspectors and teachers. A similar situation obtains in New Zealand, and means that considered changes can be implemented with little delay. Another important requirement of classroom innovation appears to be the freedom of teachers to experiment in teaching method and content rather than being subject to rigid central direction. In both Australia and New Zealand, teachers have been taking the ideas and structures of programs developed at Imperial College and Exeter, and adapting them to local examples and requirements, using locally-preferred microcomputers. Following the Exeter example, teachers in Australia and New Zealand are improving their links with research group in logic programming and artificial intelligence, and organizing national conferences and workshops.

In France the research traditions in history and the humanities, what are called in France the "human sciences", are wholly consistent with the classroom history teaching approach taken in Exeter. Research methodologies that are deemed radical in Britain attract little astonishment in France. This is hardly surprising, as the Cambridge history tradition which has produced the "new history" approach in the classroom can trace its ancestry from the methods of Louis Henry, Marc Bloch and the Annales School of French social historians. The French structuralist tradition remains strong, but has had little influence on British research methodology. In contrast, however, the French classroom remains traditional, with a centrally-directed curriculum, and difficulties in the path of a would-be individual innovator. There are national laboratories for computers in the human sciences (LISH) (Griffiths, 1985), but the emphasis is on knowledge representation and expert systems, and there has been little thought of secondary education. There are signs of change, with the publication by LISH of the Journal *Education Telematique Informatique* which is taking a growing interest in PROLOG and education, sometimes including French translations of British work on PROLOG in the history classroom. National programmes have been somewhat restrained after the unfortunate experiences with Papert and LOGO at the Centre Mondial in Paris. Marseilles, as the site of the original PROLOG implementation, has maintained a lead through Marc Bergman, who is involved with numerous governmental education-funding agencies as well as initiating the EEC project in the educational use of micro-PROLOG.

In Bulgaria the lead has been taken by Levcho Zdravchev, of the International Department of the Ministry of Education in Sofia. He organizes a seminar series on modern trends in education in Plovdiv, and is now initiating a series of conferences on computers in education, held in alternate years with an international conference series on the subject in Varna, Bulgaria has had access to less microcomputer hardware than Western countries, but is clearly determined to take a leading role, with a strong tradition of work in psychology and pedagogy. A government software house is being established to develop educational software in PROLOG, and numerous visitors are sent to Britain through the British Council. The Exeter software is in use.

The work of educational psychologists

It is easier to produce impressive-sounding research results from a particular pilot group than to undertake a rigorous evaluation of the impact and effectiveness of a particular educational innovation such as the use of PROLOG in education with microcomputers. The original Imperial College project did not involve educational psychologists, and no formal evaluation exercises were included in the brief. Instead, it has seemed appropriate for evaluations to make use of the tools in hands and locations other than those of the originators. Such an activity is not necessarily straightforward, as appropriate criteria need to be established and appropriate instruments need to be chosen or developed.

In some cases projects have included an evaluation component. The Exeter Project (Nichol & Dean, 1984a, b) focused on pupil-generated questions, analysed by university researchers from lessons and recordings, and compared with the published literature. Carole Cole, in her New Zealand Primary Science Project (Cole, 1985), followed the approach of illuminative evaluation that has grown out of Piagetian developmental learning theory, and has become accepted as appropriate for evaluation of computer-based projects.

Geoff Cumming of the Department of Psychology at La Trobe University, Melbourne (Cumming, 1983) has taken a more thoroughgoing approach. He regards micro-PROLOG, and logic programming in general, as a potentially powerful instrument for the educatonal psychologist. He regards much current psychological theory as mere assertion, and a number of orthodoxies can all too easily survive unchallenged. In particular he regards micro-PROLOG, starting with the mode of use first tried at Imperial College, as a potentially powerful instrument for testing Piagetian views of cognitive development. His project is concerned both to identify interesting behaviours and, where necessary, to construct appropriate instruments for quantification.

Paul Light and Chris Colbourn of the Department of Psychology at Southampton University (Light, Colbourn and Smith 1986), working with David Smith of the Computing Service, had a different psychological theory to test. They were concerned with peer interaction in the classroom in problem-solving tasks, and again saw micro-PROLOG, starting with the mode of use of the original Imperial College project, as a potentially powerful tool.

Tim O'Shea and Eileen Scanlon of the Open University were interested in comparing the difficulty for novice programmers in learning procedural and declarative languages. In a workshop at the 1983 Computer Assisted Learning Conference in Bristol, and at subsequent experiments, novices were set the same tasks for both kinds of language, and the performance of novices in one style of language was assessed to explore the effects of previous experience of the other style. In general they concluded that it is easier to reach a descriptive level of competence in a declarative language such as PROLOG, but harder to reach an advanced level with full operational understanding. It was harder to learn PROLOG after previous experience of a procedural language, but the reverse did not hold.

Tim O'Shea and John Self (O'Shea & Self, 1983), in a critical review of educational computing, asked questions of the use of PROLOG that were cited by Cole earlier. Self, in the Department of Psychology at Lancaster University, carried his analysis further in a later book (Self, 1985), where PROLOG emerges relatively unscathed by comparison with conventional educational computing, but with the need for improvements to its user interface. Thomas Green, of the Department of Psychology at Sheffield University, placed similar stress on the need for improvements in a critical review (Green, 1983).

Some of the above challenges were accepted by Marc Eisenstadt of the Open University Human Cognition Research Laboratory, responsible for the Open University cognitive psychology course unit in artificial intelligence. In the past, the unit has been taught using SOLO, a friendly but limited language based on semantic networks. Hank Kahney's (Kahney, 1983) evaluation of the novice user's experience of SOLO suggested that it would be preferable to provide an introduction to artificial intelligence in a language that was both friendly to beginners and powerful enough to undertake complex tasks. In the summer of 1985, following work to improve the PROLOG interface (Eisenstadt et at., 1984), Open University Summer Schools started using MACPROLOG (McCabe, 1985). A mass of experimental evidence should result.

At Edinburgh University and Sussex University research has been directed to improving the environment for the learning of PROLOG. At Edinburgh, Alan Bundy and Helen Pain (Bundy & Pain, 1985) have analysed the mistakes of novices, and at Sussex Josie Taylor has described their difficulties. Bundy has been assembling a library of software tools, developed on Edinburgh DEC 10 PROLOG, and at Sussex PROLOG is incorporated into a more general artificial intelligence environment, POPLOG, which also provides POP-II and LISP, together with extensive on-line help facilities.

The work of philosophers and logicians

Logic programming holds considerable theoretical attractions for philosophers and logicians, as it offers the opportunity of putting rigorous formal concepts and notation to practice use. There are already a number of different directions pursued by projects.

Steve Torrance of Middlesex Polytechnic is a philosopher with experience of the field of artificial intelligence (Torrance, 1984). He had support from the Nuffield Foundation to develop materials for "Thinking through PROLOG", which he has given as courses at Middlesex Polytechnic and Sussex University, offering insights for philosophers into artificial intelligence.

Tom Richards of the Department of Philosophy, La Trobe University Melbourne, is an experienced philosopher and logician (Richards, 1978) who has the support of the Australian Research Council for work teaching logic through PROLOG, in courses involving both philosophers and computer scientists at La Trobe.

Jim Hopkins of the Department of Philosophy, Kings College London, developed proof-checking systems to aid in the teaching of propositional and predicate logic, using an Apple microcomputer. With the involvement of his colleagues, there is now a research project led by Richard Spencer-Smith with the support of Mark Sainsbury, developing computer-assisted learning to assist in the teaching of logic to undergraduates, supported by the University Grants Committee.

All of the above projects are intended to culminate in the publication of books with a largely undergraduate audience. The software and documentation may also be of use for senior secondary students in particular cases, or for further education. Interest in logic programming and the teaching of logic is broadening, and certainly includes the work of Barry Richards of Edinburgh, Peter Gibbins of Bristol and Wilfred Hodges of Queen Mary College London.

Logic programming and training

There has been a significant convergence in recent months in the field of logic programming and training. Until recently it did not appear that advanced research involving logic programming was being carried out on computer equipment that is in regular commercial use. American research in artificial intelligence has typically involved the use of LISP machines and other high-cost high-performance workstations, and it has been hard for commercial trainers or data processing staff to see the applicability to their situation.

Particularly in the United Kingdom, there has been a proliferation of implementations of PROLOG for microcomputers, particularly for the IBM-PC which has emerged as an industry standard. In addition there is now a choice of expert systems shells available, and a number of companies, such as ICI and British Telecom, can report successful commercial use of PC-based systems. Finally, workers in the field of intelligent tutoring systems have realized that although they may want to use a high-performance workstation for system development, a high-specification personal computer can perform as a delivery system, possibly in combination with interactive video.

An attempt has been made at the Information Technology Development Unit at Kingston College of Further Education to draw together some of the strands of previous work to apply them to the practical world of further education and training. Following a report to the Further Education Unit of the Department of Education and Science *Fifth Generation Computers: The Implications for Further Education* (Ennals & Cotterell, 1985, see Chapter 3.1) the unit was established with additional support from Nuffield Foundation, and with staff who had gained experience on other projects described above, particularly those at Imperial College and Exeter. There has been experience over the years in running courses for industry using materials developed on research projects, and this should continue.

Under the Alvey Programme, the National Computing Centre have assembled an "Expert Systems Starter Pack", comprising cut-down versions of expert system shells for commercial use to raise awareness of the potential of intelligent knowledge-based systems. At Kingston, the ITDU is developing an analogous pack of expert systems for tutorial use in different aspects of further education, such as catering, building and business studies. Using PROLOG, the unit are building on the experience of the Exeter software toolkits.

Another part of the Alvey IKBS Awareness Programme is the IKBS Journeyman Scheme, based at Imperial College and Turing Institute in Glasgow. People are seconded from industry to work in leading research centres for a period of six months, returning to apply and disseminate what they have learnt. Experience has been encouraging, and the reports submitted by Journeymen are giving us a clearer insight into problems of technology transfer. An analogous scheme is being established in Kingston, whereby trainers are seconded to work in the Unit, participating in the development of new logic programming-based training materials.

An important focus for these activities is the Alvey Knowledge-Based Engineering Training Project, which involves Logica, the Engineering Industry Board, Imperial College and Exeter University, with the bulk of the work to be undertaken at Kingston. At Logica, a group led by Lindsay Ford has developed the TUTOR shell for intelligent tutoring systems, written in PROLOG (Davies *et al.*, 1984). This is to be adapted and extended for the domain of control and maintenance of CNC milling machines, with work on user modelling to be conducted at Exeter under Ford.

There has been related work on intelligent tutoring systems, this time for language teaching, which has potential for training. Masoud Yazdani and collaborators at Exeter University (Yazdani, 1985) have designed a system for teaching French which builds on previous work by Ben du Boulay and colleagues at Sussex University, both using PROLOG. Du Boulay has long experience in the field, having worked in Howe's group in Edinburgh (du Boulay 1979; Howe & du Boulay, 1981) and more recently applied concepts from intelligent tutoring systems to the teaching of PROLOG.

A partial agenda for future activities

Extension of national research programmes to education and training

Stimulated by the example of the Japanese Fifth Generation Programme, many countries, including Britain, have instituted national programmes in advanced information technology. Initially logic programming was not assigned a major role in Britain's Alvey Programme, founded in 1983, desite its importance in Japanese plans. From July 1984, however, a national initiative in logic programming was assembled, coordinated first by Bill Sharpe of the Rutherford Appleton Laboratory and then by Richard Ennals of Imperial College.

Just as a great deal of research and activity in education and training has flowed from the initial project at Imperial College and the inputs from associated projects on databases, expert systems, and man-machine interaction, we can look for further benefits from the logic programming initiative, not least because of the commitment of education and training showed by many of the Alvey-supported researchers. Some of the possible benefits can be itemized:

1. The work on developing new logic languages, with greater expressive power involves Logica, Cambridge University, Lancaster University, Open University, ICL, Edinburgh University and Imperial College. It should provide benefits for those teaching logic and philosophy, and for those concerned with knowledge representation in the classroom.
2. Work on developing parallel logic programming languages, such as PARLOG, to run on parallel architectures such as FLAGSHIP, involves ICL, Imperial College and Heriot-Watt University. PARLOG is implemented today for microcomputers, and its use should encourage understanding of computing with non-Von Neumann architectures. New work is increasingly concerned with knowledge representation and applications building.

3. Work on developing an improved logic programming environment involved Systems Designers, Logic Programming Associates, Expert Systems International, Edinburgh University, Sussex University, Imperial College and the Open University. Many of the participants are conscious of the needs of novice users, from their experience on other projects and are also collaborating on a "PROLOG Fluency" course coordinated by the Open University as a distance learning component in IKBS of an advanced MSc course.

4. Work on developing logic databases involves ICL, Imperial College, Turing Institute, Bradford University and Heriot-Watt University. The training world should benefit from their development of large rule-based systems for income tax regulations, with an inductive rule-learning component deriving from the research of Donald Michie.

Existing Alvey projects with a logic programming component offer considerable potential for training applications. Two examples are:

1. The large Demonstrator Project in intelligent decision support led by ICL with the DHSS, Logica, Imperial College, Surrey University and Lancaster University has a training component which has so far had little emphasis. The Logica TUTOR system is likely to be given experimental use, together with adapted versions of early software systems developed on the project to aid claimants in completing forms.

2. The project building an intelligent front end to the GLIM statistical modelling system, involving the Numerical Algorithms Group and Imperial College.

Other lessons from the Alvey Programme concern the value of collaboration in common projects and of communication within a research community. The PROLOG Education Group (PEG) was established with this in mind.

Extension of international collaboratin

Whereas there has been a tradition in advanced research of international conferences and collaboration, the world of education and training has lagged behind. The projects described earlier were established through the initiatives of individuals, often on an unfunded basis. Common interests and emphases are now emerging, and it would seem sensible for governments and funding agencies to take note of the considerable accumulated experience when making plans for future agreements for bilateral or multilateral activity.

ESPRIT, EUREKA and other initiatives of the European Economic Community should provide support for the use of advanced information processing in training, as well as support to extend the EEC project on micro-PROLOG in education. Bilateral agreements could be made with France and Italy in particular, where approaches have been made.

In other international cases, governments are often reluctant· to make commitments in sensitive areas. The British Government enjoys good relations with the governments of Japan and Bulgaria, and all sides could benefit from collaboration in education and training.

In relations with Third World countries, little emphasis has been given to date to the potential for education and training assisted by low-cost computers with advanced software. Exporting technology can imply, as had been the case in la Reunion with American computer technology, covert exporting of cultural values. Bodies such as UNESCO and IFIP should give attention to an approach to computers and education which does not impose a culture or philosophy, but is able to strengthen the local choice. There has been valuable experience at Imperial College and in Kingston in developing interfaces in different languages for foreign pupils, and in allowing individual users to use the language of their choice (a Kingston vocational student wrote his adventure game in Spanish).

New research themes

Early discussions of PROLOG in Education were very taken up with issues of syntax. Advances such as Frank McCabe's MACPROLOG make such concerns redundant, as surface syntax can be changed at any time at the click of a button. The new BSI PROLOG standard should assist those who are teaching or learning the language, as well as providing a common base for advanced environment tools such as graphical tracers and debuggers.

We should be able to move on to consider such deeper issues of knowledge, structures and knowledge representation. At this stage we will benefit from closer relations with French colleagues, for whom these issues have long been important. Subject specialists, philosophers and educationists should be seeking to be involved increasingly as the barriers between them and the system are removed. It is becoming clear that logic and logic programming are not enough: we need a better understanding of what it is to be an expert, how people modify their belief systems in the light of new knowledge. We need a greater awareness of models of pedagogy, and styles of explanation, often involving techniques in the use of natural language. We are still, for example, a long way from reproducing the patterns of dialogue and reasoning from the Socratic dialogues as reported by Plato.

One theme that stands out from all of the projects described above is that computer is seen as an aid to the teacher, and not a replacement. Even in its current state of imperfection logic programming can offer aid in education and training in different ways in different subject areas, age groups and cultures. Cost at the point of learning need be no object – a national license could cover all schools or colleges; one hopes that teachers and their pupils will not have to pay to be able to think more effectively.

A number of questions are unanswered at present. How does one progress from a naive descriptive use of logic as a computer language to fluency in PROLOG programming? How close to natural language should we go in communicating with the system, or is that likely to introduce confusions and ambiguities? How will declarative graphics in PROLOG be used in the classroom? When can we expect to use logic programming on parallel computers in education? Will speech input systems be useful and realistic when used with logic programming? How will computer science and what we teach about computers in schools change as the new generation of computers comes into use? What will we have to teach those people who are accustomed to conventional computers? How will businesses, institutions and society in general be affected by the changing approaches to computing and education outlined above?

Whatever the fifth generation of computer turns out to be like, their future users are currently in our classrooms and training courses. We should pay attention to their needs and abilities, and we should bear in mind that we are part of the problem that they will have to solve.

References

Alty, J.L. & Coombes, M.J. (1984). *Expert Systems: Concepts and Examples.* Manchester; NCC Publications.

Ball, D. (1982). Arise, graphics in PROLOG. *Computers in Schools*, Vol 5 No 3.

Bergman, M. & Kanoui, H. (1973). Application of mechanical theorem proving to symbolic calculus. *Third International Symposium on Advanced Computing Methods in Theoretical Physics*, Marseilles.

Berk, A.A. (1985). *Micro-PROLOG and Artificial Intelligence.* London; Collins.

Boomer, G. (1983). *Zen and the Art of Computing.* South Australia; Wattle Park Teachers Centre.

Bottino, R.M., Forcheri, P. Molfino, M.T. (1985). *Experimenting with PROLOG in High School.* Genoa; University of Genoa.

Briggs, J.H. (1982). Teaching mathematics with PROLOG. BSc thesis, Imperial College.

Briggs, J.H. (1984). *Micro-PROLOG rules!* London; Logic Programming Associates.

Brough, D.R. (1982). *Loop Trapping for Children's Logic Programs.* Logic Working Paper. London; Imperial College.

Brough, D.R. (1984). Problem solving using logic programming. *Microcomputers in Education 2,* ed. E. Ramsden. Chichester. Ellis Horwood.

Bundy, A. (1984). Intelligent front ends. In *Research and Development in Expert Systems,* ed. M. Bramer. Cambridge, Cambridge University Press.

Bundy, A. & Pain, H. (1985). *Evaluating PROLOG Environments.* Edinburgh; University of Edinburgh.

Bundy, A. Byrd, L. Luger G. Mellish, C. Milne, R.F., & Palmer, M. (1979). Solving mechanical problems using meta-level inference. *Expert Systems in the Micro-electronic Age,* ed. D. Michie. Edinburgh; Edinburgh University Press.

Bundy, A., Byrd, L. & Mellish, C. (1982). Special purpose, but domain independent inference mechanisms. *Proceedings of the European Conference on Artificial Intelligence,* Orsay.

Clark, K.L., & McCabe, F.G. (1984) *Micro-PROLOG: Programming in Logic.* London; Prentice-Hall.

Cole, C.M. (1985) *Using a Microcomputer to Process Data for Classroom Scientific Research.* Hamilton, New Zealand; Massey University.

Colmerauer, A. (1982). *PROLOG II Reference Manual and Theoretical Model.* Groupe Intelligence Artificielle. Luminy; University of Aix-Marseille.

Conlon, T. (1985). *Start Problem-Solving with PROLOG.* London; Addison-Wesley.

Coombs, M.J. (ed) (1984). *Developments in Expert Systems.* London; Academic Press.

Cumming, G. (1983). *Logic Programming and Cognitive Development.* Melbourne; La Trobe University.

Darlington, J., Field, A. & Pull, H. (1986). The unification of functional and logic languages. To appear in *Functional and Logic Programming.* (ed De Groot & G. Lindstrom). Englewood Cliffs, Prentice Hall.

Davies, N.G., Dickens, S.L., & Ford, L (1984). TUTOR – A prototype ICAI system. in *Research and Development in Expert Systems,* (ed. M. Bramer). Cambridge; Cambridge University Press.

De Saram, H. (1985). *Programming in micro-PROLOG.* Chichester; Ellis Horwood.

du Boulay, B (1979) "Teaching teachers mathematics through programming" DAI Research Paper No 113 University of Edinburgh.

Eisenstadt, M., Hasemer, A. & Kriwaczek, F. (1984). An improved user interface for PROLOG. *First IFIP Conference on Man-Machine Interaction*, Imperial College.

Ennals, J.R. (1983). *Beginning Micro-PROLOG*. Chichester; Ellis Horwood and Heinemann. Second edition, 1984, also Harper and Row.

Ennals, J.R. (1984). Teaching logic as a computer language in schools. In *New Horizons in Educational Computing*, ed. M. Yazdami. Chichester; Ellis Horwood. and in *Logic Programming and its Applications. Eds. M. Van Canegham & D. Warren*. San Francisco; Ablex, 1986.

Ennals, J.R. (1985). *Artificial Intelligence: Applications to Logical Reasoning and Historical Research*. Chichester; Ellis Horwood.

Ennals, J.R., & Cotterell, A. *Fifth Generation Computers: Their Implications for Further Education*. London; DES Further Education Unit.

Ennals, J.R. Boucelma O, & Bergman, M. The French connection. In *Micrcomputers in Education 2*, ed. E. Ramsden. Chichester; Ellis Horwood.

Goldberg, A. & Ross, J. (1981) Is the Smalltalk-80 System for children? *Byte*, Vol 6 No 8.

Gregory, S. (1985). Design, application and implementation of a parallel logic programming language. PhD dissertation, Imperial College.

Green, T. (1983). Review of micro-PROLOG. *SWURCC Bulletin*.

Griffiths, M. (1985). Computing and the humanities. In *The Role of Programming in Teaching Informatics*, ed. M. Griffiths & Tagg, E.D. Amsterdam; North-Holland.

Hammond, P. (1982). *APES User Manual*. London; Imperial College.

Hepburn, P. (1986) *Programming in micro-PROLOG made simple*. Chichester; Ellis Horwood.

Hogger, C.J. (1985). *Introduction to Logic Programming*. London; Academic Press.

Howe, J.A.M. & du Boulay, B. (1981). Microprocessor-assisted learning: turning the clock back?. In *Selected Readings in Computer-Based Learning*, ed N.J. Rushby. London; Kogan Page.

Hurst, R. (1984). An information technology course using PROLOG. In *Microcomputers in Education 2*, ed. E. Ramsden. Chichester; Ellis Horwood.

Kahn, K. (1984). A grammar kit on PROLOG. *New Horizons in Educational Computing*, ed. M. Yazdani. Chichester; Ellis Horwood.

Kahney, H. (1983). Problem solving by novice programmers. In *The Psychology of Computer Use: A European Perspective*. ed. T.R.G. Green, S.G. Payne & G.C. Van der Veer. London; Academic Press.

Kanoui, H. (1982). *PROLOG II Manual of examples*. Luminy; Groupe Intelligence Artificielle, University of Aix-Marseille.

Kowalski, R.A. (1979). Logic as a Computer language for children. Draft case for support from SERC. November 1979 (personal communication).

Kowalski (1979) *Logic for Problem solving*. Amsterdam; Elsevier North-Holland.

Kowalski, R.A. (1984). Logic as a computer language for children. *New Horizons in Educational Computing* ed. M. Yazdani. Chichester, Ellis Horwood.

Latham, J.O. (1984). PROLOG and English teaching. In *Microcomputers in Education 2*, ed. E. Ramsden. Chichester; Ellis Horwood.

Light, P. Colbourn, C, Smith, D (1986). Peer Interaction and Logic Programming PEGboard Vol 1 Issue 1. University of Exeter.

McCabe, F.G. (1985). *MACPROLOG*. London; Logic Programming Associates.

Nichol J, Dean, J. (1984a). Pupils, computers and history teaching. In *New Horizons in Educational Computing*. ed. M. Yazdani. Chichester; Ellis Horwood.

Nichol, J. & Dean J. (1984b). Computers and children's historical thinking and understanding. *Sussex Conference on AI, Education and Child Development*, Sussex.

Nichol, J. Dean, J. Tompsett, C. & Briggs, J.H. (1984). Computing for everyman, or computer applications in micro-PROLOG In *Microcomputers in Education 2*, ed. E. Ramsden. Chichester; Ellis Horwood.

Nichol, J., Dean, J., & Briggs, J.H. (1985). PROLOG – A revolution in education?. *Times Educational Supplement*, 25th October, 1985.

Ormerod, T.C., Manktelow, K.I. Robson, E.H. & Steward, A.P. (1985). Content and representation effects with reasoning tasks in PROLOG form. *Behaviour and Information Technology*, June 1985.

Orwell, G. (1957). Politics vs literature: An examination of Gulliver's Travels. In *Inside the Whale and other Essays*. London, Penguin.

O'Shea, T. & Self, J. (1983). *Learning and Teaching with Computers*. Brighton; Harvester.

Papert, S. (1980). *Mindstorms*. New York; Basic Books.

Pasero, R. (1982). A dialogue in natural language. In *Proceedings of First International Logic Programming Conference*, ed. H. Van Caneghem. University of Aix Marseilles, Marseilles.

Pask, G. (1975). *Conversation, Cognition and Learning*. Amsterdam, Elsevier.

Richards, T.J. (1978), *The Language of Reason*. Sydney; Pergamon.

Robinson, J.A. (1983). Logical Reasoning in machines. In *Intelligent Systems*, ed. J.E. Hayes & D. Mitchie. Chichester; Ellis Horwood.

Robinson, J.A. & Silbert, E.E. (1982). LOGLISP: an alternative to PROLOG. *Machine Intelligence 10*, ed. J.E. Hayes, D. Mitchie & Y.H. Pao. Chichester; Ellis Horwood.

Self, J. (1985). *Educational Computing Software*. Brighton, Harvester.

Sergot, M. (1984). A query the user facility for logic programming. In *Integrated Interactive Computing Systems*, ed. P. Degano & E. Sandewall. Amsterdam; North-Holland and in *New Horizons in Educational Computing*. ed. M. Yazdani. Chichester; Ellis Horwood.

Shapiro, E. (1982). *Algorithmic Program Debugging*. Cambridge, MA. MIT Press.

Tallon, W., Ball, D., & Tomley, D. (1982). BASIC or PROLOG: choosing the right language for a biology teaching task. *Computers in Schools* Vol 5 No 1.

Torrance, S. (1984). *The Mind and the Machine.* Chichester; Ellis Horwood.

Vogel, C. (1983). *Language and Creativity: the Creole Connection.* Research Report University of la Reunion.

Yazdani, M. (1984). *New Horizons in Educational Computing.* Chichester; Ellis Horwood.

Yazdani, M. (1985). *Intelligent Tutoring Systems: An Overview.* Exeter; University of Exeter.

4.2
Logic Programming in Systems Development

Introduction

Logic programming has become extremely fashionable in recent years following its adoption as the basis of the Japanese fifth generation of computer systems and its increased prominence in national and international research and development programmes. Numerous implementations of PROLOG are in current commercial use, in the hands of inexperienced users with diverse backgrounds. This chapter seeks to assess the achievements, the potential and particularly the limitations of logic programming in system development.

What is logic programming?

Logic programming offers the basis for a fundamental reassessment of approaches to system development. Through a proliferation of implementations of the language PROLOG, first implemented by Colmerauer in Marseilles in 1972, some of the ideas and techniques of logic programming are becoming available on conventional mainframe, mini and microcomputers, ranging from the Sinclair Spectrum and BBC micro systems running CP/M, MSDOS and Unix, to IBM mainframes. There is more to logic programming than PROLOG, which is itself constrained by the Von Neumann architecture of

First published in the proceedings of the Online Conference on *Knowledge-Based Systems 1986*.

current computers, which imposes compromises on logical power and purity in favour of ease of sequential execution.

The fundamental insight of logic programming, developed by Kowalski and his colleagues in Edinburgh and then at Imperial College, was that a description of a problem expressed in the notation of predicate logic could be regarded by the computer as a program to be used to solve the problem. Logic programming offers assistance in all areas of system development:

> problem description;
> executable specification;
> rapid prototyping;
> top-down program development;
> database design, development and interrogation;
> program analysis, synthesis and maintenance

Logic programming offers a common language for previously diverse branches of computing as:

> databases;
> expert systems;
> natural language processing;
> artificial intelligence;
> data processing;
> VLSI design;
> education and training.

Logic programming offers assistance; it does not provide solutions, and indeed may raise new unexpected problems. The basic requirement remains that of clear thinking, driven by a deep understanding of the relevant knowledge areas. Knowledge-based systems require a basis of knowledge. Expert systems are empty without an expert. The availability of the power of logic as unleashed in the form of logic programming systems of increasing sophistication may prove to be a mixed blessing. One does not normally hand a child an electric power drill when he has no understanding of carpentry and wants to make some shelves. To a hammer everything can come to look like a nail. Just as a blunt axe is of little use in sharpening a pencil, ten blunt axes are of no greater use. Often we might prefer an old-fashioned pencil sharpener, as long as it works and satisfied our requirements.

Logic programming requires us to describe our current state and our goal state, and to reason about each in terms of the other. The precise mechanism by which the transition is accomplished from the current state to the goal state, from the input to the output, is of secondary theoretical interest, and will vary according to the computational model and architecture of the computer system used. It is, however, of great practical importance to the commercial systems developer, whose concerns are likely to be for optimal performance and efficiency for the task in hand at the expense of elegance and logical purity.

Recent years have seen the emergence of a body of logic programming methodology which demonstrates the performance benefits from conceptual rigour. This imposes new intellectual demands on the logic programmer; artificial intelligence must be preceded by the use of natural intelligence, itself a rare commodity which requires careful nurture through education, training, and appropriate experiences during its development. This forms part of the context for my work with Kowalski at Imperial College developing "Logic as a Computer Language for Children", my subsequent work as Research Manager at Imperial College and in the Alvey Directorate, and my work with overseas research groups led by Colmerauer at Marseilles, Robinson at Syracuse and Shapiro at the Weizmann Institute in Israel. I am currently seeking to test and clarify this emerging methodology as a consultant on applications projects and as a producer of distance learning materials in logic programming and intelligent knowledge-based systems.

The results of international research in logic programming appear at all levels of system development:

experimental sequential and parallel architectures;
implementations of PROLOG and its successor logic programming languages;
the emergence of standards for PROLOG which offer portability of tools and programme code across implementations;
richer programming environments on affordable hardware;
applications building tools;
expert systems shells;
intelligent front ends and interfaces to conventional systems;
a choice of surface syntaxes and user interfaces;
documented self-explaining working applications programs;
tutorial texts directed at different levels of users.

A sequence of words is not adequate; now we can begin to show what we mean. Some problems can be solved by being reduced to sub-problems which are themselves soluble. Other problems may be shown to be insoluble, at least under the description which we may have available. Wisdom may be defined as knowing the difference between the two cases, and living with our continuing inadequacy.

The logical limitations of logic programming

By virtue of its derivation from traditions of work in logic, language processing (both natural and computer languages) and explanation, logic programming should properly inherit many of the theoretical discoveries of its ancestors. It is regrettable and arguably extremely dangerous that few users of logic programming systems appear to be aware of their inherent limitations, and that claims and expectations are stated, the realization of which is not coherently conceivable.

Logic programming has a basis of formal logic, not of magic. As Robinson has shown, processing logical facts and rules can be viewed as a form of higher order data processing, but we cannot expect the full power of first order logic to be mechanized. There are, for example, insuperable obstacles concerning negation: we cannot assert negative information without computationally explosive consequences. Instead logic programming systems tend to incorporate the results of Clark's work on negation by failure, though system developers and users may be unaware of the inevitable consequences of that decision for the applicability of the system. Logic programming systems normally assume a closed world: they reason and reach conclusions purely on the basis of the information that is explicitly available in the system, whether it has been pre-programmed or acquired during the course of an interaction with users. They do not necessarily tell us anything about the real world, but reflect the structures and details of the artificial models (or micro-worlds) which they have been given, which become potentially self-explanatory through their declarative implementation in logic.

These limitations are, of course, compounded as we seek to build complex structures on the basis of the Horn Clause subset of formal logic. We can offer "rational reconstructions" of many of the features and facilities of temporal logic, modal logic, and natural language, without the prospect of their full realization. When we embark on "mixed-language" or "mixed-paradigm" programming we cannot thereby escape the underlying logical limitations of our underlying logic programming system.

Much of the theoretical work of mathematical philosophers has very practical consequences of which we should be aware. Godel showed that we cannot prove all the theorems of a system using only the system itself. His results derived from a study of arithmetic, but apply also to object level logic programming, and to object level natural language. Meta level logic and language structures are an area of active current research, but to implement meta level facilities in the object level PROLOG system does not provide an escape from Godel's conclusion, but merely carries his conclusions up to the meta level. On the other hand, with the addition of the closed world assumption, questions about the contents of our logic database are known to be decidable. We have a powerful tool with which to increase our understanding of systems if, and only if, we are aware of the limitations of our understanding.

The general systems fallacy

The fallacy underlying all systems which purport to be generally applicable in the real world is not new, nor is it peculiar to systems based on logic programming.

The descriptive emphasis of the declarative style of logic programming may have provided a snare for the unwary, who may have the illusion that complex issues of problem-solving are finessed by providing the computer with a description of our problem which it takes as a programme.

Kowalski's early work emphasized the concept of:

Algorithm = Logic + Control.

This has been satirized, not always unfairly, as:

Logic programming = Algorithm − Control.

Work at Imperial College on IC-PROLOG, a relational language for parallel programming, and PARLOG, has focussed attention on control issues, with the development of a process interpretation of logic programming by Clark, Gregory and Ringwood. Related work has been conducted at ICOT in Tokyo, at the Weizmann Institute in Israel, and in the rigorous LISP-based community in the USA. Our very concepts of algorithms are undergoing revision with the advent of parallel computer architectures necessitating parallel algorithms and tools such as the language OCCAM with which to reason about sequential and concurrent processes.

Such work on parallel execution of logic programming does not offer the prospect of saving us from the general systems fallacy, which we now describe in schematic form:

1. If we cannot give a complete and correct description of a problem,

we are not entitled to expect another person, or a computer system, to provide a solution.

2. Even if we believe that we have given a complete and correct description of a problem, it does not follow that our description, in the terms in which we have stated it, can be given a procedural interpretation in the real world which provides its solution. There may be many equivalent descriptions, each of them arguably correct, only one or none of which gives rise to a procedural solution. We cannot neglect issues concerning knowledge structures and intelligent problem-solving strategies.

3. If we take a human expert in a given domain, with imperfections in his knowledge and understanding, and embody his knowledge in an expert system, we preserve all his imperfections, and, in an automatic system, forfeit the benefits of his control over the problem-solving process.

4. Our scientific tradition, and indeed the survival of our planet, may be imperilled by our abdicating our responsibility for solving problems and placing undue reliance on the efficacy of a system which, though it may be internally consistent, cannot reflect or encompass the detailed circumstances of the real world in real time. This argument applies both to the naive acceptance of ideologies of whatever variety, and to the reliance on the man-made automatic technology of complex computer systems. In this sense it may prove to be one of the early axioms of the new theory of "computational politics". Problems in the real world are not in general amenable to general solutions in real time.

Practical implications for system development

At this stage we can suggest some practical rules of thumb, or hints for the unwary, concerning the use of logic programming in system development:

1. There is a sense in which any system should be regarded as provisional, a prototype which reflects the state of knowledge of the designer at the time of implementation. New information may necessitate the updating or modification of the system.

2. In order to make sense of the behaviour of a system, for example to debug it in case of perceived malfunction, we have to know the description of the problem it was originally intended to address, as well as the description of the problem it was addressing at the time of malfunction, and the process of reasoning in which it was

engaged. The system itself cannot provide all of this information, and we need a higher level set of models.

3. System developers can reason by analogy in a manner that is not coherent to ascribe, or think of ascribing, to machines or computer systems. We tend to see problems as examples of a general type with which we have some experience, by reference to common logical or structural characteristics, or through a less direct process of association involving external circumstances extrinsic to the problems themselves. There are therefore limits to the extent to which we can expect systems to solve problems for which they have not been given explicit information, and to the benefits we can expect from the addition of expert rule-sets.

4. Building a system can be a very effective way of increasing our understanding of the problem which it is intended to model, raising new questions which lead to the continuation of the process of exploration.

5. System development is increasingly a matter of collaboration between members of a team, some of whom may be computer systems. The process of interaction or conversation that is involved can be regarded as a form of knowledge elicitation, where knowledge has to be made explicit in order to be shared and incorporated in the overall system model. Some knowledge is not capable of being made explicit and described in detail, but is taken as given or accepted as not needing to be questioned. For this to be a viable arrangement we must have models of those with whom we are dealing, in the context of which we can make sense of their questions and answers.

6. System development in the artificial intelligence tradition may not have as its prime objective the production of a completed system for commercial sale. The investigation may be the end in itself, as is often the case in education and training where one does not aspire to achieve perfect performance, merely to move closer to full understanding. We should be cautious regarding commercial pressures to produce premature finished products.

7. We may have much to learn from experience with expert systems shells, which will typically support work in a given field by the intelligent user up to a certain point, after which he or she will feel the need to extend, modify or adapt the shell to his or her own special circumstances. The same is likely to prove true of systems in general as their life-cycle progresses.

8. Using logic programming does not in itself offer a panacea for such problems of knowledge, but a notation and way of thinking which

may be of assistance to the thinking problem-solver.

9. We have much to learn in the field of knowledge-based systems before our dialogues can be compared with those of Socrates as reported by Plato. Perhaps we have more powerful tools with which to approach old problems, but the nature of the problems has changed little since the Ancient Greeks first devised systems of formal logic with which to tackle complexity. We could be well advized to read what they had to say, animating their arguments as programs in order to enhance our understanding.

Suggestions for further reading

Benson, I. (ed) (1986). *Intelligent Machinery: Theory and Practice*. Cambridge; Cambridge University Press.

Campbell, J.A. (ed) (1984). *Implementations of PROLOG*. Chichester; Ellis Horwood.

Clark, K.L. and Tarnlund, S-A. (ed) (1982). *Logic Programming*. London; Academic Press.

Clark, K.L. & McCabe, F.G. (1984). *Micro-PROLOG: Programming in Logic*. London; Prentice-Hall.

Clocksin, W. & Mellish, C. (1981). *Programming in PROLOG*. Berlin; Springer-Verlag.

Conlon, T. (1985). *Start Problem-Solving with PROLOG*. London; Addison-Wesley.

Ennals, J.R. (1983). *Beginning micro-PROLOG*. Chichester; Ellis Horwood and Heinemann. 2nd edition 1984 also Harper and Row.

Ennals, J.R. (1985). *Artificial Intelligence: Applications to Logical Reasoning and Historical Research*. Chichester; Ellis Horwood.

Gregory, S. (1985). *Design, Application and Implementation of a Parallel Logic Programming Language*. London; Department of Computing, Imperial College.

Hogger, C.J. (1985). *Introduction to Logic Programming*. London; Academic Press.

Kowalski, R.A. (1979). *Logic for Problem-Solving*. Amsterdam; North-Holland.

Ringwood, G. (1986). The Dining Logicians. London; Department of Computing, Imperial College.

Robinson, J.A. (1979). *Logic: Form and Function*. Edinburgh; Edinburgh University Press.

Van Caneghem, M. & Warren, D. (eds) (1986). *Logic Programming and its Applications*. San Francisco; Ablex.

The Training Access Points (TAPS) Development A Question of Balance Within Various Dimensions

Introduction

On my resignation from Imperial College and the Alvey Directorate I accepted consultancies with the Council for Educational Technology, Manspower Services Commission, Open Tech and the Engineering Industry Training Board, assisting them in the development of new national strategies and programmes for the use of advanced information technology in education and training. This is a matter of great concern to government, further exacerbated by reports from the National Economic Development Office (NEDO), the Advisory Council for Applied Research and Development (ACARD), the Information Technology Advisory Panel (ITAP), the Confederation of British Industry (CBI), and the Organization for Economic Coooperation and Development (OECD). My role has been to contribute the results of practical experience and to introduce interested parties to each other. Another appendix which I contributed to the TAPS Feasibility Study was entitled "Related National Artificial Intelligence programmes 1986–1990 and contacts in the Field".

Following the British government complicity in the American

First published as an appendix to "Training Access Point: A Feasibility Study", carried out by the Council for Educational Technology for the United Kingdom on behalf of the Manspower Services Commission, May 1986.

bombing of Libya I resigned all government consultancies, including technical responsibility for the coordination of the Manpower Services Commission Programme in Artificial Intelligence and Training, which has yet to be announced.

The application of artificial intelligence to problems of training is a complex and long-term task, for which few people as yet have relevant experience. The purpose of this analysis is to spell out some of the options and choices along 26 continua. The Information Technology Development Unit at Kingston College of Further Education (see chapter 3.1 for an account of its rationale) is now the focus for a national programme supported by the Further Education Unit of the Department of Education and Science and the Manpower Services Commission. In my new post as Senior Lecturer in Educational Technology at Kingston College of Further Education I will be able to contribute to the development of distance learning materials, to be made available through new institutional structures such as the recently-announced College of the Air.

The TAPS programme seeks to offer training advice, information and support to industry, with particular emphasis on the needs of small businesses. Appropriate use is intended to be made of different levels of available technology. The following contribution was intended to help in decisions regarding appropriate uses of expert systems hardware and software, on which I was lead consultant for the feasibility study.

Hi-tech computer equipment and the intelligent user

The emphasis should be on the user and on his or her "applications pull" rather than on "technology push" which tends to be easier to organize and pay for, but ultimately less successful. The Alvey Initiative has shown the need for a coordinated approach to the technology development, pushing a line of development in advance of the short-term views of user companies.

It is not clear what the role of a user is in the new generation of declarative systems, although it must be a mistake to assume that current approaches from traditional systems are all carried over unchanged. It is likely that the user is increasingly concerned with describing his or her problem and less with the procedural computing aspects of problem-solving (i.e. use will commence with the asking of a question, not with the command "run").

It is assumed that the user will have a far more active role where the computer is a tool to help him or her solve a problem collaboratively, rather than the user being a passive spectator. The computer may act as a catalyst, but the real work is done away from the computer.

Computing power and ease of use

There is a pragmatic decision to be taken regarding the trade-off between computer power and ease of use. One method is to build systems in a modular manner so that at each stage the user can choose which interface, syntax and support tools to have available, using some for system development which are then discarded at run-time.

To an increasing extent the system can be made to look and behave as one wishes: the problem then is to describe what one wishes and, to a large extent, this issue is independent of the computer, concerning instead the applications domain and tutorial style chosen.

It may be helpful to look at the overall systems architecture in levels, with agreed interfaces between them, enabling specialists to address the problems that concern them most in a way that supports the requirements of others, e.g.

  user interface;
  tutorial model and interaction style;
  knowledge representation for subject domain;
  applications building environment;
  mixed language programming environment;
  language implementation;
  compiler target language;
  computational model;
  underlying architecture;
  VSLI.

Optimization for particular tasks and general flexibility

The emphasis should be on the development of an executable, running specification, which then can be customized to the user's requirements regarding performance, interface, extensibility, etc. Again, this is a question of identifying the appropriate system level, and ensuring compatability with the levels above, preserving a declarative approach to issues at the relevant level and observing interface protocols.

It should be noted that this approach to systems development presupposes collaboration within a mixed-expertise team, and between teams. This raises interesting issues of the management of large-scale software systems, software life-cycles, configuration control, version management, access to databases, security and confidentiality, as well as Intellectual Property Rights.

Capability and cost

Here again, there are trade-offs to be made, with one answer being portability of code and users between systems of different sizes and costs. Using micro-PROLOG and sigma-PROLOG, the user can move through all machines from Sinclair Spectrum, Amstrad and BBC to IBM–PC, Nimbus, Vax, SUN, IBM and DEC mainframes, Cray and FLAGSHIP with a common interface, or take advantage of the different host facilities.

The computer manufacturer plays a relatively minor role in an ideas and software-driven approach to systems development. This allows us to delay our decisions regarding components of delivery systems, both hardware and software, as long as we have taken a coherent and consistent view of our problems.

However, in Britain little emphasis has been given to issues of knowledge representation, structuralism, modes of reasoning, formal pedagogics, theories of learning and communication.

Formal structures and near natural language interfaces

It is incoherent to talk of full natural language understanding from computers. There is a case to be made for emphasizing the unnatural nature of interaction with computers in order to educate the expectations of users. Near natural language can be used when interacting with intelligent databases and other IKBS systems, but this presupposes some understanding of the levels of complexity of subject matter, syntax and vocabulary.

System capability and user needs

It is crucial to have well-formulated pilot projects with close attention paid to detail, and careful scaling of effort and expectations.

System control and user control

When a learner takes control of his or her learning his or her attitude to work and authority may be changed. He or she may ask questions away from the computer, and expect reasoned answers from supervisors, managers and colleagues. This could have a dramatic and complex effect on the workplace, industrial relations, training and production methods.

System initiative and user initiative

Who asks the questions? What counts as an answer? What does one do if one does not agree with the official answers? What does one do if crucial information is not made available, or if its acquisition involves cost and effort? All these questions have a new significance in the presence of the technology with which ignorance may no longer be bliss, and with which knowledge is power.

Sequential computer operations and human reasoning

We naturally solve problems in parallel. Many of our computational concepts are wedded to conventional architectures; even the supposedly pure concept of algorithmic thinking will have to undergo revisions.

Central processing power and logical processing power

For the user it should not necessarily matter whether the processing power is local or central. For the systems engineer it may be crucial with such issues as access to updating of databases, inconsistencies of non-monotonic reasoning and temporal problems of updating and subsequent justification. Problems of large systems cannot be avoided just by opting for a distributed model. You have to deal with the relations between the modules of what is in total a system of the same overall complexity, though with a different internal architecture.

Central memory and local memory

Memory is becoming very cheap, but there remain enormous technical problems with reasoning about large, distributed, non-homogenous databases. Issues of consistency, truth maintenance and meta-level reasoning are raised in this context.

Computer networks and human networks

In theory all researchers in advanced projects are linked by computer networks. In practice there are numerous inconsistencies and incompatibilities, defective protocols and missing systems software. Human networks remain of paramount importance.

Software engineering and social engineering

Software project management is social engineering. Software engineering is still at an early stage of development.

Computional structures and social structures

There is a danger of assuming that technology can solve all our problems. There is a need to take what we know we can do and to apply it in a careful and considered way in order to help us to describe and solve some of our training needs.

Strong AI (computer brains) and weak AI (human brains)

Put crudely, the European approach is to emphasize human brains, while the American approach is to prefer computer brains!

Expert systems and human experts

It is not coherent to think of a computer expert system fulfilling more than a fraction of the functions of a human teacher. An expert needs to be able to perform the tasks on which it is advizing, and, by and large, this will not be true for a computer system in other than a trivial sense. By the same token, it makes little sense to talk of replacing experts by expert systems, but expert systems should be able to increase the effectiveness of a human expert, and to assist in the training of experts.

Instructional delivery systems and human learning

There is an increasingly clear cultural divide between Europe and the USA in the area of education and training with computers. Europeans give more emphasis to the intelligent student, trainee, teacher and trainer whereas the American emphasis is on systems that are teacher-proof and can be delivered by satellite.

Long-term goals and short-term needs

In the field of logic programming in education and training there has been a flow of software for existing computer systems as a by-product of continuing long-term research. Evaluation of the current materials will be in terms of the degree to which they satisfy the needs of their current users. Collaborative national programmes have had to amalgamate the long- and short-term concerns, mapping out a development path with benchmarks which can help the interface of separate but communicating projects.

Within TAPs, companies are concerned with short-term survival, and are not used to spending on research, development, training, education, and planning. They are unaccustomed to describing objectives beyond the end of the current financial year, so have to be offered systems and schemes which can deliver something of practical utility in the shortest possible timescale, preferably immediately, and with the minimum reliance on intelligent trained users, who are in short supply in British industry at present.

Systems that are placed in the hands of companies and government agencies for practical use must have been running smoothly for some months in laboratories, and must have full documentation when sent to beta test sites. This suggests the need for a full time TAPs expert systems documentation team, developing a unified consistent style, and monitoring feedback in a professional manner, possibly commissioning and scripting support videos, etc. British industry must be pandered to in the short term if it is to exist in the longer term.

Hype and hard-nosed reality

TAPs has to deliver, and demonstrate working systems in the hands of real people.

We would benefit from a suite of training demonstrator packages using ESP-Advisor (ESI) and the new successor they are currently building, and from a training package for companies such as Currys, Dixons, Rumbelows, to enable their sales staff to mount in-shop demonstrations of shells and TAPs fragments from March 1987.

Expensive "knowledge engineers" and lost cost "unemployed"

Considerable emphasis has been placed on the role of the "knowledge engineer", a highly paid specialist, to construct the knowledge-based system using knowledge elicited from mere mortals. This can only have a finite degree of success, as the bases for such inductive systems tend to be statistical rather than derived from the structure of the knowledge area itself.

In the training context, where we do not have the aim of achieving a perfect system to replace the expert, but intend instead to strengthen the capacity of the human problem-solver, we can instead choose to build on the foundations of clear understanding of parts of the problem, by working through a series of rapid prototypes, at the end of which the problem may have been solved by it no longer appearing to be a problem, or by some underlying issue emerging which diverts our attention. A major task is to describe and redescribe our problem, in the language most natural for it, and the expert system may simply serve as a catalyst for this.

Computer technology can now be regarded as disposable, cost free, and only meriting value to the extent that it contributes to the solution of human problems. The focus of our work in TAPs must be the human predicament; we must not regard small business (wo)men as disposable and cost free. The unemployed (wo)man has ideas and insights which must be built on, strengthened with confidence, and attributed social value.

Academic aspirations and commercial survival

Expert systems technology has already proved subversive of the normal order of things. We are at a dangerous stage where there is a shortage of academic criteria by which to judge new expert systems, and where too much store is set by the output of computer systems. Companies that are using the technology to their genuine commercial advantage suddenly stop publishing details of what they are doing, and regimes of classification and censorship are applied to academic work on collaborative projects with industry.

"Intelligent systems" and available systems

Overblown claims are being made for current systems: that they are user-friendly, can be addressed in natural language, that they are in some sense intelligent. An "intelligent system" would by definition offer a higher level of behaviour than one is accustomed to, for "intelligence" is a moving target, drawn from the analogy with human behaviour. We need to be aware of the limitations of any system we use.

Knowledge engineering tools and affordable PC software

Powerful things can be done with PCs when the user is aware of what he or she is doing and what the system is doing. We do need demonstration sites where the scope of powerful knowledge engineering tools can be explored, and companies encouraged to purchase them as appropriate.

Mainframe-based systems and PC-based systems

The gap between the mainframe and the PC using communities has closed. Today's PCs have more memory and capability than yesterday's mainframes.

Central control and individual autonomy

Central control and individual autonomy are an organizational concern as different social and management systems take on the technology with different consequences for control, access and power. They need to be monitored.

Database consistency and ease of updating

Database consistency and ease of updating is a critical issue. The easier it is to update the database, such as by asserting and retracting facts, the easier it may be corrupted, lose its consistency and its logical integrity.

4.4
Diagnosing problems with micro-PROLOG

A doctor asks: "How is he feeling?"
The nurse says: "He is groaning."
A report on his behaviour. But need there be any question for them whether the groaning is really genuine, is really the expression of anything? Might they not, for example, draw the conclusion "if he groans, we must give him more analgesic" – without suppressing a middle term? Isn't the point the service to which they put the description of behaviour?
(L. Wittgenstein, *Philosophical Investigations*. Blackwell, 1968, p. 179)

The argument of this paper is that recent research advances have greatly enhanced our capacity to bring computing power to bear on problems of medical decision-making, but that in addition to enabling us to describe and explain medical phenomena, the computer has laid bare deeper problems of knowledge which require our attention.

In the first section we review the contribution made by micro-PROLOG to the application of computer technology to issues of medical expertise and decision support on personal computers. This is regarded as a diagnostic exercise, as we uncover problems that are amenable to treatment within our present body of knowledge and meta-knowledge. Micro-PROLOG represents new generation computing in infant form: in the second section we seek to assess its potential future contribution to the resolution of problems which are as old as mankind itself.

Some light is cast on the problem by previously obscure writings of Wittgenstein, little consulted by users of personal computers. In his *Philosophical Investigations* he made certain assumptions that might now be reassessed by workers in artificial intelligence:

> Only of a living human being and what resembles (behaves like) a living human being can one say: it has sensations; it sees; is blind; hears; is deaf; is conscious or unconscious. (p.97)

We are concerned here with human behaviour, and in particular the behaviour of the medical expert, which we are seeking in some sense to replicate or support. First it must be described. We should not assume that a fluent description denotes a deep level of understanding. Wittgenstein draws the analogy of children playing with trains:

> When children play at trains their game is connected with their knowledge of trains. It would nevertheless be possible for the children of a tribe unacquainted with trains to learn this game from others, and to play it without knowing that it was copied from anything. One might say that the game did not make the same sense to them as to us. (p.97)

In a manner that is particularly relevant to our consideration of the declarative use of micro-PROLOG in developing expert systems, Wittgenstein draws attention to the different uses to which descriptions are put:

> What we call "descriptions" are instruments for particular uses. Think of a machine-drawing, a cross-section, an elevation with measurements, which an engineer has before him. Thinking of a description of a word-picture of the facts has something misleading about it: one tends to think only of such pictures as hang on our walls: which seem simply to portray how a thing looks, what it is like. (These pictures are as it were idle). (p.99)

When we give an account of micro-PROLOG in terms of facts and rules, there is a danger of minimizing the difficulty of representing and resolving problems of knowledge. In particular, we often gloss over the distinction and relationship between the problem area and its description. In Wittgenstein's words:

> Don't always think that you read off what you say from the facts; that you portray these in words according to rules. For even so you would have to apply the rule in the particular case without guidance.

We make no apology for raising difficult problems which have preoccupied philosophers over the ages. Possession of a supposedly powerful personal computer equipped with modern state-of-the-art software does not obviate the need to think about problems of knowledge. Indeed, one of the messages of new generation computing is that to a large extent the computer itself drops out of consideration except in as much as it can assist, as in solving real problems. Wittgenstein, when asked to describe his aim in philosophy, replied: "To show the fly the way out of the fly-bottle". The computer makes it possible for us to show what we mean, to animate our descriptions, to release a few flies.

Describe problems with micro-PROLOG

Micro-PROLOG has brought the power of logic programming to the personal computer. Originally implemented in Marseilles in 1972, PROLOG (PROgramming in LOGic) was confined to the nursey of artificial intelligence laboratories before being allowed into school in the hands of the next generation of computer users. Professor Robert Kowalski at Imperial College was concerned to explore the potential of logic as a computer language for children, (see Chapter 4.1) and it was essential to remove the obstacle of expensive or inaccessible computer hardware. Frank McCabe implemented micro-PROLOG in 1980, originally for the Exidy Sorcerer, then for microcomputers with the CPM operating system used in British schools, such as Research Machines and North Star. It is now widely available for personal computers such as Sinclair Specturm, Apple II, BBC micro, Commodore 64, IBM-PC, Apple Macintosh, and computers running the MSDOS PCDOS and Unix operating systems. The user interface can be the same in each case, reducing the importance of the hardware and its manufacturer, though the different implementations take advantage of the memory and other facilities offered on different host machines.

After five years of classroom and research use there is a growing library of introductory and advanced texts for programmers who wish to use micro-PROLOG, and for users who do not wish to be reduced to programmers, preferring to use a range of high level tools that have resulted from different research projects. The speed of development has been accelerated by thousands of users with compatible systems which enable the same micro-PROLOG code to be used irrespective of underlying hardware. Micro-PROLOG has been widely used in a number of styles in diverse applications.

We are particularly concerned here with the declarative use of logic and logic programming in addressing problems of medical knowledge. This can be approached at the direct language level, representing medical knowledge as facts and rules in micro-PROLOG, or through a diverse collection of front end programs which can facilitate knowledge exploration in different contexts and with different user interfaces. We can gain an insight into both approaches through a closer examination of one such front end, APES (augmented PRO-LOG for expert systems), implemented by Peter Hammond and Marek Sergot at Imperial College, which has been used in medical applications. APES is implemented for microcomputers with the MSDOS and Unix operating systems. It uses the same surface syntax as SIMPLE, an introductory front end program which is available for all micro-PROLOG implementations, but offers extended facilities and behaviour.

Peter Hammond of Imperial College and Peter Alvey of the Imperial Cancer Research Fund have studied the approach to expert systems taken in the renowned MYCIN diagnostic system and its empty shell version EMYCIN, and have re-implemented such a system in APES on personal computers. EMYCIN, originally implemented in LISP, largely takes the form of production rules with references to other data such as context trees and certainty factors. In APES, the knowledge, both diagnostic rules and contextual information, is expressed in the uniform notation of facts and rules.

Let us take a simple case of recommending treatment for particular physical symptoms. In simplified EMYCIN the rules could appear as:

If problems entered = pain and
not aspirin – unsuitable
then aspirin – recommended

If problems entered = diarrhoea and
not lomotil – unsuitable
then lomotil – recommended

If suffers from peptic ulcer
then aspirin – unsuitable

If suffers from impaired liver function
then lomotil – unsuitable

When translated into APES and generalized, the program can read:

_drug recommended-for _patient if
    _patient complains-of _symptom and
    _drug suppresses _symptom and
not _drug unsuitable-for _patient

```
_drug unsuitable-for _patient if
    _drug aggravates _symptom and
    _patient suffers-from _symptom

    aspirin suppresses pain
    lomotil suppresses diarrhoea
    aspirin aggravates peptic-ulcer
    lomotil aggravates impaired-liver-function
```

The APES version offers considerably more flexible access to the knowledge expressed in the program. We can query it in a number of ways:

English: What is recommended for Peter?
APES: find (_drug: _drug recommended-for Peter)

English: Who is recommended to take aspirin?
APES: find (_person: aspirin recommended-for _person)

English: What drugs suppress what symptoms, according to our knowledge base?
APES: which (_drug _symptom: _drug suppresses _symptom)

English: Which drugs suppress pain and inflammation?
APES: which (_drug: _drug suppresses pain and
                    _drug suppresses inflammation)

This description of drugs, symptoms and side-effects can be used as a free-standing program or as a component of a larger system. As our knowledge is represented explicitly and declaratively it can be used extremely flexibly.

Such a translation of medical knowledge into declarative logic for execution on personal computers offers both advantages and dangers. Rules can be expressed with great economy and concision, making previously complex areas of knowledge explicitly represented and intelligible. Easy access is provided to factual information, which is open to flexible manipulation. The danger is that the medicine, or other areas of expertise, can be made to appear over-cosy. The fact that a representation of a knowledge area can be so easily manipulated may cloud our perception of the real problems of that knowledge area. Diagnostic systems based on hierarchical structuring of signs and symptoms are made easier to construct, but medical knowledge is not inherently hierarchical as such systems might have us believe. Different medical authorities use different taxonomies, and have different models of causation and cure. This is not to decry the power of logic and logical description, but to say that deep problems remain, perhaps approachable for the first time.

Foucault, in *The Archaeology of Knowledge*, has addressed the problem of describing and articulating medical discourse. He wrote (p.34):

> If there is a unity (to medicine), its principle is not therefore a determined form of statements; is it not rather the group of rules, which simultaneously or in turn, have made possibly purely perceptual descriptions, together with observations mediated through instruments, the procedures used in laboratory experiments, statistical calculations, epidemiological or demographic observations, institutional regulations and therapeutic practice? What one must characterize and individualize is the co-existence of these dispersed and heterogeneous statements; the system that governs their division, the degree to which they depend upon one another, the way in which they interlock or exclude one another, the transformation that they undergo, and the play of their location, arrangement and replacement.

We can begin to tackle such questions in micro-PROLOG in personal computers using logic at the object level and at the meta-level, and in combination in the same programmes. Knowledge assimilation can be seen as meta-level, deductive, and involving belief revision. Meta-level definitions of provability can be used to model medical approaches to knowledge assimilation, and can simulate object level provability, all in the same language. Such logical power and descriptive clarity at each level has great potential for demystifying problems of medical knowledge and for enhancing medical training without incurring inordinate expense.

Foucault's analysis of medical discourse seems to be addressing many questions now being raised on large software engineering projects, where distributed processing occurs according to varying models, and issues of version management and configuration control arise. Indeed, the modern concept of the software life-cycle has the ring of medicine about it. Foucault's application of mathematical logic and clarity to such knowledge domains has much to teach us: the tools of declarative logic programming on low-cost personal computers may help.

As an illustration, let us examine the use of Kowalski's "Demo" predicate in medical diagnosis. Given a full case history, we can set out to diagnose some illness, using the notation:

Demo (case-history _illness)

More demandingly, we could seek to diagnose some interesting illness:

Demo (case-history _illness) and
   interesting (_illness)

Given a known likely diagnosis G, and a partial case history P[1]
(containing variables) we could seek to complete our diagnosis:
Demo (P[1] G)

Using meta-variables in PROLOG we can combine the object
language and the meta-language. For example, we could say:

Demo (database whooping-cough) if whooping-cough

where the first argument of Demo is identical to the current global
state of the database. This allows us to use mixed sentences such as:

clear (_person) if
Not-Demo (database "whooping-cough (_person)")
   and relevant-facts (database)

Such formal concepts have been shown to be useful, on personal
computers, when studying legislation such as the British Nationality
Act (Kowalski, 1984). The author is not aware of such formal analysis
in medical domains, where knowledge structures are not accepted as
absolutes, and there has been less attention to the formal characteristics of reasoning methods. Absolute answers will not be available, but
our argument is that the tools of object level and meta-level logic,
articulated through tools such as APES, have considerable potential
in supporting medical reasoning and decision-making.

Diagnosis and prognosis

Donald Michie and Rory Johnston, in their book *The Creative
Computer* set out the prospectus of what is required from new
generation computing systems as they graduate to adulthood:

> It will require a complete reversal of the approach traditionally followed
> by technology, from one intended to get the most economical use out of
> machinery, to one aimed at making the processes of the system clearly
> comprehensible to humans. For this, computers will need to think like
> people. Unless the computer systems of the next decade fit the "human
> window" they will become so complex and opaque that they will be
> impossible to control. (p.12)

Addressing the medical sphere in particular, they maintain:

> Computer systems are needed that incorporate the expert knowledge of
> specialists in the developed countries, not only so that correct diagnoses

can be made by less skilled people in remote areas, but also so that those people can acquire more of this knowledge through machine-aided learning.

We can identify the respects in which our current systems on personal computers fall short of the requirement stated above, and describe progress in attaining the objective of practical systems for use by less skilled people in less developed countries. The improved strength of our technology offers potential benefits for the health of the world. Elsewhere we have proposed a "Strategic Health Initiative" in place of the current emphasis on Strategic Defence, or Star Wars (see Gill, 1986 and Chapter 3.3). Within the constraints of personal computers we can begin to assess practical possibilities: to-day's clear description should give rise to tomorrow's system.

It is essential to focus our attention on those aspects of medical decision support that are open to support from personal computers equipped with appropriate systems. It will be a mistake to regard such computers as powerful expert diagnosticians: even MYCIN is not used for practical diagnosis, and it proved more difficult than anticipated to adapt MYCIN to the role of an expert tutor, equipped with a model of the learner and capable of carrying out the task that the learner is assigned.

The range of data and knowledge which could be contained in a personal computer-based medical system is wide. At the "hard" end there would be factual data about medicine, services available and patient registration. At the "soft" end there would be the problems explored earlier, representing the consensus of professional wisdom and experience about managing patients' problems. This wisdom is not always supported by clear evidence, and changes as new knowledge is assimilated.

Attempts will be made to offer integration over the whole range of knowledge, but the argument of this chapter is that such attempts are doomed to failure. Medical knowledge is not sufficiently stable, not sufficiently satisfying the criteria of an established science, for the whole to be handled by a computer system. On the other hand, doctors have to operate in diverse medical domains and would benefit from the availability of specialized tools to enhance their effectiveness.

Two examples of such tools may suffice. The World Health Organization is to support the development of an expert system to aid the production of measles vaccine in Third World countries. This will involve a process of knowledge elicitation from experts who are preparing a text manual for measles vaccine production, and the production of a system to be delivered on personal computers for use in Third World medical and social conditions. The project will benefit considerably from the experience at London New Technology Network and St Thomas' Hospital in developing an expert system in PROLOG for diabetes patient management. Such a system, developed under Unix, could be delivered on the new generation of personal computers.

Fifth generation computer technology will improve the user interface to our medical expert systems, will progressively permit voice input in natural language to desktop parallel computer workstations such as the ICL/Plessey FLAGSHIP, and will facilitate speedy access to complex databases, as is envisaged by the proposed "Oxford System of Medicine." The underlying problems of medical knowledge will continue, though the computer itself is a crucial tool in their diagnosis and clarification.

Wittgenstein wrote (*Philosophical Investigations II*, ix):

> Correcter prognoses will generally issue from the judgements of those with better knowledge of mankind.
>
> – Can one learn this knowledge? Yes- some can. Not, however, by taking a course in it, but through experience.
>
> – Can someone else be a man's teacher in this? Certainly. From time to time he gives him the right tip.
>
> – This is what "learning" and "teaching" are like here.
>
> – What one acquires here is not a technique; one learns correct judgements. There are also rules, but they do not form a system, and only experienced people can apply them right. Unlike calculating rules.

References

Foucault, M. (1972) *The Archaeology of Knowledge*. London; Tavistock.
Foucault, M. (1973). *The Birth of the Clinic*. London; Tavistock.
Gill, K. (ed.) (1986). *Artificial Intelligence for Society*. Chichester; Wiley.
Michie, D. & Johnston, R. (1984). *The Creative Computer: Machine Intelligence and Human Knowledge*. Harmondsworth; Penguin.
Wittgenstein, L. (1968). *Philosophical Investigations*. Oxford; Blackwell.

4.5
Building an Expert System for Training Needs Analysis

Written with Diane Whitehead and Nigel Tipping, co-collaborators on the Stewart Wrightson Embedded Computer-Based Training Project, supported by Open Tech and the Manpower Services Commission, this paper describes work that forms part of the third phase of the project, where two teams are addressing issues of training needs analysis, and the introduction of expert systems techniques.

The principal application area for the project is insurance, providing training support for the IBA (Insurance Broking Accounting) software system which has recently been implemented on the Wang VS100 mainframe. Particular attention is given, as with the example described here, to generic aspects of training and training needs analysis, with a view to applications across the broad range of projects supported by the Manpower Services Commission in youth and adult training and the support of small businesses. The expert systems technical group is currently developing a range of prototype systems on the Wang Personal Computer, using PROLOG, in association with the industry support group at Kingston College of Further Education, supported by the Manpower Services Commission. Products of the group include distance learning training materials.

A number of kinds of knowledge are required in order to provide intelligent training for staff in the insurance industry as they use the

From a paper given at the IEE colloquium on Knowledge Elicitation on 25th March 1986.

computer-based IBA system. In the third phase of the project the objective is to build a system which will match records of actual performance against idealized performance goals and suggest possible actions to improve performances towards that ideal. The system requires knowledge of:

the subject domain: *object level*;
how the subject domain is organized: *data dictionary*;
how the subject matter can be assimilated and modified: *meta level*;
the state of knowledge of the user: *user/learner model*;
how the subject can be taught: *tutorial model*.

By virtue of their complexity, such systems must be built by teams drawing together diverse areas of expertise. Their knowledge must be elicited and represented if it is to be used for practical training, whether or not it is to be computer based. The method described here is that of the development of rapid prototypes to aid in the understanding of different aspects of the problem, which can themselves be used in training. As a precondition to training needs analysis of the particular problem, we first have to understand and describe the problem.

In this paper we discuss a particular case study with generic interest and urgent applicability across industry and commerce. The Data Protection Act of 1984 requires all companies which keep personal data about individuals to register their activities by 11th May 1986. There are serious penalties for non-compliance, both for companies and individual employees. In order to train employees in appropriate procedures for compliance under the Act, it is necessary to arrive at an understanding of its provisions. The group addressed the question: "The Data Protection Act – Do we need to comply?"

Roger Wiggin, Training Manager at Stewart Wrightson, has prepared a resource pack for company guidance on the Act. Together with distance learning materials in logic programming developed by Richard Ennals, and expert system shells from the Information Technology Development Unit at Kingston College of Further Education they provided the basis for a two-day workshop.

There follow illustrative excerpts of running prototype systems developed at the workshop. Nigel Tipping and Steve Smith used MITSI, a front-end programme to micro-PROLOG (from LPA Ltd), to enter facts and rules concerning the Data Protection Act:

someone is data-user if someone user-of personal-data.
someone is data-user if someone provides-service-using-personal-data.

somedata is personal-data if somedata about someperson and
    someperson is living-individual and
    somedata identifies someperson and
    not somedata exempt yes.

someone must register if someone user-of personal-data.

someone user-of somedata if someone uses somesys and
    somesys about somedata.

somedata not-accessible anyone if somedata about research.
somedata not-accessible anyone if somedata about consumer-credit.

somedata accessible no if somedata held-for exception.
somedata accessible no if someotherdata about somedata and
    someotherdata held-for exception.

somedata exempt yes if somedata about payroll-account.
somedata exempt yes if somedata about personal-domestic.

Diane Whitehead explored the potential of interactive systems using
APES (from Logic Based Systems Ltd):

data-protection-act applies-to _system if _system about people and
    _system automatic and
    not _system exempt
training-system about people
_company must register if _company runs _system and
    data-protection-act applies-to _system

Stewart-Wrightson runs training-system

_company incurs _penalty if _company must register and
    not _company does register and
    penalty can-be _penalty
_person incurs _penalty if _person employed-by _company and
    _company incurs _penalty

Diane employed-by Stewart-Wrightson

penalty can-be unlimited-fine
penalty can-be deregistration

The group reached the following summary conclusions on the
second day of the workshop:

1. APES is a more powerful and flexible tool than MITSI.

2. The extraction of relevant facts and rules from a body of text is not as simple as it may seem.
3. The extraction of such facts and the discipline of converting them into logical rules exposes any shortcomings and ambiguities very quickly.
4. Yes, the system should be registered.

References

Bentley, T.J. (1986). *Stewart Wrightson – ECBT Phase 3: Training Needs Analysis*. Project report; Stewart Wrightson Project.

Ennals, J.R., Tipping, N. & Smith, S. (1986). *A Spoonful of Sugar: Introducing Expert Systems Ideas to Small Businessmen*. Project report; CNJ Systems.

Wiggin, R. (1985). *The Data Protection Act*. Company Report; Stewart Wrightson Project.

4.6
Artificial Intelligence and Educational Technology

"Artificial intelligence" and "educational technology" are two names for what is fundamentally the same activity: using technology to help people to think and learn.

In artificial intelligence research we seek to give concrete form to abstract ideas by representing them as programs, which can be run, observed, amended, and used as components of subsequent larger systems or activities. Programs should be regarded as the side-effect of the process of active thinking for which the computer has been a crucial catalyst. The true objective of artificial intelligence is to come to a more mature understanding of our thinking processes and activities, and of the way in which we make sense of our world. Everything man-made can be described as artificial, in the sense of being artefacts. Artificial intelligence programs have to be preceded by the use of natural intelligence: a program can only offer a correct or comprehensible representation of a problem once it has been tackled by a human expert whose knowledge is then made explicit in the form of a program.

In educational technology we use technological devices to support and extend our capacities to think and learn. Since Marshall Mc-Luhan's work *Understanding Media* on the mass media we have become accustomed to the concept that "the medium is the message", and for some self-indulgent educational technologists the medium has also been "the massage", bringing tired ideas back to life. Research in social anthropology has revealed details of past approaches: primitive societies would often make reference to external phenomena or technologies in order to rationalize and make sense of their world. Cave paintings show a preoccupation with hierarchies and control structures in the animal kingdom. The contents of the stomach of "Pete Marsh", the body found in the Lancashire peat bog, reveal a set of religious practices based on the mystical qualities of spring seeds and herbs. Modern man uses computers – the language of computers permeates our descriptions of individual and social behaviour, providing a uniquely powerful metaphor in that we can also use the metaphorical objects ourselves.

In planning future political or military decisions, a Roman general would consult the entrails of a chicken. His modern day equivalent might consult an expert system. The answers would be equally unreliable, but the chicken could not explain its reasoning (unless we are to regard entrails as a primitive "entailment structure" in the terms outlined by Professor Gordon Pask of Brunel University). Farmers have for millennia inferred a weather prediction from the posture of cattle: modern inductive systems do the same with more technical language.

The children of Israel were given a rule-based system with which they could learn to order their lives, including details of food preparation and hygiene, which would be the envy of the Hotel and Catering Industry Training Board. They should read the Book of Leviticus, or seek to emulate its clarity in modern training technology for kitchen staff.

Medieval and Renaissance princes would take expert advice on the conduct of their affairs. Machiavelli and Castiglione, among others, recorded their advice in the educational technology recently made available by Gutenberg, the printed book. Project managers of large software engineering projects would do well to read Machiavelli's "Il Principe", recently described as a "sixteenth century data processing management manual". Social engineering and software engineering turn out to be closely linked, and software engineers neglect the educational technology of the book at their peril.

Muslims tend to describe themselves, Christians and Jews collectively as "The People of the Book", governed by a common educational technology for life and life after death derived from the books of the Old Testament. Devotees of modern Western technological culture may come to be called "The People of the Machine". On this technological analogy, should we divide people into "The People of the Flipchart" (sales executives),, "The People of the Chalk" (classroom teachers), and "The People of the Moving Image" (film and television producers and audiences)? Does Twentieth Century

Science have as great a significance for modern man as Twentieth Century Fox? Have politicians entered a fantasy world of technology, dazzled and almost educated by the technology of "Star Wars"? Is "the medium" now become "the massacre"?

It is becoming clear from the above that neither artificial intelligence nor educational technology can be validly considered in isolation from their cultural, social and political context. Such technologies can themselves be innovative (the tradition of leadership by chickens set in Roman oracular science has been followed, for example, in chicken jokes, chicken soup with rice, Kentucky Fried Chicken, "Kentucky Fried Movie", and the "Chicken Song" on the television series *Spitting Image*, by comparison with which the Sunday dinner is a pale cardboard imitation). Why did the chicken cross the road? We may well ask.

Chickens provide a metaphor for understanding the current frenetic pace in City institutions where high technology is being installed at great expense in time for the "Big Bang" in October 1986 when economic regulations will be changed. Data processing managers and commodity traders are rushing around like chicken with their heads cut off, not realizing that they are about to get more than their fingers burnt, and that they are likely to be stuffed and eaten by their predatory rivals.

There has been an unresolved contradiction in educational technology practice in recent years. At the same time as giving lip-service to the Piagetian ethos of encouraging questioning behaviour in our students, we have been proceeding apace with the Skinnerian model of training people in repeatable processes. Our technological language reflects this: we talk of word processing, data processing, information processing, text processing, knowledge processing.

Artificial intelligence may be able to contribute to the reform of the language and the practice, deriving also from Piaget but concerned to pay more than lip service. If we genuinely want to encourage questionning, hypothesis formation, experimental activity and cultural diversity in our younger generation, we need some new terms to authenticate existing practice. For "process" read "protest". Let us give the initiative to the learner, as we have been saying from the secure position of those who are always ignored. Let us start to talk of "word protesting", "data protesting", "information protesting", "text protesting", "knowledge protesting". We cannot stand aside from debate; rather we can facilitate it with our educational technology. It enables us to reach the parts of problems other technologies cannot reach.

The following example derives from the union of the fields of artificial intelligence and educational technology. It is concerned with de-mystifying and explaining for the learner the complexities of a system involving sequential and concurrent events and processes, abstracting from the real world case whose technical complexity is intimidating, and simulating critical aspects with the eminently available technology, not sufficiently used in education, of a snooker table, balls and cue.

The eighteenth century Scottish philosopher David Hume used to illustrate his theories of causation by reference to the game of billiards. The twentieth century Austrian philosopher Ludwig Wittgenstein demonstrated ideas of rules and games using basketball. In each case the objective of the players is to control the final resting-place of a single ball, though the intermediate stages vary considerably. In the case of billiards interactions are required between the cue and a ball, and between ball and ball. In basketball, the critical interactions are between players of a team, and between players of opposing teams. In neither case do players or managers ever expect that a game will run precisely according to plan, and considerable importance is given to the skill and judgement of the individual human player at the time of play.

We can approximate more closely to the complexity of general systems such as that envisaged under the American Strategic Defence Initiative by considering the example of snooker, where it is possible for a player to score a maximum break of 147 by potting every ball on the table in the optimal sequence, making no mistakes that allow his opponent to take over the initiative. While one player is maintaining a break his opponent is not allowed to intervene. It is extremely rare for the maximum break to be recorded, even by players with many decades of experience, and the confidence of tournament organizers in the difficulty of the task is confirmed by the lucrative prizes that are often offered to the successful player, who will typically describe himself as lucky. During the early stages of such a potential break, tension can be observed to rise, the tone of voice of television commentators changes, sweat breaks out on the forehead of the man with the cue, extra chalk is applied to the end of the cue after each shot, and the player displays an unconvincing nonchalance in his demeanour as he walks around the table, weighing up all the options before making an irreversible decision to pot a particular red ball. The process can be long and drawn out, lasting well over half an hour, as even the most "hurricane" of players realizes the importance of the task ahead of him.

Attempts have been made to teach robots to play snooker, with a conspicuous lack of success to date. Even in the distinctly closed world of the standard size green baize-topped table and the fixed number and combination of coloured balls, a great variety of outcomes are possible, exceeding chess in computational complexity.

In this context, the official prospectus of the Strategic Defence Initiative can be seen as ludicrous in the original sense of the word. An automatic system is to be required to pot all of the "balls" (tens of thousands of incoming missiles), in a universe devoid of "pockets", whose physical characteristics are far from fully understood, and whose performance in terms of speed of travel, degrees of deflection and other variable factors is likely to be affected by what is happening to other "balls". The system cannot be tested, and each "cue" is a hydrogen bomb to be detonated in space, dispersing "balls" of directed energy to bounce off space-based mirror platforms or "cushions". The time available before a "break" would have to begin is likely to be measured in terms of minutes. A three minute decision phase would not give time to seek guidance from any human "players". The opponents cannot be relied upon to stand back until the "break" is complete. Commencing a "break" is overwhelmingly likely to cause in itself the destruction of the "table" and the end of the "game". SDI, in short, should be regarded as a load of balls, cues and pockets, and could become the last game in town.

Further reading

Machiavelli, N. (1961). *The Prince*. Harmondsworth; Penguin.
McLuhan, M. (1964). *Understanding Media: The Extensions of Man*. London; Routledge & Kegan Paul.
Toffler, A. (1971). *Future Shock*. London; The Bodley Head.

COMPUTATIONAL POLITICS

5.1
Computational Politics

Introduction: interpreting and changing the world

As an undergraduate student of Moral Sciences at Cambridge I attended two lectures given by Noam Chomsky in 1970. Taking his themes from Marx's *Theses on Feuerbach*, the lectures were entitled:

1. "On Interpreting the World."
2. "On Changing the World."

Chomsky's work has been of fundamental importance for the discipline of computational linguistics, and has been described by Alain Colmerauer in conversation as providing the basis for the original implementation of PROLOG in Marseilles in 1972.

In this paper I want to explore the computational realization of the other side of Chomsky's work, where structures are used to understand, make sense of and participate in the world. I call this field computational politics, and maintain that it enables us to cast new light on a great body of past academic work in the field of political science and social theory, as well as offering powerful tools for political analysis, which have been put to the test in real-time experiments in recent months.

Metaphors to aid political understanding

People need metaphors with which to give coherence to the world

An earlier version of this paper was published in *AISB Quarterly*, Spring 1986.

around them, the world of which they are a part. For centuries the metaphors have been drawn from biology, with phrases such as:

    the body politick;
    the head of state;
    the executive arm.

entering normal parlance. Shakespeare is a rich source of such metaphors (see Menenius' speech in *Coriolanus*), and it was a recurrent preoccupation of Queen Elizabeth I in her speeches to Parliament.

Leach has argued that societies have always depended on external phenomena to provide metaphors for their world – early societies made great reference to animals, we make use of computers. The underlying rationality is likely to be the same, so the tools of one society can often be used to assist in making sense of the actions and structures of another.

Participating in a mythical structure

As a member of the College Council of King's College Cambridge, serving under Leach as provost, I was presented with Cornford's *Microcosmia Academica*, the guide for the aspiring academic politician, which should now be compulsory reading for students of whatever discipline. Consistent with Machiavelli, contemporary with Rupert Brooke, and anticipating Wittgenstein, Monty Python, Bernard Williams, and Douglas Adams, it sums up a stream of Cambridge thinking where the clock is set at "ten to three", and there is still "honey left for tea". The lavatory on my staircase in my final year was immortalized by Brooke:

    O spot where I was taken short,
    Oh Bodley's Court, Oh Bodley's Court,

and over the door was the phrase from Dante's *Inferno*: "Lasciate ogni speranza, voi ch'entrate".

I come from the European cultural tradition so beloved by Matthew Arnold and F.R. Leavis, which predates and will outlive computers. My first night as an undergraduate at King's as English scholar was spent in the company of E.M. Forster. His theme for much of his writing was "only connect". It is a theme which is missed by computer scientists who disregard their cultural context: the connections which matter, the only networks which work, are human. The playwright Steven Poliakoff, a fellow history undergraduate at King's, has explored these themes in his plays. Another Kingsman, Tam Dalyell MP, has lived out these themes in his courageous political life. The mysteries of the Belgrano have been followed by the tragic death of Hilda Murrell and the sinister visits to our shores of Clarence Robinson from the Pentagon. For those wishing to talk to Mr Robinson, Tam Dalyell has kindly recorded his home and office telephone numbers in Hansard. Government appears to prefer to rely on electronic and official channels.

A structuralist framework

Surviving texts and other cultural objects offer a mediating representation that was addressed by the human objects of our study, and are open to our critical and empathetic examination. This is a version of the structuralist thesis as applied to work in the human sciences, including literature, archaeology and history. Controversy has raged in Cambridge over the case of Colin McCabe, a radical English lecturer, Kingsman and structuralist critic. He was a founding member of the Cambridge Radical Philosophy Group through which I first became acquainted with the work of Foucault.

I have previously explored such ideas in writing in a variety of domains over a period of 20 years as a student, teacher and researcher; (Shakespeare's History Plays, the work of T.S. Eliot, the pottery of Josiah Wedgwood, the history of mental illness and of town planning, the United Nations, the League of Nations, the House of Commons and the European Parliament, the local history of Barnes and Sunbury, the Russian Revolution, nineteenth century immigration to the United States, political and social change in Kano (Northern Nigeria), the roles of individuals inside and outside institutions, disability in Inner London, life in small communities, the Quaker approaches of John Bellers and Peter Bedford, politics and language in Andorra, housing in eighteenth century Marseilles, Danish archaeology, Machiavelli, Leonardo da Vinci, Voyages of Discovery, the Norman Conquest and Domesday book, the Cold War and nuclear diplomacy). My work has been greatly influenced by the work of Dunn, Skinner, Macfarlane, Laslett, Giddens, Foucault, Leach, Collingwood, Laing, Goffman, Carroll, Stoppard, Pinter and Wittgenstein.

With the computer we can put some concrete form to what were previously complex abstractions, explain what we mean and come to model and understand the views and beliefs of others. An enormous amount of work remains to be done as both new questions and the means of beginning to answer some of them are now available.

Computing and politics

It is no part of the argument here to maintain that computing offers an adequate set of metaphors for politics, or indeed, vice versa. Rather I want to argue that both cultures inhabit the same world, and that each would benefit from a greater understanding of the other. From that synthesis a number of interesting consequences could flow, beyond simply an enrichment of the language of discourse.

Politics offers a rich description language, and an awareness of social structures and modalities of human interaction. It suffers from a general incapacity to implement its specified objectives, and a tendency to take a partial and over-simplistic view of complex problems, tailored to suit the belief system of the individual concerned. Often disagreements can be reduced to disagreements over the use of political language, often stemming from unrealized ideological origins (see the work of Mannheim, Marcuse, Lukacs, Sartre, Camus and Raymond Williams).

Computing offers an environment where clear descriptions can be regarded as specifications, and executed as programs. Ideas can be put to the test, and debugged. Theories can be developed incrementally, and refined in a stepwise manner. The growing discipline of software engineering displays a concern for what is known as "the whole software life-cycle", and an awareness that programs, like political policies, have an ongoing life after they are formulated, during which the context within which they are applied will change, and their own behaviour will need to be modified in the light of experience. In a manner familiar to traditional educators, software engineers place a great emphasis on sound structures, robust and flexible enough to support later enhancement and modification. All too rarely are computer scientists familiar with the workings of the real life domains and structures within which their systems are to be used, often by uncomprehending users.

Artificial intelligence and politics

The artificial intelligence tradition has included a number of attempts to reconcile the two areas of computing and politics. The United States in the Vietnam War period contained many thinking human and computer scientists who were unhappy with the direction of government policy (such as Chomsky, Spock and researchers at Yale such as Colby and Abelson). They had concerns which they wished to be able to bring to the attention of colleagues and the general public, straightforward demonstrations carrying placards, or the writing of pamphlets seemed inadequate to the task. During this period I was an exchange student in the United States, at the same school and taught by the same historians as David Schwartz of the American State Department, until recently in charge of American Strategic Nuclear Defence Policy. We share a continuing interest in peace and arms control, issues that are shrouded in complexity.

The computer offered potentially a much more powerful tool. In 1969 I was exploring the potential of the computer as a tool for the moral philosopher, studying the work of Braithwaite, Von Neumann and Rapoport, Bentham, Mill and Arrow, hampered by only having access to BASIC on a terminal link to Dartmouth College. Abelson had more powerful tools at Yale, and has described, in work published in 1973, the construction of his "Ideology Machine", a computer simulation of a Cold War ideologue such as Barry Goldwater, whose ideas had much in common with the current President, Ronald Reagan. A system was built which could be subjected to the "Turing Test": it was to be asked a series of questions on American foreign policy as put to a State Department spokesman. From their experience Abelson was able to define a "master script" which could be seen as underlying such political behaviour. I spent part of the summer of 1969 with friends and colleagues of Barry Goldwater in Arizona, and came to understand, but not share, their views.

Keeping artificial intelligence out of politics

Why have such ideas and techniques not become more widespread in the political world? There are a number of explanations which individually and in concert help us to make sense of practice in recent years.

Computer scientists and political scientists have been seen as coming from different cultures, united only by the term "scientist" which arguably sits uneasily in both cases. Artificial intelligence researchers have been seen as nonconformists or heretics within computer science, and as impossibly obscure and remote by political scientists. All concerned have been busy with their own work, and unprepared to learn the new tricks of an unfamiliar discipline.

The American artificial intelligence tradition has assumed the availability of powerful high-performance workstations, beyond the financial imaginings of impecunious political scientists outside the United States. In addition there has developed a perceived "artificial intelligence priesthood", with a visible hierarchy of gurus, all terrifying, competent and young.

Artificial intelligence and military funding

The radical cutting edge of artificial intelligence work has been blunted by the dependence of many of its exponents on military funding. Artificial intelligence research is now seen as critical to the successful execution of the Cold War ideology which it had been used to unmask. As the techniques become more understood they become incorporated into the amorphous body of computer science, and cease to be "artificial intelligence" in a professionally threatening sense. For many "artificial intelligence" has become merely the name for a set of techniques, rather than a framework for asking awkward, and often uncomfortable, questions. We have even reached the stage where "applied artificial intelligence" is to be used almost as a matter of course to automate weapons design at Georgia Tech. As they become more dependent on high levels of funding and computer equipment, artificial intelligence researchers are faced with the dilemma which faced nuclear physicists who worked on the Manhattan Project. Their work is seen as central to the success of projects with enormous global consequences, on which they were not consulted. To withdraw from such work would jeopardize their personal funding and career prospects.

Freedom of information

Bureaucratic and goverment structures feel threatened by the asking of awkward questions. Even where there is officially "freedom of information" there is understandable trepidation regarding policy modelling tools in the hands of potential critics and opponents. If civil servants, instead of implementing policies, were to start questionning them and considering alternatives, there would be serious implications for government. To quote Tennyson, writing before the Northcote-Trevelyan Report established the professional basis of the Civil Service:

> Theirs not to reason why,
> Theirs just to do and die.

Computer scientists have applied such ideas themselves all too rarely in other areas which might be open to public scrutiny. Whereas a core master script may be tantalizing and provocative, extending and refining such a script to correspond to individual cases tends to be hard. Furthermore, in so doing, the artificial intelligence researcher is inclined to make use of "frames", or stereotypes, a mode of descriptive analysis that is not always favoured in social and political science.

Computers and the professions

A more fundamental reason may involve the relationship between the professional and the computer. Computers have for too long been associated with job replacement and unemployment, and professionals have only recently seen the potential of the computer for job enhancement. Early computer systems in commercial and professional use failed to live up to their claims, but there is growing use of word processing, databases and spreadsheets on personal computers. Expert system shells are now beginning to have an impact, as professionals find they can build applications systems of their own without specialist computing knowledge. Research groups are now engaged in policy modelling: for example, different economic policies are simulated on the treasury model of the economy. To move from such numerically-based work to more knowledge-based modelling is a major change. We have gained some insight into this in building a logic-based front end to a large statistical modelling system (GLIM), where the problem is to capture the statistical knowledge of the expert statistician in a programme. Capturing and representing expert knowledge is a major research problem. Unless it is done well other professionals in a subject domain will not want to use the resulting system.

Demonstrating artificial intelligence

Attempts are being made to bring expert systems technology and artificial intelligence techniques into use in the political world, in collaborative research programmes such as the Alvey Programme in the United Kingdom. For example, the large Demonstrator Project led by International Computers Ltd is concerned with intelligent decision support in the Department of Health and Social Security. Part of the project is concerned with modelling different policy options, including representing the law and regulations as logic programs. Work is also conducted with claimants completing official forms: conclusions could have radical implications for future policy and practice, if they are allowed to. It will be instructive to monitor the extent to which research results percolate into practice: this should be one of the concerns of the Alvey Evaluation team at the Science Policy Research Unit, Sussex University.

Politics and software engineering

There are a number of respects in which politics and political science could contribute to the development of computer science. In particular, software houses are now facing major problems in setting up and managing large software projects, running on multiple sites with large teams of diverse professionals. They are addressing new questions of group management, version and configuration control, access to information, rights to amend and update the central database, control over design, subdivision of tasks, and confidentiality. These can all be seen as political questions, in the sense of questions of management of humans in groups, concerning decision-making and resource allocation. Few managers of software projects have a background in social and political science: when looking for authorities on project management they are unlikely to turn to Machiavelli. They should.

Machiavelli plays Star Wars in PROLOG

In a recent conference report for *AISB Quarterly*, Masoud Yazdani described the public presentation in Genoa of a game entitled "Machiavelli plays Star Wars". He was hampered by his lack of fluency in Italian, but noted that the game was played half in PROLOG. An English version of the game follows below, playable by anybody with access to a PROLOG system and a human brain (their own).

The specification as given below will run on any microcomputer with micro-PROLOG, such as Sinclair Spectrum, Amstrad 6128/8256, Apple 2, Commodore 64, BBC micro, or any microcomputer with the CPM, MSDOS or Unix operating systems.

The syntax used below is that of SIMPLE (for smaller machines) or APES (for MSDOS or Unix machines). If the programmes are run using APES there is a richer interaction, and explanation of answers given. If preferred, the programmes can be written using MITSI, which has been provided with recent releases of micro-PROLOG. Only the surface syntax requires modification for any system that will conform to the new BSI/ISO PROLOG standard abstract syntax. If the reader has no access to a computer, the written word, as translated from Machiavelli's Italian into PROLOG, has some descriptive power. To give a procedural interpretation to what follows, and facts to taste and then stir it. And-parallelism, Or-prallelism and requirements for co-routining are there in abundance in this rich domain for artificial intelligence action research.

The program constitutes a rule-based representation of facets of the complex world of politics, diplomacy, and warfare. It forms part of an attempt to explore computational politics. Users will need to add their own facts to see the power of the rules. Examples are given, but part of the point of the exercise is to explore the interaction of facts and rules, progressively amending the model to offer a closer approximation to reality.

The first rules are taken directly from Machiavelli's *Il Principe*, the section entitled "Il Golpe e il Leone". Later rules are more contemporary in derivation. This re-animation of Machiavellian expert systems has been presented in lectures at King's College London, Oxford University, the University of Genoa, and conferences in Odense, Elsinore and Paris, and I am grateful for earlier comments.

```
x oppresses y if x must-be (tough to y)
x bribes y if x must-be (tender to y)
x bribes y if y accepts-money-from x
x must-be (tough to y) if  x  wants-to-rule z and
                           y  citizen-of z and
                           x  wants (obedience from y)
x must-be (tender to y) if  x  wants-to-rule z and
                            y  citizen-of z and
                            x  wants (support from y)

x wants (obedience from y) if  x  newly-arrived-in z and
                               y  citizen-of z and
                               X  previous-ruler-of z and
                               not y opposed-to X

x wants (support from y) if  x  newly-arrived-in z and
                             y  citizen-of z and
                             X  previous-ruler-of z and
                             y  opposed-to X

x wants (obedience from y) if  x  established-ruler-of z and
                               y  citizen-of z

x accepts-money-from y if  y  wants z and
                           x  can-provide z and
                           y  makes-military-use-of z
```

```
x  accepts-money-from y if  y wants z and
                            x can-provide z and
                            y makes-civil-use-of z

x  works-for y if  x wants-to-do z and
                   y permits z and
                   x accepts-money-from y

x  seen-as dissident if not x accepts-money-from y

x  dissident-to y if  y offers-money-to x and
                      not x accepts-money-from y

x  wants-to-do y if not x opposed to y

x  opposed-to y if  x principles z and
                    y contrary-to z
```

The most difficult part of the problem comes at the end. How can one give an adequate representation of one's principles, or belief system, in a manner that is powerful enough to face the challenge of new facts and rules with differing structures and representations? How do we determine whether a particular action would be contrary to one's principles, or in conflict with one's belief system? This is not simply a matter of clear description but also of procedures. Do we sometimes look the other way when a difficult case comes along? Do we subtly redescribe our actions in order to have an easier life? Can negation and contradiction take an uncomfortably practical form?

It is not suggested that computers are going to solve age-old problems of politics, morality and ethical judgement. It seems possible however that by regarding a piece of analytical writing as a programme, taking a set of postulated rules as a prototype expert system, we can cast new light both on the problems that are being described, and on the thinking of the writer whose text we are animating, as we are obliged to make explicit those pieces of the argument which are left implicit. For example, using the above example derived from Machiavelli, there are some interesting questions:

1. How did a Prince know when he was safely established as a ruler?
2. Was a Prince regarded as a citizen of the place he sought to rule?
3. Was there a hierarchy of city-states and kingdoms governed by the same set of rules?

Looking at the rules of more modern origin:

1. To what extent does the use of money take over from traditional forms of power?
2. How can we make sense of alliances and power blocs?
3. Can one only afford to have principles if one has attained a particular political, social or financial position?
4. How is one deemed to be dissident in different political systems?

Further research: a Memorandum of Misunderstanding

We have been participating in recent months in a real-time experiment in the field of computational politics. Some artificial intelligence researchers, aided by powerful tools and metaphors to extend their powers of analysis, have embarked on a programme of action research, involving techniques of participant observation. It is hoped that as computational politics achieves more visible coherence, researchers may feel able to participate in the effort to preserve the world of which we make humble attempts, in our ivory towers, to make sense. Questions need to be asked. Ours is to reason why.

SDI and new generation computing

The Japanese Fifth Generation Programme is stated as having wholly civil objectives, and follows in a long tradition of national collaborative programmes organized by MITI. By contrast, the American Strategic Defence Initiative and the preceding Strategic Computing Initiative have military objectives, and follow in a long tradition of programmes organized by the Pentagon with the aid of DARPA. The British Alvey Programme started in the former manner, but with the government's agreement to participate in the American SDI the management of research is likely to follow more of the American pattern. The European ESPRIT Programme has a similar origin to the Alvey Programme, and will be similarly affected by British participation in SDI. The European EUREKA Programme is itself now threatened by the emerging attitudes of the British and French Governments, and could be transformed from its initial civil market orientation into a European Defence Initiative. There are similar dangers as the work of the Japanese Fifth Generation Programme falls into the hands of the American SDI Programme.

The underlying enabling technology can be deployed to civil or military work. The technology of logic programing, both sequential and parallel, has been developed by researchers in a civil context, who

---

2

elestial Poker at the Summit

e big game

 will never fully know what happened in the Hofdi House in ykjavik, when President Reagan and General Secretary Gorbachev peared to have come close to a wide-ranging agreement on arms ntrol, only for discussions to break down over the issue of Star ars. In the weeks since the sudden raising and dashing of hopes in land the events of those two days have been variously described in ms of triumph and disaster by both sides.

We can probably approach an understanding of the situation and of critical issue of Star Wars if we think in terms of two players in a ne of "celestial poker". The leaders of the two superpowers had h assembled a formidable military and diplomatic hand of cards, their advisers had arranged for a private game at short notice. he stakes could hardly have been higher. Each player wanted ularity at home and the continued public respect and compliance is alliance partners. Each player had domestic economic problems se solution would require the diversion of resources from arms butter. Each had established a public posture of negotiating from gth, and had demonstrated their prowess in token military ities on the territories of Third World nations. After experience evious major conflicts in Europe, it was supposed that world war ace would depend on arms arrangements in that continent which etween them, but which was not represented at the meeting.

have sought to describe their problems, ask questions, explain their conclusions and expand their knowledge with the aid of logic. When embedded in military systems the logic is likely to be stripped of much of its flexibility: some questions will not be askable as military authority is not tolerant of dissident opinions. The hierarchy of military officialdom militates against the free process of question and answer which is the basis of knowledge exploration with logic. Having launched a missile it is too late to backtrack: human decisions are made in real time and are not fully reversible, even with the help of an intelligent computer system.

SDI spells the end of the age of innocence for computer science research. It is no longer possible, and the thesis of this book is that it never was truly possible, to separate the elegant formalism and manipulative techniques applied to structures from the real world in which they are applied. Instead of artificial intelligence being deemed unfit even for toy example domains, as at the time of the 1973 Lighthill Report, it is now deemed to be a reliable component of military defence systems running to millions of lines. The truth is probably somewhere between the two positions. Perhaps it is time to reassess the definition of artificial intelligence research, which should be seen in terms not only of the construction of computer programmes, but of the exploration of problems of knowledge with the aid of the computer. We have come to realize the relative severity of different classes of problems, and that some problems cannot be solved with our current state of knowledge. We have a new respect for the human ability to perform certain straightforward tasks that turn out to be computationally extraordinarily complex. In some senses human knowledge has shrunk as we begin to realize how little we know. At the same time computer scientists can be offered large sums of money to pretend expertise and competence in constructing "peace shields" that defy simple description or formal specification.

Is it possible to pursue both SDI and New Generation Computing?

The civil objectives of the Fifth Generation Programme are contradicted by SDI. The Japanese talk in terms of increasing productivity in low productivity areas such as agriculture and fishing, of caring for an increasingly aged population, of saving energy, and of cultivating information itself as a resource. Computing power needs to be available to the people, rather than remaining the exclusive preserve of a technical or military elite. It needs to be low cost, reliable, and easy to use, preferably using natural language. Cultivating and ex-

changing information sits uneasily with military secu[rity]
Official Secrets Act. The devotion of vast financial r[esources]
skilled manpower to military programmes undoubted[ly]
efforts in agriculture, fishing, and caring for the aged. A c[hoice must]
be made, and it is a choice that cannot be left simpl[y to]
Ministers and Secretaries of State for Defence. Individua[ls]
have to make their own decisions about their individua[l]
work. The skilled scientists are few in number: much d[epends on]
their decisions. Can one use logic while abdicating contr[ol]

Von Neumann rules OK?

It was a classic two-person confrontation of the kind studied by John Von Neumann in his days of work in decision theory and economic behaviour, before his attention was diverted into computing and the design of machines. It was not, however, a zero-sum game, for the consequences of a wrong move in the game of nuclear diplomacy and warfare could be the extinction of our planet, whereas the right position by both sides could usher in a new era of peace and prosperity.

Neither side could afford to lay all their cards on the table before the meeting, or even in the early stages of talks. Each had to probe the position of the other, protected by a news blackout just as an amorous couple may take the telephone off the hook for an evening. Each had to try to think himself into the position of the other – no easy feat for two leaders who spoke through interpreters, had only met on one previous occasion, and whose advisers had only recently entered into close conversations.

Practice beforehand improves the fun

Was this like some championship bridge game, where the hands of cards are dealt out by the experts and the players are then watched as they play and try to take as many tricks as they can? In the complex world of modern superpower diplomacy this must to a large extent be so: a President or General Secretary cannot be left in sole charge of detailed negotiations when he has to be a master of so many other diverse areas of policy.

We have then to assume that advisers had played practice hands with the same or similar cards, and had arrived at a mutually satisfactory conclusion. Mr Shultz and Mr Sheverdnadze are unlikely to have persuaded their leaders to play the game without having personal confidence that their process of diplomacy could be advanced, following many long months of work at official level in Geneva and preparatory meetings in Moscow and Washington in July and August 1986.

President Reagan believes in constructive debate on defence and foreign policy within his administration, and finds that alternating between the positions held by the State Department and the Pentagon can be a good investment in domestic terms in a Congressional Election year, as well as keeping foreign governments usefully confused regarding American intentions. Thus, although the diplomatic cards for Hofdi House had been prepared by Secretary of State

Shultz, President Reagan took with him his own personal joker in the form of Richard Perle, Assistant Secretary for Defence, who has never favoured playing friendly games with the Soviet Union, and who has been the most resolute and coherent public supporter of Star Wars.

Endgames

Public expectations had been kept low before the "Pre-Summit" which however rapidly achieved the status of a historically significant Summit encounter while the world watched the closed doors on their television sets.

After early skirmishing it appears that the real business began in earnest on the Sunday, when both sides began to play using cards which they had retained up their sleeves. General Secretary Gorbachev followed a succession of spectacular concessions on inter-continental ballistic missiles and intermediate nuclear forces with the revelation that all of his concessions were contingent on American concessions on Star Wars, and that his position had to be regarded as a package. President Reagan made it clear that he was not prepared to make the required concessions on Star Wars, and the meeting ended without agreement, with all the interim understandings arrived at and drafted by teams of advisers condemned to limbo.

When the bargaining chips are down

One major outcome has been that the world has wanted to look more closely at Star Wars, which was regarded by President Reagan as being worth keeping at the expense of an unprecedented set of break-throughs in arms control and disarmament agreements. People have asked whether it might not be easier to get rid of nuclear missiles through current negotiation than through expensive exotic tech-nology not yet devised.

President Reagan's Congressional and NATO allies had suppressed their undoubted deep reservations in the cause of maintaining public NATO unity and in order to retain a powerful bargaining chip for use in a superpower Summit. The bargaining chip had not been played, and European governments were left open to the ridicule of the Peace Movement and opposition parties for remaining adherents of a policy which they had never seriously attempted to defend.

The American public was treated to an unprecedented propaganda offensive in the run-up to the Congressional elections, with support for Star Wars being equated with patriotism. Proper informed debate is almost impossible in such an election atmosphere.

Allegations of hypocrisy have been flying to which Western governments have been dangerously slow to respond. Established NATO strategy is in some disarray, with conflicting voices speaking about the future of missile systems such as Cruise, Pershing and Trident, and new support is emerging for a non-nuclear approach to the defence of Europe.

The Western media have tried to seek out advocates of Star Wars, and have failed. No scientists can be found to speak in favour, so the media have in many cases understandably but lamentably sought to minimise embarrassment to themselves and to their governments by writing about something else, anything else.

Silencing the Sherpas

British civil servants are debarred from public comment on such matters, and the British Government has even ruled that civil servants should no longer give evidence to Parliamentary Select Committees. In their reaction to the House of Commons Defence Select Committee Report on the Westland Affair Government has revealed its intense embarrassment over a number of recent events which it would rather not have discussed further.

The same committee has yet to publish the results of its inquiries regarding Star Wars, which included taking evidence from senior civil servants from the Department of Trade and Industry in December 1985. The SDI Pariticipation Office in Whitehall has maintained a prudent silence. Theirs has been a difficult and misunderstood task in recent months.

The 1972 Anti-Ballistic Missile Treaty

It is not known precisely what General Secretary Gorbachev insisted should be done about Star Wars in his final Hofdi House package, but it is clear that he could not have been demanding an unenforceable end to all research. In general terms he wanted research and experimentation confined to the laboratory, and he wanted no tests in space that would be in breach of the Anti-Ballistic Missile Treaty, which was approved by the US Senate and the USSR Supreme Soviet and ratified by Presidents Nixon and Podgorny in September 1972.

Article 5 of that treaty reads as follows:

1. Each party undertakes not to develop, test, or deploy ABM systems

or components which are sea-based, space-based or mobile land-based.

2. Each party undertakes not to develop, test or deploy ABM launchers for launching more than one ABM interceptor missile at a time from each launcher, nor to modify deployed launchers to provide them with such a capability, nor to develop, test, or deploy automatic or semi-automatic or other similar systems for rapid reload of ABM launchers.

Article 9 of the treaty reads as follows:

> To assure the viability and effectiveness of this treaty, each party undertakes not to transfer to other states, and not to deploy outside its national territory, ABM systems or their components limited by this treaty.

President Reagan's NATO allies meeting in Brussels and then Gleneagles gave a public endorsement of his position over Star Wars, and also confirmed their adherence to the 1972 ABM Treaty. Indeed, continued adherence to this treaty had been one of the conditions laid down by Mrs Thatcher in 1984 for British participation in Star Wars research. The issue apparently revolves around interpretations of what constitutes laboratory research, and regarding the narrowness or breadth with which the ABM Treaty should be interpreted. The Pentagon's broad interpretation, whereby the United States is free to test Star Wars technology in space, is contested by the American diplomats who negotiated it with a narrow literal interpretation in mind.

NATO countries are under pressure from the American advocates of each position, and tend to bear in mind that Star Wars offers little if any prospect of significant defence for Europe, even if it turned out to be feasible to build a "peace shield". Indeed an interpretation of article 9 of the ABM treaty would be that to transfer technology or deploy system components outside the territory of the United States is forbidden.

Consulting within NATO

NATO generals are complaining about lack of consultation before and after the Summit, and their politicians are paying the price for not having spoken out sooner, in numerous meetings since President Reagan launched his Strategic Defence Initiative in March 1983. Few contracts have been agreed with European companies despite the public image of participation, and they are not even compensated with the prospect of future lucrative contracts following the Senate

Amendment by Senator John Glenn restricting contracts to American firms unless it could be demonstrated that they did not have the necessary technology. The last minute agreements by Japan and Italy to participate appear to have been token gestures to strengthen SDI as a bargaining chip, rather than signalling major collaborative activity.

A face-saving formula

It should not be hard for a face-saving formula to be found that salves the feelings of all but the hardest-bitten hawks in the Pentagon and the Kremlin. Many apparent hawks would probably argue that they too are playing celestial poker as a way of life. A formula should be found soon as the American Congress has already cut the 1986–87 budget for Star Wars to $3.5 billion, and Democrats are seeking further cuts to assist in balancing the federal budget, within which the defence budget is under considerable pressure. The bargaining chip could diminish in value within weeks.

A possible formula could be as follows:

Both President Reagan and General Secretary Gorbachev have demonstrated by their concessions at the Summit and in subsequent diplomatic exchanges that they are earnestly seeking world peace and arms control.

Both the USA and the USSR are entitled under the 1972 ABM Treaty currently in force to have one anti-ballistic missile system in service. The USA has not exercised this option to date.

Both the USA and the USSR have conducted laboratory research on a new generation of strategic defensive systems.

Both the USA and the USSR have conceded that advances in verification technology mean that effective monitoring of nuclear tests is now straightforwardly possible, and have consented to the installation of the relevant equipment by international scientists.

Article 12 of the ABM Treaty concerns verification:

1. For the purpose of providing assurance of compliance with the provisions of this treaty, each party shall use national technical means of verification at its disposal in a manner consistent with generally recognized principles of international law.
2. Each party undertakes not to interfere with the national technical means of verification of the other party operating in accordance with Paragraph (1) of this article.
3. Each party undertakes not to use deliberate concealment measures which impede verification by national technical means of compliance with the provisions of this treaty. This obligation shall not

require changes in current construction, assembly, conversion or overhaul practices.

Both the USA and the USSR have expressed willingness to remove all intermediate nuclear weapons from Europe, and to move to the removal of all intercontinental ballistic missiles, with the ultimate objective of removing all nuclear weapons.

Both the USA and USSR concede that, though it is not feasible to construct a leakproof "peace shield", powerful new generations of weapons could be built with Star Wars technology.

The concept of strategic defence and an end to nuclear weapons is indeed attractive. It cannot be achieved through some magic of defensive military technology, but by continuing the process of talks between nations, and by using communications and verification technology to monitor the peaceful conduct of research and diplomacy.

In this sense the United Nations Organisation and in particular the Security Council is concerned with the strategic defence of us all. It is needed in 1986 every bit as much as it was in 1945. As Winston Churchill put it, it is better to "Jaw Jaw, rather than War War". Great powers who were allies together in 1945 against a common enemy should remember how to get along together in time of peace. The alternative is all too obvious and terrible. To adapt the words of Neil Kinnock, Leader of the British Labour Party "I am prepared to die for my world, but not that my world should die for me".

Stop playing games in space

As Mr Kinnock said when he launched the Coalition Against Star Wars in June 1986:

> The disparity between expenditure of money, talent and technology on armaments and that spent on development is now so great as to be contrary to the material advantage of the world as well as being in breach of all our ideas of moral obligation.

His views have been echoed by David Steel, Leader of the Liberal Party, who has described the analysis presented in this book and the work of The Strategic Research Initiative in general as having:

> demonstrated the threat posed to British advanced research by this ill-conceived and destabilising programme.

There are better games to play than celestial snooker and celestial poker. After all, in the words of Tam Dalyell:

> we do not have a spare planet

In memoriam

The work described here has been carried on independently over many years, and is dedicated to the memory of Hugh Anderson, President of the Cambridge Union Society, founder of Students for a Labour Victory, outstanding student debater and politician of his generation, and my friend. The last two debating speeches he gave were on the subjects:

1. Computers tell no lies.
2. The best things in life are not free.

He died of cancer in the summer 1970, but will not be forgotten by those who knew him.

Name Index

Subject Index

1. To what extent does the use of money take over from traditional forms of power?
2. How can we make sense of alliances and power blocs?
3. Can one only afford to have principles if one has attained a particular political, social or financial position?
4. How is one deemed to be dissident in different political systems?

Further research: a Memorandum of Misunderstanding

We have been participating in recent months in a real-time experiment in the field of computational politics. Some artificial intelligence researchers, aided by powerful tools and metaphors to extend their powers of analysis, have embarked on a programme of action research, involving techniques of participant observation. It is hoped that as computational politics achieves more visible coherence, researchers may feel able to participate in the effort to preserve the world of which we make humble attempts, in our ivory towers, to make sense. Questions need to be asked. Ours is to reason why.

SDI and new generation computing

The Japanese Fifth Generation Programme is stated as having wholly civil objectives, and follows in a long tradition of national collaborative programmes organized by MITI. By contrast, the American Strategic Defence Initiative and the preceding Strategic Computing Initiative have military objectives, and follow in a long tradition of programmes organized by the Pentagon with the aid of DARPA. The British Alvey Programme started in the former manner, but with the government's agreement to participate in the American SDI the management of research is likely to follow more of the American pattern. The European ESPRIT Programme has a similar origin to the Alvey Programme, and will be similarly affected by British participation in SDI. The European EUREKA Programme is itself now threatened by the emerging attitudes of the British and French Governments, and could be transformed from its initial civil market orientation into a European Defence Initiative. There are similar dangers as the work of the Japanese Fifth Generation Programme falls into the hands of the American SDI Programme.

The underlying enabling technology can be deployed to civil or military work. The technology of logic programing, both sequential and parallel, has been developed by researchers in a civil context, who have sought to describe their problems, ask questions, explain their conclusions and expand their knowledge with the aid of logic. When embedded in military systems the logic is likely to be stripped of much of its flexibility: some questions will not be askable as military authority is not tolerant of dissident opinions. The hierarchy of military officialdom militates against the free process of question and answer which is the basis of knowledge exploration with logic. Having launched a missile it is too late to backtrack: human decisions are made in real time and are not fully reversible, even with the help of an intelligent computer system.

SDI spells the end of the age of innocence for computer science research. It is no longer possible, and the thesis of this book is that it never was truly possible, to separate the elegant formalism and manipulative techniques applied to structures from the real world in which they are applied. Instead of artificial intelligence being deemed unfit even for toy example domains, as at the time of the 1973 Lighthill Report, it is now deemed to be a reliable component of military defence systems running to millions of lines. The truth is probably somewhere between the two positions. Perhaps it is time to reassess the definition of artificial intelligence research, which should be seen in terms not only of the construction of computer programmes, but of the exploration of problems of knowledge with the aid of the computer. We have come to realize the relative severity of different classes of problems, and that some problems cannot be solved with our current state of knowledge. We have a new respect for the human ability to perform certain straightforward tasks that turn out to be computationally extraordinarily complex. In some senses human knowledge has shrunk as we begin to realize how little we know. At the same time computer scientists can be offered large sums of money to pretend expertise and competence in constructing "peace shields" that defy simple description or formal specification.

Is it possible to pursue both SDI and New Generation Computing?

The civil objectives of the Fifth Generation Programme are contradicted by SDI. The Japanese talk in terms of increasing productivity in low productivity areas such as agriculture and fishing, of caring for an increasingly aged population, of saving energy, and of cultivating information itself as a resource. Computing power needs to be available to the people, rather than remaining the exclusive preserve of a technical or military elite. It needs to be low cost, reliable, and easy to use, preferably using natural language. Cultivating and exchanging information sits uneasily with military security and the Official Secrets Act. The devotion of vast financial resources and skilled manpower to military programmes undoubtedly weakens efforts in agriculture, fishing, and caring for the aged. A choice has to be made, and it is a choice that cannot be left simply to Prime Ministers and Secretaries of State for Defence. Individual scientists have to make their own decisions about their individual lives and work. The skilled scientists are few in number: much depends on their decisions. Can one use logic while abdicating control?

5.2
Celestial Poker at the Summit

The big game

We will never fully know what happened in the Hofdi House in Reykjavik, when President Reagan and General Secretary Gorbachev appeared to have come close to a wide-ranging agreement on arms control, only for discussions to break down over the issue of Star Wars. In the weeks since the sudden raising and dashing of hopes in Iceland the events of those two days have been variously described in terms of triumph and disaster by both sides.

We can probably approach an understanding of the situation and of the critical issue of Star Wars if we think in terms of two players in a game of "celestial poker". The leaders of the two superpowers had each assembled a formidable military and diplomatic hand of cards, and their advisers had arranged for a private game at short notice.

The stakes could hardly have been higher. Each player wanted popularity at home and the continued public respect and compliance of his alliance partners. Each player had domestic economic problems whose solution would require the diversion of resources from arms into butter. Each had established a public posture of negotiating from strength, and had demonstrated their prowess in token military activities on the territories of Third World nations. After experience of previous major conflicts in Europe, it was supposed that world war or peace would depend on arms arrangements in that continent which lay between them, but which was not represented at the meeting.